ALSO BY BENJAMIN WOOLLEY

Virtual Worlds
The Bride of Science

THE QUEEN'S
CONJURER

THE QUEEN'S CONJURER

THE SCIENCE AND MAGIC
OF DR. JOHN DEE,
ADVISER TO QUEEN ELIZABETH I

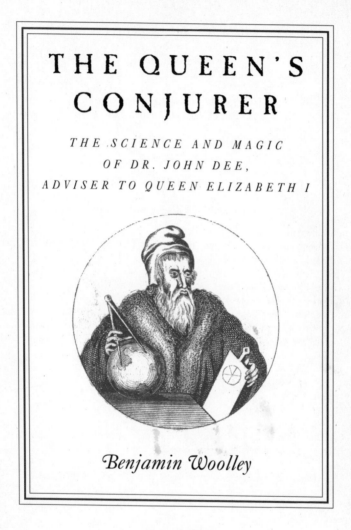

Benjamin Woolley

An Owl Book

HENRY HOLT AND COMPANY

New York

Henry Holt and Company, LLC
Publishers since 1866
115 West 18th Street
New York, New York 10011

Henry Holt® is a registered trademark
of Henry Holt and Company, LLC.

Distributed in Canada by H. B. Fenn and Company Ltd.

Library of Congress Cataloging-in-Publication Data

Woolley, Benjamin.
  The queen's conjurer : the science and magic of Dr. John Dee, adviser to Queen
Elizabeth I / Benjamin Woolley.—1st ed.
    p.   cm.
Includes bibliographical references (p.) and index.
ISBN 0-8050-6510-5 (pbk.)
    1. Dee, John, 1527–1608. 2. Occultists—Great Britain—Biography.
3. Scientists—Great Britain—Biography. 4. Astrologers—Great Britain—
Biography. 5. Great Britain—History—Elizabeth, 1558–1603—Biography.
I. Title.

BF1598.D5 W66 2001
133'.092—dc21   00-053919
[B]

Published by arrangement with HarperCollins Publishers Ltd.

First published in hardcover in 2001 by Henry Holt and Company

First Owl Books Edition 2002

DESIGNED BY FRITZ METSCH

Printed in the United States of America

1 3 5 7 9 10 8 6 4 2

He cometh unto you with a tale which holdeth children from play, and old men from the chimney-corner.

SIR PHILIP SIDNEY,
Defence of Poesy

Dee's journey
across Europe

- - - - - Holy Roman Empire

DENMAR

North Sea

ENGLAND

Harlingen

Dokkum

Emden

Osterho

Oldenburg

Delmenhorst

Bremen

London
Mortlake • • Greenwich
Gravesend •

Enkhuizen

Haarlem

Amsterdam

Brielle

Rotterdam

LOW COUNTRIES

Hess

Kassel

FRANCE

Frankfurt

HOLY ROMAN

W E

S

AUTHOR'S NOTE

❖

FOR CLARITY and consistency, the spellings used in quotations have generally been modernized. I have also adopted the modern Gregorian calendar for dating events, including those occurring when the old-style Julian calendar was still in use. The Gregorian system or "new style" was introduced on 4 October 1582, making that month ten days shorter. It also standardized on 1 January as New Year's Day. England continued to use old-style dates, and celebrated New Year on Lady Day, 25 March. This means for example, 1 March 1584 old style converts to 11 March 1585 new style. Where an old-style date identifies an original document (such as a letter), it has not been converted.

Following Dee's example, I have also anglicized the names of some of the people and places he encountered during his travels.

The primary source material for this book is a collection of diaries written by Dee. The personal diaries are preserved in the Bodleian Library at Oxford, the diaries recording the angelic "actions" at the British Library in London. Selections of these diaries have been published by Casaubon in *True and Faithful Relation*, Halliwell in *The Private Diary of Dr. John Dee*, and most recently Fenton in *The Diaries of John Dee* (see the Bibliography for complete references). I would like to thank Edward Fenton for allowing me to quote from his book, and also for his help with my research and writing.

For help with research in Bohemia and Poland, thanks go to Michal Pober, György Szônyi, and Yustyne Kilianćzyk, who accompanied me during my travels, and to Václav Bůžek, Vladimir Karpenko, Lubos Antonin, Lubomír Konečný, and Denisa Kera. For suggestions, corrections, contributions, and translations, thanks go to Robin Cousins, Michal Pober, William Sherman, Stephen Clucas, Darby

Costello, Alan Stewart, William Stenhouse, and Anke Holdenried. I would also like to acknowledge the authors whose recent scholarship has been invaluable in the compilation of this work, particularly Michael Wilding, Deborah Harkness, Julian Roberts, Andrew Watson, Christopher Whitby, and Jim Reeds.

Personal thanks go to Arabella Pike, Anthony Sheil, Asha Joseph, and Matthew Woolley.

PART ONE
THE FLIGHT OF THE DUNG BEETLE

My mind to me a kingdom is
Such perfect joy therein I find,
That it excels all other bliss
That world affords or grows by kind.

EDWARD DYER,
My mind to me a kingdom is

✦

THERE is no record of the moment John Dee entered the world. He is not to be found in any parish register or private correspondence. There is no birth certificate or diary entry. There is only a series of numbers, a cosmic coordinate: 1527 July 13 4^h.2'. P.M. Lat. 51°.32'.

The data are to be found on a mysterious document now among his papers at the Bodleian Library in Oxford.[1] It is a sheet of parchment upon which is drawn a square containing a series of numbers and astrological symbols. It is a horoscope, drawn up in the ancient manner, showing the state of the heavens at the precise time and place of Dee's birth.

Some biographical information can be gleaned from the chart. He was born at 4:02 P.M. on 13 July 1527. His birthplace was 51 degrees and 32 seconds north of the equator, which is roughly the latitude of London.[2] Latitudes, which specify how far north or south a location is on the earth's surface, were not drawn on maps of early or mid-sixteenth-century England (there were barely any maps anyway; the earliest surviving map of London is dated 1558).[3] However, the information was to be found in tables of astrological data. There is one compiled by Dee himself still to be found among his papers, which identifies the location of cities and landmarks across the world, from Paris (49°10', 150 miles from London) to the "Lake of Sodome" (31°10', 2,404 miles from London).[4] In that table, Dee gives London's latitude as close to that shown on his birth chart, 51°20', which according to modern measurement falls just outside the wall or "ditch" marking the city's northern limit.

Following the practice of the time, Dee did not record the longitude (the east/west position) of his birthplace. There was no standard meridian at the time, and the methods of measuring longitude were extremely unreliable. In his table of astrological data, Dee gives London's longitude as 19°54', which would place the meridian somewhere along a line passing near Krakow, which perhaps indicates that he drew up the table while living there in the 1580s. However, from the date and the position of the Sun plotted on the birth chart, it is evident that Dee's birthplace was within a few degrees of the modern Greenwich meridian.

The most likely location is the City itself. Dee's father, Roland, was a member of London's powerful guild of "mercers" or textile merchants. His mother was Jane, daughter of one William Wild, who Roland had married three years earlier when she was just fifteen years old. John was apparently their first and only surviving child.[5]

Roland was later recorded in official papers as being a resident of Tower Ward, the area immediately west of the great Norman Tower of London, and within sight of Tower Hill, where, as the Tudor surveyor John Stow put it, there "is always readily prepared at the charges of the city a large scaffold and gallows of timber, for the execution of such traitors and transgressors as are delivered out of the Tower."[6]

Roland would in coming years find himself a "transgressor" in the Tower. But in the 1520s, he was on the threshold of a promising mercantile career, which drew him in the opposite direction, toward the teeming square mile of the City squeezed in by walls on three sides and spilling into the Thames on the fourth.

Many of the merchants in Tower Ward lived along Thames Street, close to Billingsgate Docks, where the quays bustled with barks and barges bringing herring, wine, wool, and timber into the capital. Next to Watergate, a lane leading up from the river, stood "Wool Wharf," which since the reign of Richard II had been used for the "tronage"— public weighing—of wool imports.[7] Roland Dee would perform a similar job in coming years, so he and his little boy were likely to have visited, if not actually occupied, the rickety riverside house, as bulbous packets of wool were heaved into its weighing room and dropped on the official scales or "tron."

Up from Thames Street lay the imposing parish church of St. Dunstan's in the East. Its fabric was lavishly maintained by rich local merchants, whose generous bequests were rewarded with opulent sepulchres in its nave and cemetery. Dunstan was then one of the most revered and popular saints in England (there was another church named after him in the west of the city). His name was associated with Glastonbury and early British nationalism and would feature prominently in the life of the little boy who was being brought up within its precincts.[8]

Beyond St. Dunstan's were the bustling inns and narrow streets whose very names spelled commerce: Lombard Street, just north of the church, so called since the merchants of northern Italy settled there in the twelfth century; the sign of the Three Cranes, named after a timber crane used to unload lighters carrying casks of wine from Bordeaux, and the venue for French tradesmen brokering deals with English vintners; Threadneedle, Milk, and Friday Streets, where tailors, dairymen, and fishmongers plied their trades; Cheapside, the thoroughfare for London's main market or "cheap," lined with grocers and apothecaries; Ironmongers Lane, where among the clanking wares hanging from shop fronts Roland would go to meet his fellow mercers at their handsomely refurbished hall.[9]

This was the world of John's formative years: a place filled with the babble of foreign tongues and complex numbers, of ready "reckonyngs" and tricky deals.

However, the City was not the only focus of Roland's career, and it is just possible that John was born just a few miles up the Thames, on the Greenwich meridian itself. This would certainly have been a perfect setting for the astronomer-to-be to make his entry into the world.

Greenwich Palace stood on the bank of the Thames, with Greenwich Hill rising up behind, like a tree-covered Tudor ruff.[10] It was King Henry VIII's birthplace and his main residence. Roland had a position in Henry's court as a "gentleman sewer."[11] The role, like so many court positions at the time, hovered between the ceremonial and the functional. It is unlikely Roland would have been expected to stitch the king's clothing, but he may have been involved with buying and maintaining the innumerable fabrics that furnished the king's palaces and person.

John's birth coincided with what proved to be some of the most momentous events in English, indeed European, history, all of which were taking place within the confines of Henry's privy chambers at Greenwich, and which embroiled members of the royal household such as Roland.

Just three weeks before John was born, the king, anxious for a male heir and to consummate his infatuation for Anne Boleyn, had accosted his wife Catherine "in her closet" and, reviving arguments about their union violating biblical law, announced that their marriage was invalid.[12]

In the drama that followed, a key role was played by a colleague of Roland's, a gentleman sewer in Catherine's retinue named Felipez. Catherine was desperate to get news of her situation back to her nephew and Catholic guardian, Charles V of Spain, the Holy Roman Emperor and the most powerful monarch in Europe. She told Felipez to go to the king and protest that his mistress had cruelly refused him passage to Spain, where the sewer's mother was dangerously ill. Catherine knew Henry would contradict her and dispatch the apparently disgruntled servant back to his home, where he could make contact with Charles.

Henry was prepared for such dissimulation and "did also dissimulate." He granted Felipez a license to leave the country while arranging for agents to waylay the sewer en route. But Felipez managed to give the king's men the slip and reach the emperor at Valladolid, where he broke the news of Henry's plan to have his marriage to Catherine annulled.[13] The sewer's revelations precipitated a crisis that would culminate in Henry's break with Rome and the turmoil of the Reformation, seismic events that would shape English politics for generations to come and bring danger and conflict into the life of the infant son denied to Henry and Catherine, but so recently born to Roland and Jane.

*   *   *

WHEN ALL AROUND is in a state of turmoil, the only direction in which a bewildered young boy may look for a sense of certainty and stability is up.

Standing in the pastures and playing fields that still surrounded the City's walls, gazing at a vivid canopy of stars yet to be diminished by light or atmospheric pollution, John Dee beheld a universe that had apparently remained unchanged since the Creation.

As everyone then knew, the earth was at the center of the cosmos; the Sun, the Moon, and the planets revolved around it, fixed to the perimeters of a series of concentric spheres. The outermost sphere carried the stars. Beyond lay heaven. Historians of science talk of the modern view of the universe being mechanistic, but this one was mechanistic too. The system was in a state of constant movement, but regulated by immutable laws. Change was possible only within the space between the earth's surface and the orbit of the Moon. This was the sphere of fire and air, the domain of such ephemeral astronomical phenomena as comets and meteors.

Where the modern universe is infinite, the size and age of this ancient one, this nest of glistening orbs, was more modest. Genealogies in Genesis and elsewhere in the Bible showed it to be fewer than six millennia old. As for its size, the fifteenth-century printing pioneer and encyclopedist William Caxton wrote: "If the first man that God formed ever, which was Adam, had gone from the first day that he was made and created twenty-five miles every day, yet should he not have comen thither, but should yet have the space of seven hundred and thirteen year to go at the time when this volume was performed by the very author. Or if there were a great stone which should fall from thence unto the earth it should be an hundred year ere it came to the ground."[14]

This, then, was the cosmos that Dee beheld as a child: stable, fixed, finite. There were disputes over details, but the overall view had not changed significantly since the time of the Egyptian astronomer Claudius Ptolemy, who in the second century had established the mathematical laws by which the universe operated. Ptolemy had invented a series of hypothetical entities such as "epicycles," "deferents," and "equants" that made it possible to work out with a high degree of accuracy not just the motions of the planets in the past, but their positions into the distant future, accounting even for such astronomical gymnastics as retrograde motion, when a planet appears to stop, backtrack, and then continue on its way.

Many tables of planetary positions were compiled using Ptolemy's formulas. These showed how each planet moved in relation to the stars, in particular, the constellations of the astrological zodiac. Such almanacs or "ephemerides" were among the most popular books to be produced in these still early days of printing, and Dee would accumulate more than fifteen different sets in his library over the years. It was one of these that he used to work out his birth chart.

Thanks to the mathematical nature of the heavenly motions, he could plot the positions of the planets at the moment of his birth with far more certainty and precision than the flapping scholars his father passed in the corridors of Greenwich Palace could determine the legitimacy of Henry VIII's matrimonial maneuvers.

Where birth charts are now circular, Dee's was drawn up as a square, a form that went back to the ancient Egyptians. The information it contains is basically the same as that contained in a modern chart, except that the positions of Uranus, Neptune, and Pluto are missing, as these planets had yet to be discovered. The chart is highly accurate. Dee managed to map the position of each heavenly body in the sky to within a few minutes of arc (a minute being one sixtieth of a degree), with the exception of Mercury, which is nearly two degrees adrift. The ascendant, which marks the position of the sign of the zodiac rising on the eastern horizon, is out by just under one degree.

The twelve triangles in the chart represent the most synthetic elements of any birth chart, the position of the "houses." The houses are purely astrological (as opposed to astronomical) entities, determining how the planets influence the subject's appearance, temperament, property, relationships, and so on. As the signs of the zodiac are tied to the rotation of the celestial sphere, the houses are tied to the rotation of the earth, the two becoming enmeshed by the moment of birth.

Dee left no record of his own interpretation of the chart, though he certainly knew what it meant. His counsel was frequently sought by friends and patrons, who, at a turning point in their lives, would come to him for advice. He usually performed such services for free, but when money was short, which it often was, he would sometimes accept a token of appreciation. One grateful client, for example, provided him with a pair of gilt bowls.[15]

However, he rarely committed his findings to writing. Such works could be dangerous, particularly when the subjects were of aristocratic or royal status, which many were. The only interpretation of any length that survives concerns Dee's pupil, the glamorous poet and soldier Sir Philip Sidney, for whom Dee drew up a sixty-two-page nativity that made a number of tentative predictions. He foretold that Sidney would enjoy a wonderful career between the ages of fifteen and thirty-one. Thereafter, he faced mortal danger from a sword or gunshot injury, which if survived would inaugurate even greater glories and a long life. Sidney was killed fighting in the Low Countries on 17 October 1586, aged thirty-one.[16]

Dee's own chart depicts similar contrasts. The two most powerful influences, the Sun and the Moon, the two "luminaries," are in opposition—a common enough configuration, but one that suggested a conflict of personality. More notable for Dee was the position of Jupiter, which basked with the Sun in the "serene and warm" sign of Cancer, where it was exalted. In his copy of Ptolemy, he marked the observation that Jupiter's distance from the ascendant (the sign rising on the eastern horizon) indicated that he would be skilled in science.[17] "If he should be lord alone," Ptolemy wrote, Jupiter would also promote "honour, happiness, content and peace."

Unfortunately, Jupiter was not "lord alone." He was threatened by Mars, so his benign influence was seriously compromised. The same passage in Ptolemy that promised scientific proficiency also warned of isolation and condemnation.

There were other disturbing signs, such as the presence of the star Antares together with the planet Mars. Antares has been described as the "Scorpion's heart," as it appears in the middle of the constellation of Scorpio. Mars is a troublesome presence in any chart, causing "mischief and destruction," as Ptolemy put it. Antares was by tradition taken to have an influence similar to Mars, so the presence of the two apparently acting in unison, and within the sign ruled by Mars, must have struck Dee as a threatening combination.[18]

Dee's chart thus revealed the cosmic setting of the life he was about to lead, showing him a universe and a life of schisms and oppositions, of sunshine and moonshadow, jovial humanity and Martian malevolence, a world that promised understanding, but threatened isolation.

‑✦‑

THE first hint that there might be something magical about John Dee came in 1547. He was nineteen years old and a reader in Greek at Trinity College, Cambridge. The college had been set up by Henry VIII as one of the last acts of his reign, his faintly ridiculous effigy standing to this day over the main gate to remind the many students who have passed beneath—including such notables as Isaac Newton, Lord Byron, and Stephen Hawking—of his benefaction.

Dee's selection as one of the Trinity's founding fellows reflected his success as an undergraduate student at the neighboring college of St. John's. When he had arrived in Cambridge in 1542, the university was in a state of confusion. Henry VIII's reforms had deprived it of two chancellors in less than a decade, John Fisher in 1535 and Thomas Cromwell in 1540, and enrollments had fallen to their lowest-ever levels—an average of just thirty students a year.

However, it was also a time of scholastic reform, with figures like Sir John Cheke, Dee's Cambridge teacher, Sir Thomas Smith, and Roger Ascham encouraging the adoption of the "new learning" introduced to the university by Erasmus, the Dutch scholar who brought the Italian humanism of the Renaissance to northern Europe. The medieval domination of Latin texts and Roman numerals over the curriculum began to yield to Greek ideas and Arabic arithmetic. A whole body of ancient books that for years had been ignored or forgotten, such as those of Plato and Pythagoras, were translated and studied. There was a new emphasis on teaching the "quadrivium" to undergraduates, the four of the seven "liberal arts" dealing with geometry, arithmetic, harmonics, and astronomy.[1]

Dee thrived in such an atmosphere. He was so eager to learn, he later recalled, so "vehemently bent to study," that he studied for eighteen hours a day, allowing just four hours for sleep, and two for meals.[2]

His passion was mathematics. As a subject, it was regarded in some circles with suspicion. The seventeenth-century antiquarian John Aubrey reported that during the Tudor era the authorities had "burned Mathematical books for Conjuring books."[3] Mathematics was still popularly associated with the magical "black arts," the term "calculating," sometimes corrupted to "calculing," being synonymous with conjuration. Pythagoras, the semimythical figure hailed as one of the founding fathers of mathematics, was himself considered to be a magician. It was he who argued that numbers had inherent powers, pointing out the creative vitality immanent in the first four integers, 1, 2, 3, and 4, which expressed not only the most basic elements of geometry (the point, the line, the triangle, and the solid) but also the harmonic ratios underlying music and cosmic proportions. Such ideas inspired subsequent thinkers to search for other significances, assessing the meaning of the number of elements and planets, contemplating the precedence of the number nine over ten, constructing numerical hierarchies, counting angels on pinheads. Even Kepler and Newton, the founders of modern cosmology, allowed such numerological considerations to shape their work. Kepler believed that the planets must be spheres because of the trinity of center, radius, and surface; Newton decided to break with tradition and assert that there were seven colors of the rainbow because there were seven planets and seven notes in the musical octave.[4] Like these men, Dee found the cosmic combinations thrown up by mathematics irresistible, and at the numerologically named Trinity College, he decided to undertake an extraordinary experiment to demonstrate their power.

He mounted a production of a play by Aristophanes called *Peace*. The play had first been produced in 421 B.C. It is a comedy, in style and humor much like Aristophanes' later and better-known work, *Lysistrata*, about the women of Athens holding a sex strike to stop their men fighting wars. *Peace*, which as its name suggests explores a similarly pacifist theme, is about a "vine dresser" called Trygaeus, who wishes to consult Zeus, the King of the Gods, about the military fortunes of his fellow Athenians.

The opening scenes concern Trygaeus's attempts to reach Zeus's heavenly palace. He first tries to do this using ladders, which keep toppling over. So, like the mythical hero Bellerophon who slew the fearful Chimera, he calls on the services of a flying creature to carry him up to the Olympian heights.

However, where Bellerophon had the mighty steed Pegasus, Trygaeus got a dung beetle, a giant "scarab," which takes him on a ride so terrifying, he nearly "forms food" for the creature.

Dramatically, it is a marvelous moment, but in the middle of Trinity's main hall, without electrical lighting, dry ice, or motors, virtually impossible to realize. Nevertheless, Dee was determined to find a way of bringing his giant dung beetle to life, and it was to mathematics that he turned for a solution.

In his "Mathematicall Praeface" to Euclid's *Elements* (1570), probably his most influential published work, Dee discussed an "art mathematical" he called "thaumaturgy," "which giveth certain order to make strange works, of the sense to be perceived and of men greatly to be wondered at." The word's etymology is obscure, the Oxford English Dictionary dating its origins to nearly a century after Dee first used it, by which time it had become synonymous with magical tricks.

To Dee, however, it was mathematics rather than magic that was the key to thaumaturgy. Examples he gave were feats of engineering rather than conjuration, such as the "dove of wood" built by the Greek mathematician and reputed founder of mechanics Archytas, which could apparently fly unaided, or the "brazen head" attributed to the German monk Albertus Magnus, "which did seem to speak." Dee recalled seeing something like the latter for himself at Saint Denis in Paris, an automaton that he and a friend saw "self-moving." "Marvellous was the workmanship of late days," he continued, "for in Nuremberg a fly of iron, being let out of the Artificer's hand did (as it were) fly about the gates . . . and at length, as though weary, return to his master's hand again. Moreover, an artificial eagle was ordered to fly out of the same town, a mighty way . . . aloft in the air, toward the Emperor coming thither, and following him, being come to the gate of the town."[5]

Dee believed such artificial marvels showed that, with mathematics, man could achieve miracles to rival God, and in his production of *Peace* he had his first opportunity to prove it.

On the day of the performance, the benches of Trinity's main hall were packed with students and academics, and possibly a scattering of courtiers from London. The pitch lamps were ignited, the stage was set. Trygaeus made his entrance and mounted the insect. "Now come, my Pegasus," he cried. "Come, pluck up a spirit; rush upwards from the earth, stretch out your speedy wings and make straight for the palace of Zeus; for once give up foraging in your daily food." To the audience's amazement, the creature leapt from the stage.

"Hi! you down there, what are you after now?" called Trygaeus, as he was lifted toward the eaves of the hall. "Oh! my god! It's a man taking a crap in the Piraeus, close to the whorehouses. But is it my death you seek then, my death? Will you not bury that right away and pile a great heap of earth upon it and plant wild thyme therein and pour perfumes on it? If I were to fall from up here and misfortune happened to me, the town of Chios would owe a fine of five talents for my death, all because of your damned arse."

"Alas! how frightened I am! oh! I have no heart for jests," the beetle's mount cries, adding, while peering offstage, "Ah! machinist, take great care of me."[6]

Dee's coup de théâtre had its intended effect. A "great wondring" spread through the audience. Dee left no clue as to how he actually made his creature fly around the stage, but the mechanisms mentioned in his "Praeface" include pneumatics, mirrors, and springs. He also wrote a paper on the use of pulleys.[7] An account of Trinity College's theatrical expenses for 1546 and 1547 survive, but they provide little clue, listing such commodities as pitch, "cressets" (iron vessels in which pitch-soaked tapers were burnt for stage lighting), and costumes. The only "extraordinary item" listed is a "great Rownd Candlestick for the stage in the hall," which cost four shillings and sixpence.[8]

"Many vain reports" soon began to circulate speculating on how the effect had been achieved.[9] Some believed such an act of levitation could not have been realized by stagecraft alone. Another, possibly diabolical force must have been deployed.

Dee's experience is echoed in a scene in Shakespeare's *Winter's Tale*, when Paulina tells King Leontes that she is about to bring what he believes to be a statue of his dead wife to life:

> *Quit presently the chapel, or resolve you*
> *For more amazement. If you can behold it,*
> *I'll make the statue move indeed, descend,*
> *And take you by the hand, but then you'll think—*
> *Which I protest against—I am assisted by wicked powers.*[10]

Dee was similarly accused of being assisted by wicked powers, and he too did protest. In a desperate "Digression Apologeticall" that immediately followed the passage in the "Praeface" where he discussed thaumaturgy and theatrical effects, he wrote:

> And for these and such like marvellous Acts and Feats, Naturally, Mathematically, and Mechanically wrought and contrived: ought any honest Student and Modest Christian Philosopher be counted & called a Conjuror? . . . Shall that man be (in hugger mugger) condemned as a Companion of the Hellhounds, and a Caller, and Conjuror of wicked and damned Spirits?

The answer, as Dee would imminently discover, was "Yes."

III

✦

IN 1547, the year of his dramatic debut at Trinity, Dee noted that at 10 P.M. on 10 August he and a "Master Christopherson" heard nocturnal birdsong—"whistlers."

This is the earliest surviving entry in one of Dee's most important if least appreciated works, his private diary. It is no ordinary journal. Diaries and calendars of the modern sort were not yet invented. The nearest equivalent, printed ephemerides, contained astrological tables plotting the positions of the planets for each month of the year. Dee used these to record notable events, each entry being scrawled next to the row tabulating the disposition of the heavens for the relevant period or day. Why he did this is unknown, though it is likely he was trying to identify links between his personal life and celestial events. The result is a uniquely intimate personal diary of Elizabethan life. Unfortunately, the often illegible notes are delivered in a frustratingly terse staccato and have been patchily preserved. For the years 1547 to 1554, just six entries remain, which survive because the antiquarian Elias Ashmole happened to copy them down a century later.

The entry concerning the whistlers is typical. The presence of the friend Master Christopherson is unexplained. Even his identity is a mystery, though he may have been John Christopherson, later the Catholic Bishop of Chichester (1557–1558), who in Queen Mary's reign Dee would encounter during interrogations of Protestant heretics. The significance of the birdsong is also unclear. Edmund Spenser noted in *The Faerie Queen* that the "Whistler shrill" was a bad omen, "that who so hears, doth die."[1]

Dee does not even mention where this incident took place. Given that it occurred at 10 P.M. on an August night, he and Master

Christopherson may have been in a field or garden, where Dee was preparing to take some astronomical measurements. He later recalled that it was during this period that his interest in astronomy first flourished. Each clear night he would stand beneath the canopy of stars, set up his quadrant or cross-staff, and make "observations (very many to the hour and minute) of the heavenly influences and operations actual in this elemental portion of the world. Of which sort I made some thousands in the years then following."[2]

Dee soon discovered, however, that England did not provide the best viewpoint for surveying the secrets of the universe. To behold the intellectual firmament in all its glory, he would need to look abroad, in particular to the place where the light of the Renaissance now shone with its fullest intensity: the Low Countries.

The Low Countries covered the coastal region that has since become Belgium, the Netherlands, and Luxembourg. They were termed low because so much of the land they covered was beneath the level of the North Sea. But they were also prone to floods of foreign influences, the "intertraffique of the mind," as Dee called it. Radical Protestantism had poured in from Germany, Renaissance science and art from Italy, news of navigational discoveries from Portugal, and imperial forces from Spain, whose king, the Holy Roman Emperor and custodian of Catholicism Charles V, now ruled the entire region.[3]

On 24 June 1548, Dee arrived at one of the busiest junctions of this intertraffique, the city of Louvain, near Brussels. It was home to the finest university in the region, a hub of humanism adopted by English reformers such as Dee's friend and fellow Cambridge academic Roger Ascham as a model of educational innovation.[4] The strong Protestant sympathies in the town, combined with the Catholicism of the imperial authorities, generated an intense, unsettled, exciting atmosphere in the university's schools, made all the more precarious by, as Dee noted in his diary, the recent arrival from Spain of Philip, son and heir of Emperor Charles V, who was being groomed by his father for his imperial destiny.

Dee loved it. He enrolled in a law course "for leisure," but spent his time among the mathematicians, in particular a group clustered around the eminent scientist and physician Gemma Frisius.[5] Frisius (1508–1555) was the university's professor of medicine and mathematics, and practiced as a physician in the town. However, his most important work was geographical rather than medical. He pioneered the use of triangulation in land surveying, which enabled the position of a remote landmark to be measured from two points of a known distance apart. The method relied on trigonometry, which was then almost unknown in England.[6]

Under Frisius's influence, Louvain had become caught up in a rapture of scientific measurement, a mood reflected in the Flemish picture *The Measurers*, which was painted by an unknown artist around the time Dee was there.[7] Frisius had set up one of the finest workshops in Europe for making measuring instruments run by the engraver and goldsmith Gaspar à Mirica, and apprenticed some of the leading cartographers of the Renaissance.

Among the cross-staffs and astrolabes in Mirica's workshop, Dee encountered Frisius's leading cartographer, Gerard Mercator.[8] He was laboring away on a series of globes and maps that incorporated the discoveries made by Columbus and his successors in the New World. Dee became fascinated by Mercator's painstaking work, watching over his shoulder a picture of the world emerge that to sixteenth-century eyes would have been just as startling and significant as the first photographs of Earth taken from space in the twentieth. Medieval charts usually depicted the world as a disc or semicircle comprising three continents divided by the Mediterranean, with Asia at the top, Europe to the left, Africa to the right, and Jerusalem in the center.[9] They also often located religious as well as physical features, such as the Garden of Eden and the Tower of Babel.[10] In contrast, Mercator's maps were geographical, showing a world made up of four continents, its curved surface "projected" onto a rectangular map using a mathematical method that was navigationally accurate.

It was in the midst of these measurers of Louvain that Dee's "whole system of philosophising in the foreign manner laid down its first and deepest roots."[11] He became inseparable from the thirty-six-year-old Mercator. "It was the custom of our mutual friendship and intimacy that, during three whole years, neither of us willingly lacked the other's presence for as much as three whole days," he reminisced years later. As a mark of his respect and affection, Mercator gave Dee a pair of his globes, one of the earth, the other of the heavens, objects of huge financial and incalculable scientific value. In return Dee would later dedicate his 1558 astronomical work, *Propaedeumata aphoristica*, to Mercator.

At Louvain, Dee also developed his skills in the use of such instruments as the cross-staff and astronomical rings, presumably during surveying expeditions under the guidance of Frisius and Mercator. He would also steal off into the still dark and dangerous hinterland of cosmological speculation. Just a few years before Dee had arrived at Louvain, Copernicus's heretical theory about the sun rather than the earth being at the center of the universe had started to seep out of Germany. It was first described in an account by George Rheticus (which Dee owned, though it is not clear when he bought it[12]), and later published in 1543 in Copernicus's own *De revolutionibus*. Whether or not Dee and Mercator were discussing Copernicus's ideas at this point is uncertain, but they were apparently experimenting with new models of the universe. Mercator even made one out of brass, especially for Dee. Dee called it a "theorick." At first glance it might have appeared to reflect the orthodox view of the universe, comprising a series of concentric rings made of brass representing the spheres thought to carry the planets and stars. But Dee mentions it having rings for the ninth and tenth spheres.[13] According to tradition, the universe had eight spheres: seven carrying the planets (the Moon, Mercury, Venus, the Sun, Mars, Jupiter, Saturn), and an outer shell carrying the stars, beyond which lay heaven. In some accounts there was also a ninth sphere, the *primum mobile* or divine force that drove the cosmic system. Mercator's "theorick" had ten rings, which at least suggests that it was unconventional. Unfortunately, it is impossible to know how it differed from orthodox models, as the device, like Mercator's globes, would later be stolen from Dee's house.

Mercator may have been the most influential, but he was by no means the only mathematician and cartographer Dee encountered at this time. In 1550, Dee went to Brussels to meet Mathias Haker, a musician and mathematician to the Danish court, and "by wagon" to Antwerp, to see Abraham Ortelius, Mercator's onetime traveling companion and a fellow cartographer. Dee evidently got on well with the mapmaker, who also came from a family of merchants. Some time later, perhaps when they met near London on 12 March 1577, Dee provided a fulsome entry for Ortelius's "Friendship Album," into which he added his coat of arms (first granted in 1567) and an expression of love for Ortelius, "Geographer, Mathematician, Philosopher."[14]

Dee also met Pedro Nuñez, then the leading navigator in Lisbon, from where Columbus had set off in 1492 in search for a western passage to the Indies. Nuñez evidently became a close and important intellectual friend. When Dee was struck down with a serious illness in the late 1550s, he appointed Nuñez his literary executor.

Dee generally had little to do with his fellow countrymen while he was away. He did, however, become a firm friend of Sir William Pickering, the English ambassador to Charles V's court at Brussels. On 7 December 1549 Dee began to "eat at the house" of Pickering, as he put it in his diary. He also became his host's tutor, training him in the arts that would help Pickering establish a position in the ferociously competitive court of the most powerful ruler in Europe: "logic, rhetoric, arithmetic, in the use of the astronomer's staff, the use of the astronomer's ring, the astrolabe, in the use of both [i.e., terrestrial and celestial] Globes, &c."[15]

Pickering had, like Dee, studied under Sir John Cheke at Cambridge, and that was presumably the connection that enabled the young scholar to break bread with the powerful and glamorous diplomat. Pickering was from a good family, his father having been Knight Marshal to Henry VIII. He was dashing and wealthy, "one of the finest gentlemen of this age, for his worth in learning, arts and warfare," and a future suitor to Queen Elizabeth.[16]

The two would develop a long and fruitful relationship, with Pickering occasionally sending Dee books he had managed to pick up from his foreign postings.[17] Pickering also bequeathed Dee a strange mirror that, like Pickering himself, caught the eye of Queen Elizabeth, and became enmeshed with Dee's magical experiments.

Supping at Pickering's table in Brussels, surveying with Mercator and Frisius in Louvain, Dee must have felt himself at the center of the intellectual and political firmament, a feeling that would have been confirmed when Charles V, the Holy Roman Emperor himself, offered Dee a position at court. It was the first of five such offers from "Christian Emperors," and like the others, he would decline it. He never gave a reason for this decision. It may have been anxiety about embracing Charles V's Catholicism, which would exile him from an increasingly Protestant England. It may have been loyalty to his homeland, and a heartfelt hope—indeed a presumption—that its sovereign would one day extend to him the privilege Charles V had so generously offered.

*   *   *

BY 1551, THE whole Continent seemed to lie at young Dee's feet, which now strode confidently from one great center of learning to the next. On 20 July, after five days' travel, he arrived in Paris, where, "within a few days after (at the request of some English gentlemen, made unto me to do somewhat there for the honour of my country) I did undertake to read freely and publicly Euclid's Elements Geometrical . . . a thing never done publicly in any University of Christendom."[18]

According to Dee's own account, the lectures were a sensation. Even though he was just twenty-four and unknown, he later boasted that he had packed out the "mathematical schools," with latecomers being forced to lean in through the windows. He left no record of what had attracted such numbers, but whatever it was, it apparently caused a sensation. "A greater wonder arose among the beholders, than of my Aristophanes Scarabeus [the dung beetle] mounting up to the top of Trinity Hall in Cambridge," he later wrote.[19]

More offers of royal patronage and jobs flowed in, as did invitations from learned scholars. Once again, Dee turned the work down. But he did exploit the chance to meet as many other mathematicians as he could and to start building up his nascent book collection.

One particularly precious item came into his hands at this time, a manuscript copy of Ptolemy's *Tetrabiblios*, the standard ancient work on astrology and astronomy, which came from the library of the king of France himself.[20]

Soon after his triumphs in Paris, Dee returned home to a very different England. The throne was no longer overflowing with the dominating bulk of Henry. Perched upon it now was Henry's son Edward VI, his feet not yet reaching the floor. Edward's succession in January of 1547 at the age of nine had released a surge of pent-up Protestant fervor. "Everywhere statues were destroyed in the churches," Dee noted in his diary.[21] "The great crucifix . . . on the altar of St. Paul's was a few days ago cast down by force of instruments, several men being wounded in the process and one killed," an alarmed Spanish ambassador reported. "There is not a single crucifix now remaining in the other churches."[22]

The impulses of the Reformists were not, however, purely destructive. A progressive academic mood, receptive to the sorts of ideas Dee had encountered in Louvain, swept through court, promoted by Dee's former Cambridge associates Roger Ascham, now Edward's Latin secretary, and John Cheke, Edward's former tutor and now his close aide. Cheke professed that he did not have a "mathematical head," but showed a "great affection" toward mathematicians, Dee evidently among them, as he personally supervised Dee's introduction to the upper reaches of the new Edwardian court. Among those Dee met was Cheke's son-in-law, William Cecil, the man who, ennobled as Baron Burghley, would become the foremost statesman of the Elizabethan era. Even at this early stage of his career, Cecil was well established at court, and it was he who presented Dee to the king himself.

Dee proudly pressed into Edward's hands two astronomical works he had written during his time at Louvain. They clearly showed Mercator's and Frisius's influence, one being on celestial globes, the other on the sizes and distances of heavenly bodies.[23] Neither work has survived (like a great deal of Dee's prolific output), though the very titles indicate that he was now hoping to establish himself as a British Mercator.

Dee could hardly expect the juvenile monarch to understand such works, but the dedication to the king was certainly appreciated, and Dee was duly rewarded with a pension of 100 crowns, which in March 1553 he exchanged for income from the rectory of Upton-upon-Severn. This produced £80 a year, a modest sum, but certainly comfortable for a young man of ambition living in the expectation of a decent inheritance from his prospering father.

His situation improved further when, on 28 February 1552, he was invited to enter the service of William Herbert, earl of Pembroke.[24] Herbert was at the height of his powers, the wily broker who had sided with the victorious John Dudley, earl of Warwick, in the aristocratic scramble for political domination during Edward's minority. Dee was probably retained to work as a tutor for William's sons.

It is hard to imagine how Dee got on in the household. The earl of Pembroke was no Pickering. He was wild, "a mad . . . fighting fellow," according to Aubrey.[25] It was said that he could neither read nor write, and used a stamp to sign his name.[26] His idea of good company was not a learned tutor or refined diplomat but his "cur-dog," which reputedly died as it lay in the hearse during its master's funeral procession. At Wilton in Wiltshire, where Pembroke had built a magnificent mansion out of the rubble of a dissolved abbey, his retainers were notorious for persistent brawling.

Despite the differences, Pembroke evidently came to trust his in-house scholar, as he asked him to cast horoscopes for members of his family, including his second wife.[27] He may also have recommended Dee to John Dudley, who since his seizure of the reigns of power from Edward's Protector, the earl of Somerset, had promoted himself to Lord President of the Council and duke of Northumberland.[28]

Dee joined Northumberland's household in late 1552, possibly as an adviser to Northumberland himself, or as tutor to his sons.[29] Dee would have been seen as a safe choice for either role, carrying suitable testimonials from such well-known Protestant humanists as John Cheke and Roger Ascham.

Dee was now established as an intellectual of standing. He was "astronomus peritissimus," an expert astronomer, as John Bale put it in his *Index of British and Other Writers*, published in the 1550s.[30] He was at the heart of the new Protestant order, poised to become a favorite of the king, destined to enjoy rank and wealth.

Then fortune intervened. The heavens turned hostile and, as for Hamlet, all occasions did inform against him.

IV

O N the afternoon of 6 July 1553, a terrible storm broke over Greenwich as King Edward lay in bed close to death.

He had fallen ill the year before, and the duke of Northumberland, possibly on Dee's advice, had called on the services of the Italian physician and astrologer Girolamo Cardano to treat the ailing king. Cardano was an acquaintance of Dee's, the two having met in Southwark around this time.[1] Before seeing his royal patient, Cardano had cast Edward's horoscope and discovered "omens of great calamity." A physical examination followed that confirmed the prediction, as Edward was found to be suffering from consumption. Cardano was summoned to give his opinion to the council. He did not report his grim astrological findings, as to draw up the horoscope of a monarch was potentially illegal, a form of spying through magical surveillance. All he said was that the king needed rest.

By the end of 1552, Edward was bloated and coughing up blood. He was prescribed opiates and other remedies, some quite elaborate, such as a mixture of spearmint syrup, red fennel, liverwort, turnip, dates, raisins, mace, celery, and the raw meat of a nine-day-old sow, nine spoonfuls to be taken as required. To counter rumors that the king was being poisoned, Northumberland planted the story that Princess Mary, Henry VIII's daughter by his first marriage and in Catholic eyes his only legitimate offspring, had given her half-brother the evil eye in an attempt to despatch him by witchcraft. Northumberland feared that if she became queen, England's great Protestant experiment would be over forever.

Northumberland persuaded Edward to disinherit Mary in favor of Lady Jane Grey, the Protestant great-granddaughter of Henry

VII. To protect his position further, Northumberland also married Lady Jane off to his fourth son, Guilford, and Jane's sister Katherine to Pembroke's son William, Lord Herbert. The joint ceremony was held on 31 May 1553 at Durham House, Northumberland's London palace overlooking the Thames.[2] It involved the two families that were now acting as Dee's patrons, and it is possible he attended what turned out to be a key historical event.

Two months later, on that stormy afternoon of July, King Edward prepared to die. With his final breaths, he was said to have whispered a prayer he had composed especially for the occasion, beseeching God to "defend this realm from papistry, and maintain Thy true religion, that I and my people may praise Thy holy Name, for Thy Son Jesus Christ's sake, Amen."[3] He died at 6 P.M.

As soon as Edward was dead, Northumberland attempted to install Lady Jane Grey on the throne. Popular sentiment, nimble aristocratic loyalties, and the law favored Mary. Within days, she had asserted her claim and won over most of Northumberland's allies, including the earl of Pembroke, who stood outside Castle Baynard, his London home, and threw a "cap full of angels" to the people (an angel was the name of a coin) to celebrate her accession. He also announced the annulment of his son's marriage to Katherine Grey, which he had taken the precaution of ensuring remained unconsummated.

The speed of Northumberland's fall was breathtaking. On 23 August, barely a month after Edward's death, he stood on the scaffold on Tower Hill. Stretched out beneath him was the City that had abandoned him and embraced Mary. Nearly a tenth of its population, around 10,000 people, had gathered to watch him die. They beheld a broken man, who now publicly renounced his Protestant beliefs. He was, and wanted to die, a Catholic. Having recanted, he was blindfolded and knelt before the block. Before the executioner could strike the blindfold slipped, and the duke had to get up to put it on again. He knelt again, his distress now obvious, and with a single blow he was decapitated.

In the days leading up to Northumberland's execution, Queen Mary's Privy Council had begun a purge of his sympathizers. On

21 August 1553, an order was issued to the lieutenant of the Tower of London, requesting that three prisoners be sent before the council for examination. One of the names listed was Roland Dee.[4]

Roland, like his son John, had prospered in recent years. Reforms such as the dissolution of the monasteries had released acres of new land onto London's starved property market, and set off a boom that would see the City's population nearly quadruple in the coming decades, from fewer than 50,000 to nearly 200,000.[5] Roland had directly benefited from this, being appointed by the king as one of two "packers" with joint responsibility for checking all merchandise shipped through London and its suburbs, with the right to "untruss and ransack" any consignment not packed in his presence. In return, he was to receive a "moiety" (half share) of fees payable on the shipments, the other half going to the other packer, who was to be appointed by the Lord Mayor.[6]

Now he was a wanted man, though there is no record of the precise charge. Given the date, and the fact that the Privy Council itself wanted to interview him, it seems likely he had been identified as a Protestant activist, even one of Northumberland's conspirators. On 1 September, he was released, a ruined man. Having built up a position at court, a thriving business in the City, and been rewarded with lucrative privileges—having, indeed, carefully laid the foundations for promotion to the gentry, perhaps ultimately even minor nobility—he seemed to lose everything, a misfortune that would have a devastating impact on the fortunes of his son as well as himself. By such "hard dealing," Dee later wrote in a begging letter to William Cecil, his father "was disabled for leaving unto me due maintenance."[7] In other words, having expected to inherit the sort of independent means that would enable him to continue his studies unhindered, Dee suddenly found that he would have to fend for himself.

The legacy of his father's fall was to reach further. Two years later, John Dee found himself in equal, if not greater, peril.

* * *

IN 1555, MARY's supporters began to burn heretics. The church could not execute those it convicted of heresy, so under a statute called *de Heretico Comburendo*, the civil authorities undertook this responsibility. The statute had been in force during Henry's reign, but was abolished in 1547 as part of Edward's program of Protestant reform. In January of 1555 Mary's government restored it, and within a month the fires were alight. The first victim was John Rogers, canon at St. Paul's Cathedral, who was consigned to the flames at Smithfield. Smithfield was London's meat market, as well as the venue for its grisliest executions. For four centuries traitors, witches, and heretics were brought there and, like the cuts of meat in the butchers' stalls, hung, roasted and boiled.

Rogers was a married priest, therefore by definition a heretic, and according to Protestant accounts was denied the chance to say good-bye to his wife and children before being tied to the stake. Across the country, many more met the same fate. The estimated numbers vary widely according to the religious sympathies of those reporting them, but are now put at around 300 in the five years of Mary's reign. Protestant storytellers would send a shudder through their audiences with tales of agonizing deaths, of necklaces of gunpowder worn by the victims, which ignited and blew off their heads or, worse, failed to go off, as happened in the case of John Hooper, Bishop of Gloucester, who took three quarters of an hour to expire. It was even said that a woman had given birth as she burned, her baby being thrown back into the fire by the executioner.

The flames burned fiercest in Smithfield, and the smoke from the pyres crept through the surrounding streets, stoking up rebellion as well as fear. There were reports of a mysterious voice emanating from a wall that spoke favorable words about Mary's half-sister, Princess Elizabeth, but remained silent about the queen. A dead cat dressed as a cleric was hung from the gibbet at Cheapside.[8] A dagger was thrown at one priest who criticized Edward VI's reign, and a "murderous assault" was made on another during Communion. "The Blessed Sacrament itself was the object of profane outrages, and street brawls arising out of religious disputes were frequent," as one Catholic commentary later noted.[9]

The persecution Mary had unleashed was not confined to those who meddled in the affairs of state or religious zealots; ordinary people—poulterers, linen drapers, and matrons who expressed themselves too freely—could also expect a knock at the door.

One day late in May 1555, John Warne, an upholsterer living in Walbrook in the east end of the City, looked up from his stitching to find the sheriffs at his doorway. He was dragged off to Newgate prison, where he was interrogated by Edmund Bonner, the "bloody" bishop of London. In *Acts and Monuments of these Latter and Perillous Dayes*, a chronicle of martyrdoms compiled by the exiled Puritan teacher John Foxe in Switzerland during this time, Bonner is identified as the most diligent and heartless executor of Mary's Counter-Reformation. Foxe summarized his view of the bishop in two lines of doggerel:

> This cannibal in three years space three hundred martyrs slew.
> They were his food, he loved so blood, he spared none he knew.[10]

Bonner accused Warne, presumably on the testimony of informants, of failing to attend mass and refusing to accept the doctrine of transubstantiation—the Roman Catholic belief that bread and wine was turned during Mass into Christ's actual flesh and blood. He was also reported to have seen "a great rough water-spaniel" with its head shaved in the manner of a Catholic priest. "Thou didst laugh at it and like it," Bonner said.[11] Warne was apparently unmoved by such accusations, and refused to recant his beliefs "unless he were thereunto thoroughly persuaded by the holy Scriptures"—a robustly nonconformist response, as a belief in the Bible as the sole source of divine truth and authority was central to Protestant theology.

After being examined by Bonner for three days, Warne was handed back to the sheriffs and kept at Newgate to await his fate. On 31 May, he was taken to Smithfield, where, according to Foxe's account, he was chained to the stake and burned alongside John Cardmaker, a canon from St. Paul's. As the flames leapt up around them, the two held hands and together "passed through the fire to the blessed rest and peace among God's holy saints and martyrs."[12]

The following day, the sheriffs were out again. The man they wanted this time was John Dee.

PART TWO

THE LORD OF MISRULE

✤

. . . when the planets
In evil mixture to disorder wander,
What plagues and what portents, what mutiny,
What raging of the sea, shaking of earth,
Commotion in the winds! Frights, changes, horrors,
Divert and crack, rend and deracinate,
The unity and married calm of states
Quite from their fixture!

WILLIAM SHAKESPEARE,
Troilus and Cressida

V

✤

ON 28 May 1555, a letter was despatched by the Privy
Council, ordering Francis Englefeld, Mary's Master of the
Court of Wards, to arrest Dee.[1] His house was to be
sealed, and his books and papers seized as evidence. His living from
Upton-upon-Severn was also confiscated, depriving him of his only
regular source of income.

He may have eluded the authorities for a day or two, but by 1
June he was under the custody of Sir Richard Morgan, chief justice
of the Common Pleas. He was taken to Hampton Court, where he
was to be held incommunicado "until Mr Secretary Bourne and Mr
Englefelde shall repair thither for his further examination."[2]

Dee must have suspected something like this was going to happen. Many of his closest friends had already been arrested or forced
into exile. Following an audience with Princess Elizabeth, Sir
William Pickering had escaped back to the Continent, and been
indicted for treason in his absence. John Day, one of London's most
prominent printers, who later published many of Dee's works, had
been imprisoned and, on his release, also went abroad. The arrest of
his own father, Roland, would have added to the atmosphere of
apprehension, casting suspicion over the whole family.

Dee was arrested with several accomplices: one Butler, whose
identity remains unknown; Christopher Cary, a pupil of Dee's
and possibly a kinsman of George Carey, a cousin of Elizabeth and
later made by her Baron Hunsdon;[3] John Field, a publisher and
astronomer who would soon collaborate with Dee on the printing
of a set of ephemerides drawn up according to heretical Copernican
principles; and Sir Thomas Benger, by far the most senior member

of the group, who later became auditor to Queen Elizabeth and was now one of her "principal servants at Woodstock," as Dee put it.[4]

The list of names is a telling one. It points to Dee being identified as a member of a secret Protestant cell that Mary's government believed to be clustered around Elizabeth. A week later Elizabeth herself would be brought to Hampton Court, as Mary, now married to King Philip of Spain, approached the term of what turned out to be a phantom pregnancy. Mary was under pressure to dispose of Elizabeth, whose very existence was seen as a threat to the reestablishment of Catholicism and the authority of the Pope, and there were repeated attempts to implicate the princess in Protestant schemes. In Mary's private chambers, the two sisters had a tearful confrontation, apparently within the hearing of Philip, whom Elizabeth knew to be hiding in suitably Shakespearean manner behind an arras. Mary demanded that Elizabeth reject her Protestant beliefs, and Elizabeth once more refused to do so.

The accusations against Dee were many and various, but focused not on his religious leanings so much as his links with mathematics and magic. "In those dark times," the seventeenth-century historian John Aubrey wrote of Dee's era, "astrologer, mathematician and conjuror were accounted the same things."[5] This was certainly the case with Dee. He was charged with "calculating," "conjuring," and "witchcraft" on the grounds that he had drawn up horoscopes for Mary, her husband Philip of Spain, and Elizabeth.

He was probably guilty. The remnant of his diary for this period includes an entry (inaccurately transcribed by Elias Ashmole) showing the date and time of Mary's marriage to Philip, and noting that the rising sign at the moment of their wedding—11 A.M., 25 July 1554—was Libra (a good omen, as Libra was the sign associated with marriage or partnership, ruled by Venus).

The only other entry from his diary for this period, dated three weeks prior to his arrest, simply reads "Books brought from France to London." It seems innocent enough, but may disguise an attempt to communicate with the exiled Pickering, one of Elizabeth's partisans and therefore a potential traitor. It may even suggest that Dee was acting as an intermediary between Pickering and

Elizabeth, for he was also in correspondence with the princess around this time.

Whether or not such suspicions had any grounds, the merest whiff of intrigue would have been sufficient to prompt the council's decision to arrest Dee, and if it was to keep him, it would need a stronger accusation than a suggestion he had been drawing up horoscopes.

A stronger accusation was duly found, and the nature of its source gives a hint of the political nature of the proceedings. Two informers were now cited who claimed to have evidence that Dee had "endeavoured by enchantments to destroy Queen Mary." One of them was identified by Dee as "Prideaux." There was a Catholic spy of that name who later fled to Spain, where he sought the protection of King Philip.[6]

The other informer was a rather more conspicuous and colorful character called George Ferrers, a lawyer, a member of Lincoln's Inn, and an MP, who was briefly imprisoned in 1542 for failing to pay off debts owed to various London institutions.[7] In 1553, he was appointed the capital's "Lord of Misrule," an ancient role bestowed during yuletide revelries. The tradition had been revived by the duke of Northumberland for what would turn out to be Edward's last Christmas, and it was a huge success, with Ferrers fulfilling the office admirably, decked in satin robes and presiding over a court of fools and illusionists. He was to repeat the part during Mary's reign, though no doubt the "merry disports" that formed part of the event would not, as they did in the inaugural year, include jesters dressed as cardinals.

Ferrers apparently bore a grudge against Dee. In 1578, during the reign of Elizabeth, an edition of a pamphlet entitled *Mirror for Magistrates*, which was suppressed, included a story written by him apparently lampooning Dee. It described a sorcerer hired by one Elianor Cobham to kill the queen by sticking pins through a wax effigy of her. The story had a particular poignancy at the time, as just such an effigy of Elizabeth was found (at Lincoln's Inn Fields, where Ferrers practiced as a lawyer), and Dee was asked by the Privy Council to advise upon its significance.[8]

Ferrers now accused Dee of using "enchantments" to blind one of his children and to kill another.

On 5 June, Dee, together with his codefendants Cary, Benger, and Field, was ordered to be brought before Secretary of State Sir John Bourne, Francis Englefeld, Sir Richard Read, and Dr. Thomas Hughes to be examined on his "lewd and vain practises of calculing and conjuring."

The tribunal was made up of Mary's most loyal supporters, suggesting that there was a strongly political motive behind Dee's arrest. Englefeld was the man Mary would later handpick to investigate a conspiracy against her husband, Philip of Spain.[9] Sir John Bourne was famous as "an especial stirrer up in such cases," having "marvellously tossed and examined" one of the leaders of Wyatt's Rebellion. Lord North was reputed to have scoured the streets of London in search of a pauper's baby to pass off as the male heir Mary was failing, after ten months of gestation, to produce.[10]

At the time of Dee's interview with these men, the atmosphere at Hampton Court was fraught—with fears about the true nature of Mary's "pregnancy," with xenophobia of the Spanish king Philip, with sectarian fervor, with suspicions about plots and schemes being hatched in every corridor and chamber.

The examiners demanded that Dee answer at first four articles relating to his supposed offenses, then a further eighteen. A "doctor," probably Thomas Hughes, called for him to be committed to "perpetual prison" on charges that, as Dee later put it, "he most unchristianlike and maliciously had devised."[11] But none of the charges could be substantiated.

A week later, having failed to extract a confession, his interrogators ordered that he be taken under guard by boat from Hampton Court to London, where he was to face Lord Broke, Justice of the Common Pleas. Broke in turn referred the matter on to the Star Chamber at the Palace of Westminster.

By now the weakness of the case against Dee and his confederates was becoming obvious. Some members of the council were probably mindful that these men were close to Elizabeth, who despite Mary's hostility remained heir to the throne. So by July,

without a decisive conviction in prospect, they decided to relax the
conditions under which the prisoners were held, particularly for Sir
Thomas Benger, who was being held at Fleet Prison, down by the
fetid Fleet River that carried the capital's sewage past the cell windows into the Thames. On 7 July the Privy Council told the prison
warden "to permit Sir Thomas Benger to have liberty of the Fleet,
and his wife to come unto him at times convenient."[12]

On 29 August 1555, three months after his arrest, Dee was
bound over to keep the peace until Christmas 1556. However, he
did not escape unscathed. He was permanently deprived of his post
as rector of Upton, depriving him of his living, and he alone of the
group was to be handed over for further investigation on religious
matters.[13] In other words, he was now suspected of being a heretic,
and the man asked to examine him was the bishop of London—
"Bloody" Bonner himself.

VI

✦

OLD St. Paul's Cathedral was far larger than the replacement built after the great fire of 1666, an immense hulk of Caen stone that had loomed over London for centuries. During Edward's reign, it had been the focus of London's religious reforms. In 1549, in the cathedral's precincts, an ornate chapel and charnel house filled with elaborate marble monuments to the dead had been torn down by Protestant fanatics. The bones found beneath, apparently amounting to more than a thousand cartloads, had been taken out to marshlands north of the city, where they were dumped and landscaped over, creating a hill high enough to support three windmills.[1] That same year, the cathedral's altar and magnificent reredos were destroyed and replaced with a plain table, and the nave was turned into a thoroughfare between Paternoster Row and Carter Lane "for people with vessels of ale and beer, baskets of bread, fish, flesh and fruit, men leading mules, horses and other beasts."[2] Since Mary's accession to the throne, many of these alterations had been reversed, and it was a very different St. Paul's that another heretic approached one autumn morning in 1555, to be examined by Bishop Bonner. The altar had been restored, the animals ejected, and an air of reverent hush restored to the soaring nave.

The prisoner was John Philpot, and he was quite a catch for Bonner. He was the son of a knight, educated at Oxford, widely traveled and highly cultivated, having "knowledge of the Hebrew tongue." He had spent some time at Venice and Padua, but had attracted the unwelcome attentions of "a certain Franciscan friar" sent to spy on him, and was forced to leave. Back in England during Edward's reign, he advanced quickly to become archdeacon of Winchester.[3] Then Mary ascended the throne.

Philpot was arrested in 1554 for refusing to conduct Mass following a preliminary examination by Bishop Gardiner, and was imprisoned in Newgate. There he remained for a year before proper hearings began.

His first examination was with a panel of commissioners sent by Mary, who saw him at Newgate on 2 October 1555. According to Foxe's not entirely impartial account of the event in *Acts and Monuments*, the commissioners poked fun at Philpot about his weight, implying that even a Protestant with his puritan values was not immune from fleshly temptations. Philpot responded with impregnable composure that quickly drove his interrogators to distraction. A further examination followed a similar course, and ended with one of the commissioners calling him a "vile heretic knave," and ordering that he be taken away to face the more formidable inquisition of Bonner himself.

The Bishop's Palace squatted among the buttresses of St. Paul's southwest side, beneath Lollards' Tower, one of the cathedral's two bell towers. Philpot was left in the palace's coalhouse, which Bonner used as a temporary prison.

The coalhouse was already filled with a generous supply of fuel for the Smithfield fires—six suspected heretics in all, including a married priest from Essex who had withdrawn a recantation extracted from him after the bishop "buffeted" his face black and blue. As a prison, it was probably worse than Newgate. It was windowless, and despite the generous supply of coal, there was no provision for making a fire to provide warmth or light. There was only straw for bedding, and in a dark adjoining chamber, a set of wooden stocks.

The reception Philpot got from the bishop's staff was quite at odds with the meanness of his accommodation. He was given a "mess of meat and good pot of drink" and copious apologies for the inconvenience of being incarcerated; apparently the bishop had not known of his arrival. A little later, he was brought up to the bishop's private study, where Bonner, sitting alone at a table, was full of bonhomie, offering his hand and suggesting that the whole business was a frightful mistake. "I promise you I mean you no more hurt than to mine own person," Bonner said. "I will not therefore burden you with your conscience as now, I marvel that you are so merry in prison as you be, singing and rejoicing, as the prophet saith, 'rejoicing in your naughtiness.' "[4]

Bonner sent him off to be given a glass of "good wine" from the palace cellars, which Philpot enjoyed standing at the cellar door, before being taken back to the coalhouse, "where I with my six fellows do rouse together in straw as cheerfully (we thank God) as others do in their beds of down."[5]

There followed a series of other examinations, each one taking the form of a polite and learned discussion on theological particulars, conducted in the genteel surroundings of the Bishop's Palace, and each ending with Philpot being "carried" (i.e., manhandled) back to the coalhouse.

On 19 November, Philpot was once again led blinking out of his fuel cell and brought before the bishop. This time, Bonner had company: the bishop of Rochester, the chancellor of Lichfield, a Dr. Chedsey. And another, relatively young, learned scholar was also in attendance, whom Bonner introduced as one of his chaplains: John Dee.

What was John Dee, who might have been a cohabitee in the coalhouse, doing there? Had the Protestant poacher turned Catholic keeper? Unfortunately, there is no record of Dee's own interrogation with Bonner, nor of his subsequent treatment. He disappears into St. Paul's a suspected heretic, and now emerges an obedient chaplain.

The only record of Philpot's imprisonment and examination by the bishop is contained in Foxe's *Acts and Monuments*, which was first published in English in 1563, after Elizabeth had succeeded to the throne and returned the country to Protestantism. It is a significant historical document, but by no means politically or religiously neutral. Though it covers the entire history of religious persecution, it focuses with particular intensity on "the bloody murderings" of "godly martyrs" during Mary's reign. And it does not disappoint. Through the testimony of Mary's Protestant victims, often scratched onto scraps of paper and smuggled away just hours before their authors' deaths, accompanied by gruesome illustrations of beatings and burnings, Foxe embroidered a vivid but decidedly Protestant picture of Catholic cruelty. It is therefore not completely surprising that the account of Philpot's interview, based on Philpot's own account, does not portray John Dee in a flattering light.

The examination was to prove a turning point in Philpot's trial. It began with Bonner asking Philpot why he had kept his interrogators waiting. The bishop's tone was now very different from the friendly one he had adopted at their first meeting.

"My lord, it is not unknown to you that I am a prisoner, and that the doors be shut upon me," Philpot said.

This did not satisfy Bonner. "We sent for thee to the intent thou shoulds't have come to mass. How say you, would you have come to mass, or no, if the doors had been sooner opener?"

"My lord, that is another manner of question," Philpot replied. Bonner did not pursue the matter, instead engaging Philpot in a theological debate on the subject of the unity of the church and the papacy. In particular, Philpot was asked to discuss the works of the third-century philosopher St. Cyprian of Carthage, who according to Bonner declared, "There must be one high priest, to which the residue must obey," a clear endorsement of papal authority. Philpot disputed this interpretation, arguing that St. Cyprian was referring to himself, then being patriarch of Africa.

At this point Dee intervened. "St Cyprian hath these words: 'That upon Peter was builded the church, as upon the first beginning of unity.'" Philpot replied with another quote, from a book of Cyprian's that Dee himself would later have in his library: "In the person of one man, God gave the keys to all, that he, in signification thereby, might declare the unity of all men."

After a further exchange, Dee announced that he was leaving the room, whereupon Philpot, in his first display of temper, called after him: "Master Dee, you are too young in divinity to teach me in the matters of my faith. Though you be learned in other things more than I, yet in divinity I have been longer practised than you." It was a clear reference to Dee's reputation as a magician, which was obviously understood by all those present. Dee did not reply.

Dee did not attend any further interviews with Philpot, which from this point onward became increasingly hostile. However, at around the same time he did attend another examination, this with one of the newer arrivals at the Bishop's Palace, Bartlet Green. Dee had mentioned Green in an account of his arrest written many years later, in which he described himself as having been a "prisoner long" at the Bishop's Palace, "and bedfellow with Barthlet Green, who was burnt."[6]

This was an economical version of the truth. In a letter to Philpot intercepted by Bonner, Green reported the encounter as follows: "I was brought into my lord [Bonner]'s inner chamber . . . and there was put in a chamber with master Dee, who entreated me very friendly. That night I supped at my lord's table, and lay with master Dee in the chamber you [i.e., Philpot] did see. On the morrow I was served at dinner from my lord's table, and at night did eat in the hall with his gentlemen; where I have been placed ever since, and fared wonderfully well."[7] That is the only reference to Dee that Green gave in his submission.

Poor Bartlet did not fare so wonderfully well in the coming days, and neither did Philpot. Philpot evidently attempted to engineer an escape. The bishop's men discovered a dagger sewn into the belly of a roasted pig that had been delivered to Philpot. As punishment, Bonner sent Philpot to be locked up in the coalhouse stocks, and a few days later himself came to the coalhouse to see his prisoner. Bonner claimed it was the first time he had ever visited the place, and thought it too good for Philpot. He ordered his guards to seize the prisoner, and to follow. He led them to the "privy door" leading from his palace into St. Paul's, where the bishop's prison warden was waiting with orders to "place" Philpot.

The keeper led the prisoner up the nave of the cathedral, past the reinstated rites and shrines Philpot so despised, and up the stone steps leading to Lollards' Tower. Many of his fellow heretics were already incarcerated in one of the tower's chambers, forced to sit or lie with their feet and hands locked into a wall of wooden stocks, deafened by the din of the bells. But Philpot was taken along the walkway across the west side of the cathedral, into a tunnel leading into the bell tower on the opposite side of the church, the "Blind Tower." There he was confined in a chamber "as high almost as the battlements of Paul's" with a single east-facing window "by which I may look over the tops of a great many of houses, but see no man passing into them." He was body-searched and a number of letters were found hidden in his clothes, which he tried to tear up as the guards pulled them from him. One of these letters was addressed to Bartlet Green.

The interrogations did not stop for Philpot, but they were now aimed solely at incriminating rather than converting him. The letter to Green, painstakingly pieced together, contained a reference to Dee, "the great conjuror." "How think you, my lords, is not this an honest man to belie me, and to call my chaplain a great conjuror?" Bonner asked the assembled bishops. They obligingly smiled at Bonner's irony.

Philpot evidently realized that his position was now hopeless. He asked his servant, whose visits provided his only remaining link with the outside world, to procure a "bladder of black powder," which Bonner's men intercepted. Philpot explained that it was to make ink, but Bonner's suspicion must have been that it was filled with gunpowder. Philpot no doubt planned to hang the pouch around his neck in the event that he was burned, to provide an early release from the lingering agonies of incineration.

Philpot was formally condemned on 16 December 1555 and held in a small chamber in preparation for the handover to Newgate's chief keeper—the moment when the ecclesiastical authorities washed their hands and returned to their chapels, leaving the secular arm of government to conclude the business. Philpot's new keeper was a man called Alexander, whose first words to his new prisoner were, "Ah! Hast thou not done well to bring thyself hither?" These cheery words were followed by an order to hold the prisoner down on a block of stone, and lock his legs using as "many irons as he could bear," which Alexander said he would remove only if Philpot paid him £4.

An appeal to the civic authorities brought gentler treatment. The city sheriff, one Master Macham, ordered that the prisoner's irons be removed and his personal possessions restored. Philpot was then taken to Newgate, where he was given a cell to himself. The following day, he had his last meal, and was told to make his preparations for his execution. He was awoken at eight the following morning, and taken to Smithfield, being carried by his guards to the place of execution as "the way was foul." As they lifted him up, he apparently joked, "What? Will ye make me a pope?"

Bartlet Green was burned a month after Philpot. Beyond his brief encounter with Dee, little is known about his last days. He was brought into one of the final interrogations with Philpot to identify the incriminating letter, which he did. He was not to be heard of again until 27 January 1556, when he followed Philpot on the short journey from Newgate up Giltspur Street to the place of execution, still smoldering from the burning of a heretic called Thomas Whittle the day before. Bartlet was twenty-five years old when he died that day.

                              *   *   *

THE FIGURE OF Dee glimpsed through the pages of Foxe's *Acts and Monuments*, of the "great conjuror," Bonner's "chaplain," flitting in and out of interrogations, is disturbing. He had become a favored and apparently enthusiastic member of Bonner's household. Indeed, the bishop was his "singular friend," and would apparently remain so even into the late 1560s, when Bonner, removed from the episcopacy and stripped of his honors by Elizabeth's Protestant government, lay dying in Marshalsea prison.[8] A note in a book also reveals that Dee was staying, perhaps even living, at Fulham Palace, the bishop of London's Thameside residence four miles upriver from the City, between 18 and 24 September 1555, in the weeks leading up to Philpot's interrogations.[9]

Does this, then, show that Dee, so recently an enthusiastic member of Edward VI's Reformist court, was a closet Catholic?

The Reformation did not slice the world up between Catholicism and Protestantism quite as neatly as many historical accounts suggest. There were militants on both sides prepared to kill and die for their cause, but the vast majority, including many of the leading figures of the Reformation, were more ambivalent. Up to his death, Henry VIII himself clung to many Catholic rites and attitudes, even concerning divorce. His was a struggle for power rather than religious principles.[10] Queen Elizabeth, a symbol of Protestant sovereignty, told the French Ambassador André Hurault: "There is only one Jesus Christ. . . . The rest is dispute over trifles."[11] This, it seems, was Dee's view as well.

Throughout his life, Dee refused to commit himself to a particular religion. It is certain he was not an orthodox Catholic. In 1568, by which time England had reverted to Protestantism under Elizabeth, the Jesuit leader Francis Borgia received a secret report on the state of the English Hospice in Rome. The hospice provided lodging for English pilgrims and later, as the English College, became a training camp for Catholic missionaries and spies. In the paper, probably written by the exiled Catholic militant Dr., later Cardinal William Allen, a warning is issued to keep the hospice's lodgers away from certain irreligious influences, including one "Ioannes Deus, sacerdos uxoratus, magicis curiosisque artibus deditus," "John Dee, a married priest, given to magic and uncanny arts."[12] This curious note contains two pieces of information about Dee for which there is no other direct evidence: that he was ordained and that he was married. Philpot's reference during one of his interrogations to Dee being so "young in divinity" suggests it was Bonner himself who ordained Dee. This would explain the origin of the "doctor" title that became so closely associated with his name, for which Dee himself never publicly accounted. The marriage must have come later, as Catholic priests must remain celibate. This was the reason the Jesuit report ordered the English Hospice's inmates to avoid him; it proved he had renounced his Catholicism. Being connected with "magic and uncanny arts" compounded the sin. It was code for pagan heresy and unorthodox scientific interests.

However, Dee could not be counted a committed Protestant either. He showed a certain partiality for Catholic rites in later life, and was comfortable among Catholic activists, such as Sir George Peckham, whom Dee advised on setting up a Catholic colony in the New World.

Such mixed messages left many of those who met him wondering where his loyalties lay. One correspondent of Francis Walsingham's was so befuddled by Dee's theology, he concluded that the philosopher must have "disliked of all religions."[13]

In fact, Dee was a deeply committed Christian. His diaries are filled with heartfelt expressions of piety, including accounts of lengthy sessions of anguished prayer and supplication conducted in his private chapel. But he refused to accept that Protestants or Catholics, the Bible, or the Pope had the monopoly of knowledge. He believed that God's truth was in the world of nature and learning as well. It was to the movements of the stars and the pages of ancient texts that humanity must look to find the common ground upon which the church had originally been built. Only on Peter's Rock, the long lost foundation of faith, could the "first beginning of unity" proclaimed by St. Cyprian and reiterated by Dee during Philpot's interrogation be restored. This was his true mission, and his behavior following his arrest by Mary was, as subsequent events showed, aimed at its fulfillment.

᭢

FOLLOWING his brush with Bartlet Green and John Philpot, Dee appeared to be very much at home in the new Catholic order. On 15 January 1556, a few days before Green's execution, he published his "Supplication to Q. Mary . . . for the recovery and preservation of ancient writers and monuments." The "monuments" to which he referred were not the statues toppled by Protestant zealots in church naves and monastical chapels, but, to Dee, the far more precious ancient and medieval manuscripts shelved in vestries and scriptoria. The tempest of the Reformation had already scattered many of these irreplaceable pages across the country. "There was no quicker merchandise than library books," John Bale later observed of the period, noting that bundles of them were routinely to be found for sale in "grocers, soapsellers, tailors, and other occupiers' shops, some in ships ready to be carried overseas into Flanders."[1] If action was not taken quickly, England's fragile intellectual infrastructure would be blown to the four corners of the earth.

Dee's plan was to send agents across the length and breadth of the country to collect or copy these works for a new "Library Royal." This great national archive would not only preserve manuscripts and books from "rot and worms," but provide a resource to which "learned men" could turn in times of religious strife and uncertainty to settle "such doubts and points of learning, as much cumber and vex their heads." For there they would find, Dee argued, that all the most troubling issues of the day—for example, the true meaning of St. Cyprian's words concerning the unity of the church, the subject of Dee's heated argument with Philpot—"are most pithily in such old monuments debated and discussed."[2] Thus would "learning wonderfully be advanced."

This visionary scheme did not receive official backing. However, it provided Dee with a pretext for pursuing his own private version of it. There followed a period of frenetic bibliographic activity. Dee crisscrossed the country in his endless search for material, keeping notes as he went: "Remember two in Wales who have excellent monuments. Mr Edward ap Roger in Raubon 7 miles from Oswestree Northward and Richard ap Edward price at Mivod X [i.e., ten] miles from Oswestree, somewhat westwards. Archdecon Crowly and Robert Crowly sometime printer had Tully's translation of Cyropaedia."[3]

Dee's desire to preserve precious texts pushed him to extreme, even criminal, measures. He borrowed four scientific manuscripts from Peterhouse in Cambridge, promising to return them but apparently failing to do so. He acquired six manuscripts from the collection of John Leland, even though he must have known that Leland's library was supposed to be in the custody of Sir John Cheke, who had recently been kidnapped by Mary's spies while exiled in Antwerp, brought home, and forced to renounce his Protestantism.[4]

As he continued with his obsessive quest for scientific texts, Dee also started work on one of his own, the *Propaedeumata Aphoristica* (Preliminary aphoristic teachings), a series of aphorisms aimed at explaining "by rational processes" astrological powers.[5]

Dee wanted to discover the "true virtues of nature." His concern was to find out how celestial events—the movement of the Sun, Moon, and planets against the stars—influenced "sublunar," that is, atmospheric and terrestrial, ones.

In the early sixteenth century, astrology was in decline in England. This was not because of a general disbelief in its powers. Indeed, no one then seriously questioned the idea that the planets influenced earthly events, any more than anyone would now question the existence of gravity. Rather, the cause of the decline was a general "torpor," as the historian Keith Thomas put it, in English mathematics.[6] It was impossible, for example, to get English ephemerides, so they had to be imported at great expense. Dee's work was to help shake England out of this torpor, and it was his *Propaedeumata* that set the trend.

In the book, Dee theorized that every entity in the universe emanated "rays" of a force that influenced other objects it struck. An example of such rays are the forces of attraction and repulsion produced by the "lodestone," magnetized iron ore. This demonstrated in miniature what was happening throughout the cosmos. The important feature of these rays for Dee was that they could be scientifically studied. Indeed, he issued a plea for more detailed astronomical studies, so that the true sizes and distances, and therefore influence, of the heavenly bodies could be established.

This became the basis of Dee's natural philosophy, and it is very tempting to see it as anticipating by more than a century Isaac Newton's groundbreaking *Principia Mathematica*, the fountainhead of the scientific revolution and modern physics. There are certainly similarities with Newton's theory of gravity: the idea of a magnetic-like force emanating from physical bodies that acts on other physical bodies; the emphasis on mathematics combined with measurement as a way of discovering how such a force works. Furthermore, like Newton, Dee believed that the universe worked according to mathematical laws, and he also believed that the sorts of principles set out in *Propaedeumata Aphoristica* provided a way of proving it.

Other works he produced around this time, few of which have survived, reinforce the view that he was moving toward a decidedly scientific view of the universe. He wrote papers on perspective, on astronomical instruments, and on the properties of circular motions. While working for Northumberland's household in 1553, he had also written a work for the duke's wife on the ebb and flow of tides, a subject directly related to the idea of gravity, and also an interest of Newton's.

He even endorsed the observation that two bodies of unequal weight fall to the ground at the same speed.[7] The acceptance that this could be the case, even though it flew in the face of common sense and accepted theories of motion, is usually attributed to Galileo (1564–1642), and is cited as proof of the great Italian astronomer's pioneering role in making observation the keystone of scientific enquiry. However, Dee knew of it (and, as he points out, so did others before him).

The *Propaedeumata Aphoristica* was no proto-*Principia Mathematica*, however, for at its heart lay a force that was magical as much as physical. This is revealed by the title page of the book, which shows the qualities of heat and humidity, the Sun and the Moon, the elements earth and water all connected via converging lines to a mystical symbol that dominates the center of the image: the monad.

The monad was a magical sign invented by Dee. He regarded it as the key to a true understanding of the unity of the cosmos. Its appearance on the title page of a rationalist production like *Propaedeumata Aphoristica* indicates that Dee's idea of physics strayed far beyond the limits of physical reality.

Dee's belief that the "rays" emanating from physical objects could affect the human soul as well as the body shows that the *Propaedeumata* was essentially an astrological work. This is why astrologers, by applying principles abstracted from centuries of practice, could divine something about a person from the configuration of the heavenly bodies at the moment of his or her birth. And that is why, with a scientific understanding of such bodies and the rays emanating from them, so much more could be achieved.

He also suggested that the tools used to manipulate light could also be used to manipulate such emanations. Lenses and mirrors might be able to concentrate, reflect, or refract these rays. They may even be able to make them visible. Perhaps (though he was circumspect on the matter, because of its connotations of conjuration), a fortune-teller's crystal ball works as a sort of lens, the material from which it is made being of such a quality that it is able to capture and focus the invisible rays at play in its immediate vicinity.

Thus at the heart of Dee's science lay what has come to be called "natural" (as opposed to supernatural) magic. When God created the universe, itself an act that Dee accepted to be beyond scientific understanding, He let loose a divine force that causes the planets to turn, the Sun to rise, the Moon to wax and wane. Magic, as Dee saw it, is the human ability to tap this force. The better our understanding of the way it drives the universe, the more powerful the magic becomes. In other words, magic is technology.

Dee did not complete *Propaedeumata*. During the final years of Mary's reign, England was stricken by a series of disasters: bad harvests and famines at home, diplomatic failures and military blunders abroad. Meanwhile, two devastating epidemics of influenza (which got its name from the belief that it was caused by malign astrological influences) swept across the country in 1557 and 1558. Dee fell seriously ill, and thought he might not have long to live. He arranged for a draft of *Propaedeumata* to be published, and handed over the rest of his literary affairs to his friend Pedro Nuñez.

Queen Mary was also in terminal decline. At the end of 1557, six months after Philip had departed for Spain, she once again announced that she was pregnant. In February 1558, in anticipation of the imminent birth, she withdrew to her chamber. As before, a baby failed to materialize, though Mary was still expecting one at the end of March. She finally gave up hope in May, and fell into a debilitating depression from which she would never recover.

Mary died on 17 November 1558. Anyone associated with her regime and religion was now dangerously exposed, chief among them Bishop Bonner and, many must have assumed, his chaplain, John Dee.

VIII

✤

FTER all the stormy, tempestuous and blustery windy
weather of Queen Mary was overblown, the darksome
clouds of discomfort dispersed, the palpable fogs and mists
of most intolerable misery consumed, and the dashing showers of
persecution overpast, it pleased God to send England a calm and
quiet season, a clear and lovely sunshine, a quietus from former
broils, and a world of blessings by good Queen Elizabeth."[1] Thus
the chronicler Raphael Holinshed, writing in the 1570s, announced
the passing of Mary and the arrival of Elizabeth.

Elizabeth ascended the throne uncontested. In a scene that sub-
limely combines the Protestant virtues of humanism, piety, and
humility, legend records that she received the news while sitting
alone beneath an oak at Hatfield House reading the New Testament
in Greek. One of the two nobles sent to announce her succession
was the earl of Pembroke, who, having switched his allegiance from
Northumberland to Mary, managed with equal agility to switch
back again, and was rewarded with a position in Elizabeth's council, though never with her personal affection or admiration.

Elizabeth entered London less than a week after her half-sister's
death, and was received with rapture. Bonner stood in line at the
walls of the City to welcome her. She offered her hand to the mayor
and his aldermen to be kissed, but when Bonner approached and
knelt before her, she withdrew her hand and passed along. This,
everyone immediately realized, was a woman who was going to
make a clean break with the past, theologically as well as politically.

Another sign of her intentions was her decision to appoint
Robert Dudley, her intimate favorite, a radical Protestant and the

son of the disgraced duke of Northumberland, as chief organizer of her coronation.

Dudley enthusiastically accepted the role, and decided he needed the help of a scholar to set the date of the ceremony, someone who could draw on the most ancient and respected astrological and historical authorities to determine the best day. His appointment was a surprising one. He did not choose from among the ranks of persecuted exiles tentatively returning to the country. Instead he selected a man who, at least according to Foxe, reeked of the smoke from Bonner's bonfires: John Dee.

*   *   *

CHOOSING THE DATE of Elizabeth's coronation was not simply a matter of scheduling. It was a highly sensitive decision. The prospect of her reign was by no means regarded with the unbridled enthusiasm that, following the triumph of the Armada, Protestant chroniclers would retrospectively assume. England had endured two troubled experiments in monarchy with Edward, the first sovereign anointed by a Protestant church, and Mary, the first queen regnant.[2] The idea of a third that combined these apparently disastrous innovations aroused deep apprehension.

As the daughter of Anne Boleyn, the offspring of Henry's assault on the unity of the church, Elizabeth's inheritance of the divine right of sovereignty represented a challenge to the political, even cosmic, order. Indeed, Mary had found the idea of Elizabeth being Henry's child literally inconceivable, and assumed her father must have really been Boleyn's lute player, Mark Smeaton. Making her queen meant that England would be committed to a course of Protestant reformation from which it would be very hard to return.

Elizabeth's sex amplified the sense of uncertainty. The combination of femininity with majesty was still regarded by many as highly combustible. Mary had been the first English queen to rule her subjects, rather than act as their king's consort. Perhaps, some speculated, it was her gender as much as her religion that had made her reign such a difficult one, responsible for civil and religious unrest at home, and military failure abroad. John Knox had issued his famous *First Blast of the Trumpet against the Monstrous Regiment of Women* in 1558, the final year of Mary's reign. For him the idea of female government was so outrageous that it demanded a new term—"monstriferous." Calvin wrote to William Cecil that it "was a deviation from the primitive and established order of nature, it ought to be held as a judgement on man for his dereliction of his rights."[3]

The prognostications of the French prophet Nostradamus for 1559, the first full year of Elizabeth's reign, seemed to confirm Calvin's view. They were translated into English and widely read, foretelling "divers calamities, weepings and mournings" and "civil sedition" that would make the "lowest" rise up against the "highest."[4]

Thus, the selection of the date that inaugurated this experiment would have been regarded as crucial. It needed to muster all the favorable auspices that ancient authorities could provide, and counter all the doom mongers and naysayers by showing that God would bless such an ordination.

> *O, when degree is shak'd*
> *Which is the ladder of all high designs*
> *The enterprise is sick!*

observed Ulysses in Shakespeare's *Troilus and Cressida*.

> *Take but degree away, untune that string,*
> *And hark what discord follows!*[5]

Nostradamus had foretold such discord, and this is what Dee, in his selection of Elizabeth's coronation day, had to prevent.

Dee certainly had the qualifications. His *Propaedeumata* had established him as one of the country's leading natural philosophers, and revived interest in mathematically based astrology (as opposed to the sort of divination practiced by Nostradamus). His frantic bibliographic activity during Mary's reign had also armed him with a formidable array of ancient texts from which he could cite precedents and authorities.

However, this was not enough to erase the stigma of his association with Bonner, which, thanks to the work of Foxe and others, was already widely suspected, if not known. There must have been some other redeeming quality.

A clue lies in the treatment Dee received in Foxe's account of Bonner's persecutions. In the first edition of *Acts and Monuments*, which was being completed in Basel around this time, Dee's involvement with Bonner is fully documented. However, by the 1576 edition, he has completely disappeared. His words are still there, but every occurrence of his name (more than ten) has been deleted, or substituted with the anonymous label "a Doctor."

This privilege of erasure is almost unique to Dee in a work that is otherwise notable for naming names. For example, in one of Philpot's interrogations, Dee is joined by another doctor, one Chedsey, whom Foxe did not allow the same anonymity, not even when they appeared in the same sentence.[6] Perhaps Foxe removed Dee's name because he was threatened with legal action, or was pressured by the court. But this seems unlikely. *Acts and Monuments* became one of the most revered texts of the Elizabethan age, the queen commanding a copy to be lodged in every cathedral library in the country. A more probable explanation is that Foxe learned that Dee was up to something while he was in Bonner's household, and this something meant that the portrayal of him in *Acts and Monuments* as a Catholic colluder was unfair.

In a deposition made to the commissioners sent to interview him by Elizabeth in 1582, Dee clearly states that his arrest and handover to Bonner resulted from his being engaged upon "some travails for her Majesty's behalf." He had undertaken these unspecified travails "to the comfort of her Majesty's favourers then, and some of her principal servants, at Woodstock," Woodstock being the palace where Elizabeth was held under arrest. These "favourers" undoubtedly included Robert Dudley. They also included one John Ashley, who had since become Master of the Queen's Jewel House. Dudley was dead by the time Dee came to be interviewed by the queen's commissioners, but Ashley was still alive, and Dee invited them to go and ask the Master about the Bonner years should they disbelieve his claims.

Of course, these "travails" may have been an invention, made up to exculpate Dee from accusations of complicity with Bonner's burnings. But as Dee well knew, his testimonial to the commissioners would be read by Elizabeth, and she was obviously in a position to confirm whether or not, at least in this respect, it was true.

It therefore seems reasonable to assume that Dee's presence in Bonner's household was known about, perhaps even encouraged, by Elizabeth and her supporters. This would explain why, having been deprived of the rectorship of Upton following his arrest in 1553, he was now awarded the living at Leadenham in Lincolnshire, presented to him by two members of the Stanley family, Sir William and Henry, Lord Strange.[7]

Thus it was not as a shamed member of a failed regime that Dee emerged into the limelight in late 1558, but as the loyal ally of a glorious new one, as an "intelligencer," in all the possible meanings of that peculiar Elizabethan term: a seeker of hidden knowledge, philosophical and scientific, as well as political.

*   *   *

THE CHRISTMAS FESTIVITIES of 1558–1559 provided Catholic onlookers with disturbing omens of Elizabeth's religious policies. "Your lordship will have heard of the farce performed in the presence of Her Majesty on Epiphany Day," wrote a concerned ambassador to his Spanish duke, referring to a Twelfth Night masque. The poor man was appalled by the "mummery performed after supper, of crows in the habits of cardinals, of asses habited as bishops, and of wolves representing abbots." "I will consign it to silence," he added.[8]

In the midst of these revelries, Dee set about writing a long and detailed analysis of the astrological auguries for Elizabeth's reign. He chose 15 January 1559 as its start date. His reasons, along with the document setting them out, are lost, but he was no doubt swayed by such factors as Jupiter being in Aquarius, suggesting the emergence of such statesmanlike qualities as impartiality, independence, and tolerance, and Mars in Scorpio providing the passion and commitment needed of a prince.[9] Such a day would mark the nativity of a great monarch.

Having set the date, Dee was invited by Robert Dudley for an audience with the queen at Whitehall Palace, magnificently restored by her father, Henry, as his main London residence.

At the appointed time, Dee passed through the three-story entrance gate of checkered flint and stone either designed by or lived in by Henry's chief artist, Hans Holbein, and approached the Great Hall built by Cardinal Wolsey to be presented to her majesty by Dudley and the earl of Pembroke. He remembered vividly what she said to him that day: "Where my brother hath given him a crown, I will give him a noble." It was a clever play on the names of coins, the noble being a gold piece worth two silver crowns. But this was not an offer of small change. She was promising a doubling of the fortunes he had enjoyed under Edward. He was to become a favored member of her court, a player in the great Protestant era to come.

Dee might even for an instant have imagined she meant more. Was there not a suggestion, a hint—Dee's mathematical mind could have calculated the implications in an instant—that she was promising him not just a noble but *nobility*—title, money, lands, respect, reckoning for the "hard dealing" that had ruined his father and deprived him of an inheritance, the restoration of the Dee dynasty, the independence to develop new ideas, the resources to build up his library, and the influence to found his scientific academy?

There was no time to dwell on such dreams. Only a few days remained before the coronation date Dee had selected, and frantic preparations were already under way. There was such a surge in demand for crimson silk and cloth of gold and silver that customs officers were instructed to impound all available stock. Such an order would once have been carried out by Dee's father, Roland, but he was dead by 1555, before the change of regime could save him.[10]

On the coronation eve, Elizabeth processed from the Tower of London to the Palace of Westminster, where she was to make her preparations for the ceremony. A series of magnificent pageants were performed on huge scaffolds erected along the route: at Gracechurch Street a "Pageant of the Roses" represented the Tudor dynasty on a three-tiered platform, at Cornhill and Little Conduit a play on the theme of time. At Cheapside, inappropriately named for this occasion, she paused to receive a gift of 1,000 gold marks, presented by the City Recorder. She passed on toward Westminster through Temple Bar, an archway marking the City's western limit upon which had been mounted huge statues of Gogmagog and Corineus, giants featured in the story of Brutus, a legendary king of ancient Britain who would come to play a prominent part in Dee's own explorations of British mythology.

The following morning, with the streets "new-laid with gravel and blue cloth and railed on each side,"[11] Elizabeth appeared at the doors of Westminster Hall attired in her coronation robes, made of cloth-of-gold, trimmed in ermine and stitched with jewels. Her auburn hair was down, emphasizing her maidenly youth. She processed toward Westminster Abbey beneath a canopy carried by the Barons of the Cinque Ports, followed by nobles, heralds, and bishops. The carpet upon which she trod, dusted with snow, disappeared as she went, the crowds lining the route scrambling to tear off samples to keep or sell as souvenirs.

Dee would have had his place in the abbey, though not in the nave, which was reserved for the nobles who were called upon to declare Elizabeth's rightful claim to the throne. Illuminated by thousands of torches, candles, and the weak winter light penetrating the stained glass windows, standing beneath a thick canopy of tapestries amid a forest of soaring Gothic pillars, surrounded by the chants of choirs and cries of acclamation, Elizabeth then played her role in the ancient act of pagan magic that works a mortal human into a sovereign.

She emerged from the abbey bearing the enchanted instruments of government, the orb representing the cosmos, the scepter, the magic wand of authority, and the crown, the halo of monarchy. Smiling and calling to the crowd in a way that at least one observer thought indecorous, she walked back to Westminster Hall, where a great banquet was held that lasted until one o'clock the following morning, culminating with the queen's champion clattering into the hall mounted on a great steed and dressed in full armor, to challenge anyone who questioned her title.

PART THREE

THE MOST
PRECIOUS JEWEL

❧

When Faustus had with pleasure ta'en the view
Of rarest things, and royal courts of kings,
He stayed his course, and so returned home,
Where such as bear his absence, but with grief,
I mean his friends and nearest companions,
Did gratulate his safety with kind words,
And in their conference of what befell,
Touching his journey through the world and air,
They put forth questions of astrology.

CHRISTOPHER MARLOWE,
The Tragedie of Dr. Faustus

✤

SOON after Elizabeth's coronation, Dee performed a disappearing act. For nearly five years, he is absent from the historical record.[1] All that can be divined was that he spent much of his time abroad, continued collecting books, and started to explore a new field of research: the Cabala.

The Cabala was a potent combination of language, mathematics, and mysticism based around the Hebrew language. Dee had taught himself Hebrew, and acquired his first Hebrew texts around this time. Thanks to the influence of humanists such as John Cheke, there had been a growth of interest in the language along with the study of Greek, because of its potential to release the knowledge contained in ancient texts. But for the Cabalists, Hebrew was much more than another language, because encoded within it, they believed, were the secrets of the universe.

"In the beginning was the Word," as St. John put it. Dee and his contemporaries assumed that Word to have been in Hebrew, or rather in the purified form from which it was derived, before it became corrupted by Adam's Fall. Thus, to Dee, an analysis of Hebrew was a way of discovering the structure that underlay God's creation. The laws of nature were its grammar, the stuff of physical reality its nouns.

Cabalism had obscure origins going back to first-century Palestine, and by the sixteenth century was regarded in orthodox academic circles with the same suspicion as mathematics, with which it shared many features. Among the multiplicity of methods it used to study language was Gematria, which involved searching for numbers that could be substituted for each letter of the Hebrew alphabet. By then performing arithmetical operations with these numbers, for example, by "adding" two words together, it was hoped to find a mathematical relationship underlying the language that would show how one phrase related to another.

Another feature of the Cabala was its numerological preoccupation with angels. Indeed, one of the purposes of Gematria was to work out how many there were (as many as 301,655,172 according to some calculations).[2] It also provided a means for working out their names, and their relationships to each other. For example, it identified the seventy-two angels who provide a route to understanding the "sephiroth," the "ten names most common to God" that together make his "one great name." The names of such angels were derived from the Hebrew description of their function, suffixed with an ending such as "el" or "iah."

These angels live at the top, divine level of the Cabala's three-tiered universe. Below them lay the celestial level of the stars, and at the bottom the elemental level of the physical world. This structure is reflected in the Hebrew language itself, in the three parts of Hebrew speech and the twenty-two letters in the Hebrew alphabet, which are divided into two groups of nine letters and one of four, corresponding to the nine orders of angels, nine spheres, and four elements.

Such correspondences strike the modern mind as meaningless. Meric Casaubon, who would publish Dee's spiritual diaries a century later, and found his subject at turns bewildering and bewitching, warned that "some men come into the world with Cabalistical Brains, their heads are full of mysteries. . . . Out of the very ABC that children are taught . . . they will fetch all the Secrets of God's Wisdom."[3] There is no question that Dee had such a brain, and it was at its busiest during this period, culminating with a paper he wrote on the subject in 1562, which has not survived.[4]

Worse from the puritanical Meric's point of view, the Cabala was more than a theory. It had a practical, magical side too. Since language was tied into the formation of the universe, words had the potential to change it. Cabalism provided a technology for engineering incantations that could summon spirits and influence events, as prayers are supposed to do, but formulated according to the systematic, almost scientific principles of the Cabala. And, unlike prayers, such incantations would work whether you were Catholic or Protestant.[5]

There is no evidence that Dee tried to use the Cabala in this way at this stage in his career. He was, however, fascinated by another practical use, an application of particular interest in the tense political atmosphere of Reformation Europe, where governments were eager to find ways of preserving their own secrets and discovering those of their rivals: the creation of secret codes and ciphers.

*   *   *

IN FEBRUARY 1563, Dee reappears in the busy merchant town of Antwerp, staying at the sign of the Golden Angel. He was engaged in his endless, cripplingly expensive search for interesting, important, and sometimes illicit works to add to his library, and he was about to make what he considered to be the find of his life.

Antwerp was filled with the escalating clatter of printing presses. It boasted one of the world's most important publishing firms, founded by Christopher Plantin, whose "Officina Plantiniana" workshop turned out thousands of Christian and humanist works that were distributed across Europe and as far afield as the Spanish colonies in Mexico and South America. Plantin also produced several heretical works, notably those of Hendrik Niclaes, founder of the "Family of Love." This secretive sect, whose members came to be called "Familists," counted among its number Dee's friend the mapmaker Abraham Ortelius, and the Birkmanns, a powerful bookselling family based in Cologne, whose London shop Dee patronized continuously over a forty-year period, falling into conversation with anyone who happened to be there.[6]

The Familists invited all "lovers of truth . . . of what nation and religion soever they be, Christian, Jews, Mahomites, or Turks, and heathen" to become part of a learned brotherhood.[7] They also believed that members could show allegiance to any prevailing religious doctrine in order to promote the movement's aims of developing an all-embracing theology. This reflected Dee's own view, and it is likely he knew of and was sympathetic with the sect.[8]

During the winter of 1563, Dee heard rumors that a copy of one of the most secret and precious manuscripts in circulation, for which scholars from all over Europe had been searching since the turn of the century, had turned up in Antwerp. It was called *Steganographia*, and had been written by the German abbot Johannes Trithemius.

Trithemius was one of the founders of modern cryptography, the science of codes. He wrote the first published work on the subject, *Polygraphia*, which appeared in 1518. He was born in 1462 and took his name from Trittenheim, a town on the left bank of the Moselle in Germany. He claimed not to be able to read until he was fifteen. At that age he had a dream in which he was presented with two tablets, one inscribed with writing, the other with pictures. He was told to choose between them, and chose the tablet with writing because of his "longing for knowledge of Scripture."[9]

He joined the Benedictine abbey of Sponheim, which was then "poor, undisciplined, ruinous, and virtually without furniture." In July 1483, he was appointed abbot, and embarked on a complete renovation of the place, transforming it into a center of learning. He built a lodge for visiting scholars, decorating the walls with classical and contemporary prose and poetry. He also rebuilt the library, increasing its holdings from just forty-eight volumes to 2,000.

Trithemius's book-collecting drew him toward the study of the Cabala, and his work became a strong influence for many of the great mystic scholars of the early sixteenth century, notably Henry Cornelius Agrippa of Nettesheim, who was a pupil. Agrippa was the leading writer on mysticism and magic of the Renaissance. His shadow "made all Europe honour him," as Marlowe put it in his play *Dr. Faustus*.

As with Dee, Trithemius's interest in such subjects led to his being accused of "trafficking" with demons. It was even said that he conjured up the bride of the German emperor Maximilian I soon after her death so the emperor could see her once more. As Trithemius kept his work increasingly secret to avoid such accusations, so they became ever more insistent and threatening.

Dee knew of the accusations against Trithemius, and placed him alongside Socrates and Pico della Mirandola, the pioneer of a Christian form of the Cabala, as a victim of intolerance. Like Dee, Trithemius drew a sharp division between magic and superstition.

Magic was about knowledge, the study of the hidden forces, spiritual as well as physical, that rule nature. Superstition exploited ignorance. Thus Trithemius called for witches and wizards to be rooted out, and attacked the sort of fortune-telling practiced by the likes of Nostradamus as "empty and foolish."

Trithemius summed up his career as follows: "I always wanted to know what was knowable in the world. . . . But it was not within my power to satisfy the desire as I wished." This was a sentiment that Dee would one day echo. But just now, with his growing library of texts, his knowledge of languages and science, his influence at court, and friendship with Europe's leading intellectuals, Dee seemed to be poised on the very threshold of satisfaction.

And to top it all, he had within his grasp a copy of *Steganographia*.

Trithemius had started work on the book between 1499 and 1500. As he was writing it, he sent a letter to his friend Arnold Bostius, a Carmelite monk who lived in Ghent, in which he boasted that once finished it would be a "great work . . . that, if it should ever be published (which God forbid) the whole world will wonder at." He promised that it would contain a host of hidden writing systems, a way of transmitting messages over great distances using fire, a method of teaching Latin in two hours, and a form of communication that can be achieved while eating, sitting, or walking without speech, facial expressions, or signs. Unfortunately, Bostius had died before the letter arrived, and it was read with horror by his brother Carmelites, who circulated it in an attempt to discredit its author.

A further setback came around 1500 when Trithemius was visited by an officious dignitary called Carolus Bovillus. Bovillus later reported that "I hoped that I would enjoy a pleasing visit with a philosopher; but I discovered him to be a magician." It was his perusal of the *Steganographia*, in particular its lists of the "barbarous and strange names of spirits" in languages he did not recognize, that convinced him of this.[10]

Trithemius abandoned the work and died in 1516. The *Steganographia* lived on, thanks to its advance publicity, and manuscript copies of three of the four books mentioned by Bovillus were thought to have survived. They soon acquired a mythical status, and became as sought after as such legendary lost texts as Aristotle's missing dialogues.

Hence John Dee's excitement when at last he heard of the existence of a copy of the manuscript in Antwerp. Getting his hands on it proved difficult. It involved him spending all his traveling money, some £20, perhaps on bribes, and working through an intermediary, a mysterious "nobleman of Hungary," who in return demanded that Dee "pleasure him . . . with such points of science as . . . he requireth."[11] Even then, he could keep the manuscript for only ten days.

Tucked away in his lodgings at the sign of the Golden Angel, perhaps on his own, or with the distracting presence of the Hungarian noble watching over his shoulder, he began transcribing the work. It was a difficult task. Ignoring any problems of legibility, the manuscript was a difficult one to copy. It was filled with tables of numbers and endless lists of nearly identical and apparently meaningless names. He had to work round the clock to get the job done in time.

On 16 February 1563, his marathon job completed, he managed to force his tired fingers to pen one further document: a letter to William Cecil, Queen Elizabeth's key minister, reporting the discovery of this, "the most precious jewel that I have yet of other men's travails recovered," and begging for some recompense to his costs, which had left him virtually penniless.[12] This discovery, he wanted to show Cecil, demonstrated why Elizabeth's regime needed someone with his contacts and understanding scouring the Continent for new texts and ideas, and why it was worth paying him to allow him to continue.

*   *   *

WHEN DEE WROTE his letter to Cecil, he knew that when he passed it into the hands of his messenger—perhaps a weary English traveler on his way home, or a Dutch merchant shipping "fattes and mawndes" to London—it was about to embark on a long and perilous journey that could last a few days or several weeks. Furthermore, he had no means of knowing when or even if it would reach its destination.

As every sixteenth-century prince and general knew, distance was the first enemy. Roads were often impassable, "noisome sloughs," "so gulled with the fall of water that passengers cannot pass."[13] Despite such barriers and discomforts, despite the enormous and, in Dee's case, crippling cost, Tudor nobles, scholars, and merchants craved travel. There was a constant traffic of people and goods across Europe, and as a result, growing interdependence between regions. A system that promised instant communications over unlimited distances was of obvious importance, and that was one of the many innovations that Trithemius had boasted to Bostius the *Steganographia* contained.

When Dee finally managed to read the manuscript for himself, he found that Trithemius was apparently equal to his word. The work was divided into three books, the last of which was incomplete and of a rather different nature from the first two. Books I and II describe an enormously elaborate system for sending messages between two people using unintelligible incantations.

Trithemius gave several examples of how the system would work. For instance, the sender of a message first writes it out, using any language he chooses, on a piece of paper, after a preamble of paternosters and other such supplications. He then speaks a special formula to summon one of the many spirits identified by Trithemius, say, Padiel:

> Padiel aporsy mesarpon omeuas peludyn malpreaxo. Condusen, vlearo thersephi bayl merphon, paroys gebuly mailthomyon ilthear tamarson acrimy lon peatha Casmy Chertiel, medony reabdo, lasonti iaciel mal arti bulomeon abry pathulmon theoma pathormyn.[14]

Padiel should then appear, whereupon the sender hands over the message. The spirit takes it to the recipient, who must speak another incantation, thus causing the original message to be revealed.

To complicate matters, the sender must learn the "places, names, and signs of the principal spirits, lest through ignorance one calls from the north a spirit dwelling in the south; which would not only hinder the purpose but might also injure the operator."[15] There are hundreds of thousands of spirits, some of which appear in the day, others of which prefer the dark of the night, some subordinate to others, each with its own sign. Books I and II of the *Steganographia* list many of them, giving details of their powers and peculiarities and the conjurations needed to call them.

Book III, which is incomplete, is very different. It begins by promising even greater feats of communication than the first two books, which are based on the discoveries of an ancient and apparently fictional philosopher called Menastor. In the tradition of occult knowledge, the findings have been, Trithemius warns, presented in a way so that "to men of learning and men deeply engaged in the study of magic, it might, by the Grace of God, be in some degree intelligible" but not to "thick-skinned turnip-eaters."[16]

Instead of endless epistles, Book III is filled with tables. They are messily laid out, except for the first, which appears in the book's preface. This assigns numerical values for twenty-one spirits, each of which is associated with one of the seven planets. There will, Trithemius promises, be seven chapters in the following book, one for each planet.

Chapter 1, the only chapter to survive, duly follows with a description of how to call on the help of Saturn to communicate with a fellow adept. It is accompanied by a series of numerical tables that are apparently to be used to perform astronomical calculations.

It would be another forty years before the manuscript that Dee now had in his possession would be published. It first appeared in 1606 in Frankfurt, together with a shorter work called the *Clavis* or "key" to the *Steganographia*. It was the *Clavis* that revealed Trithemius's true purpose. The apparently nonsensical spiritual incantations in the first two books turned out to be coded messages. For example, in the case of the call for Padiel:

Padiel aporsy mesarpon omeuas peludyn malpreaxo

the message, or "plain text" as cryptographers now call it, was encoded in the alternate letters of alternate words:

padiel aPoRsY mesarpon oMeUaS peludyn mAlPrEaXo

which yields the words "Primus apex." The *Clavis* thus showed that Books I and II of the *Steganographia* were not really about magic. They were full of ciphers, for which Europe's political tensions had produced a growing demand. However, the *Clavis* did not include a key for Book III. Did this mean it was really a work of magic? Or was it, too, a code book? The question remained unresolved for centuries. Gustavus Selenus, the pseudonym of Duke August II of Brunswick-Lüneburg, reprinted Book III in his definitive 1624 study, *Cryptomenytices et Cryptographiae*, establishing Trithemius's position as a founding father of modern cryptography, but offered no solution. W. E. Heidel claimed to have cracked the code in 1676, but published his results in the form of a series of equally indecipherable cryptograms, thereby managing merely to add to the mystery.

By the late twentieth century, most scholars seem to have given up on the task, and have consigned the work to the realm of the occult.[17] Then, in the late 1990s, two people settled the matter once and for all, one in 1993, the other in 1996. The first to succeed was a German linguist working in America, Thomas Ernst.[18] The second, who had no idea of Ernst's success until he had published his own paper, was Jim Reeds, working in the Mathematics and Cryptography Research Department at the American communications company AT&T. Reeds's diligent efforts at analyzing this and other mysterious texts associated with Dee have proved extraordinarily successful.

What Ernst and Reeds discovered was that the third book of the *Steganographia* did indeed contain a code. There were hints as to how it might work in the tables and the text. For example, Reeds noticed that the first column of the table in the preface contained multiples of twenty-five. What was the significance of this number? There was also a passage in the first chapter that seemed to be suggestive:

If you wish to operate in Steganography . . . you must first of all acquaint yourself with [Saturn's] various and diverse motions; and first the various motions, pure, proper, mixed, direct, retrograde and perplexed.

Using a combination of skill and guesswork, Reeds worked out that the numbers in the tables seemed to represent letters of an alphabet, with each letter being represented by a number added to a multiple of twenty-five. Lengthy analysis revealed the alphabet to comprise twenty-two of the Roman characters (A to Z minus J, K, and W), supplemented by three other symbols. It was also in reverse order, which was perhaps what Trithemius was hinting at in his reference to the "retrograde" motions of Saturn.

Reeds confirmed that the key was correct by trying it out on various sections of the book. For example, a series of numbers in the first table spelled out "Ioannes," the Latin form of John, Trithemius's first name. A selection of words in one of the tables in chapter 1 contained some German words that translate into the phrase "the bringer of this letter is a bad rogue and a thief." Reeds found another puzzling phrase, this one apparently in Latin. It was repeated several times: "Gaza frequens Libycos duxit Carthago triumphos." It turns out to be a pangram, a phrase that contains all the letters of the alphabet (like "the quick brown fox jumps over the lazy dog").[19]

Having broken the code, he found that the tables could be made to yield up their secrets for the first time in half a millennium. Unfortunately these secrets proved not to be particularly informative. Besides one or two gnomic phrases, the remainder of the plain text seemed to be unintelligible nonsense. This may be because the plain text is itself in some way encoded, or because the tables became corrupted over their years of underground circulation in manuscript form.

Nevertheless, the discovery of the true purpose of Book III of the *Steganographia* was a breakthrough, proving for the first time that it was primarily a work of cryptography, not magic.

But one question remains unanswered: whether Dee realized that the *Steganographia* was a code book. It is not even clear whether he had seen the *Clavis*, the key to Books I and II. So when he so excitedly commended the work to William Cecil as "meeter" (i.e., more suitable or useful) and "more behoveful" (more beneficial) to "your honor or a Prince" (Queen Elizabeth) than any other, what did he mean? Meet and behoveful for what, exactly? Spiritual communication is a possibility, but an unlikely one. As Dee well knew, Cecil was a very practical and conservative man, and, though he undoubtedly accepted the existence of spirits, was unlikely to have been persuaded to practice the sorts of elaborate rituals Trithemius described.[20]

Dee was fascinated by and evidently expert in cryptography. He owned several copies of Trithemius's *Polygraphia*, which was explicitly about codes, and studied other key texts on the subject, notably Jacques Gohorry's *De usu & mysteriis notarum* and Jacopo Silvestri's *Opus novum*, the latter of which Dee used to practice writing in cipher for himself.[21] Thus, when he promised Cecil that the book would advance the "secret sciences," he was not necessarily referring to the occult.

At the time Dee sent his letter, Cecil was just beginning to put in place the espionage network that, under Francis Walsingham, his successor as spy master, would become one of the most formidable and effective in Europe. This network came to rely heavily on codes.[22]

However, Dee did not see the *Stegonographia* as just a political or diplomatic tool. He considered the text to have other, more esoteric uses as well. Cryptography, particularly of the sort practiced by Trithemius, was closely connected to the Cabala, and it was conceivable that the same techniques used in the *Steganographia* could be used to decipher other texts written in forgotten or corrupted languages. One that would arouse particular excitement was called the "Book of Soyga," an anonymous tome that Dee came to believe contained an ancient, even divine message written in the language originally spoken by Adam—in other words the true, unspoiled word of God. Another was a mysterious volume attributed to Roger Bacon that in coming centuries would become notorious among cryptanalysts as the Voynich Manuscript.[23] It has yet to be deciphered. The study of codes, which was also the study of the structure of language, might yield the magic key to decoding such texts and revealing the messages they contained.

Beyond even that, Dee was commending the *Steganographia* to Cecil because it was an example of the sort of intellectual treasures that the Continent held and that England so conspicuously lacked.

In his letter to Cecil, he deplored the lack of an English philosopher able to produce works "in the Science *De Numeris formalibus*, the Science *De Ponderibus mysticis*, and ye Science *De Mensuris diuinis*: (by which three, the huge frame of this world is fashioned . . .)." His travels, his scholasticism, his access to rare texts and Europe's leading thinkers, his observations, and his studies meant that he could be such a philosopher, and thus open up to the English court the riches of the Renaissance.

X

❧

WHEN infancy and childhood are past, the choice of a future way of life begins to present itself to young men as a problem," Dee wrote while he was still in Antwerp. "Having hesitated for some time at the crossroads of their wavering judgment, they at last come to a decision: Some (who have fallen in love with truth and virtue) will for the rest of their lives devote their entire energy to the pursuit of philosophy, while others (ensnared by the enticements of this world or burning with a desire for riches) cannot but devote all their energies to a life of pleasure and profit."[1]

From this earnest assessment, it is clear in which direction Dee imagined he would go. But when he returned to England after his lengthy Continental tour, he was to find the choice was not as clear-cut as he had assumed it to be.

He arrived at Greenwich Palace on 14 June 1564, accompanied by Elizabeth, the marchioness of Northampton, and a slender volume entitled *Monas Hieroglyphica* (The hieroglyphic monad).

The marchioness had arrived in Antwerp in April, just as Dee was preparing to come home. She was suffering from breast cancer, and was there to consult physicians, hoping to benefit from the more advanced state of medical knowledge to be found in the Low Countries. Dee offered to accompany her home, and in return she promised to help reintroduce him to the court.

The first thing he did was show Elizabeth the *Monas*. He considered it to be his most important work to date. He had felt "pregnant" with it for seven years, and then had written it in a fit of intellectual and mystical rapture lasting just twelve days.

For a man once arrested for "calculing," and still arousing suspicion because of his interest in the "uncanny arts," the presentation of such a work as the *Monas* to the queen was a risky one. It was filled with magical ideas, deeply influenced by Continental thinking, dangerously preoccupied with what churchmen, of both Catholic and Protestant persuasions, considered to be pagan matters, combining numerology, the Cabala, astrology, cosmology, and mathematics. This may explain why Dee decided to dedicate it not to the queen, but the newly crowned Holy Roman Emperor, Maximilian II, nephew of Charles V of Spain. As Dee had discovered during a stay the previous year at the emperor's court in Bratislava, Maximilian was broad-minded and shared an interest in the sorts of ideas the *Monas* explored. Dee had no guarantee that Elizabeth would show such a broad-minded attitude.

Perhaps he presented the work to her as a test, to see if the queen and her realm were ready to embrace the sort of philosopher skilled in the science *De Ponderibus mysticis* that he had told Cecil England lacked and that he had now become.

Elizabeth's response was encouraging. She was intrigued, if baffled, by the *Monas* and promised she would become Dee's "scholar" if he disclosed "unto her the secrets of that book."[2] The two of them sat together "perusing" the mysterious work, queen and subject, pupil and master, magician and apprentice, adept and novice. She became, he later proclaimed, a "sacred witness" of its secrets.[3]

The title refers to a symbol or hieroglyph. The same symbol appeared on the title page on the *Propaedeumata*. Like *Propaedeumata*, *Monas* also comprises a series of theorems. However, there the similarities between the two works end. Where the *Propaedeumata* is about observation and experimentation, the *Monas* arises out of pure thought and mystical intuition.

A clue to its meaning is contained in a question Dee posed in his dedication to Maximilian: "Is it not rare, I ask, that the common astronomical symbols of the planets, instead of being dead, dumb, or, up to the present hour at least, quasi-barbaric signs, should have become characters imbued with immortal life and should now be able to express their especial meanings most eloquently in any tongue and to any nation?"[4] It was "as if in an age long past they had been the same, or as if our forefathers had wished that in the future they would be such."

In other words, Dee thought that the "astronomical" symbols appeared to be the relics of a long lost universal language that transcended national and, by implication, religious barriers. The aim of the *Monas* was to test this hypothesis by looking for suggestive structures within the symbols themselves.

What he claimed to have discovered, the "very rarest thing of all," was that all the symbols could be combined into one, a variant on the sign for Mercury. This was the symbol that formed the central motif of the *Monas*, a symbol exemplifying the unity of the universe.

Despite the book's inherent dangers, or perhaps because of them, Elizabeth seemed to be drawn to the *Monas*. She even suggested she might act upon its findings.[5] In the dedication, Dee wrote that if Maximilian "will look at [the book] with attention, still greater mysteries will present themselves such as we have described in our cosmopolitical theories."[6] Presumably the same would apply to Elizabeth.

Unfortunately, the nature of these "cosmopolitical theories" remains obscure, as the work in which Dee expounded them has apparently gone missing. Dee later used the term "cosmopolitical" in the sense of cosmopolitan, referring to the idea of a more global perspective of political affairs. In one book he described himself as being a "Cosmopolites," a "Citizen and Member of the whole and only one Mystical City Universal."[7] Perhaps these theories in some way related to his ideas on imperialism, a vision of the emergence of world government run according to universal Christian principles.

Whether or not these were the "cosmopolitical" concerns that Dee discussed with Elizabeth, she was beguiled by them, and she "in most heroical and princely wise did comfort me and encourage me in my studies."

He needed all the comfort and encouragement he could get, as the book received a less welcome reception in other quarters. "University Graduates of high degree," Dee later wrote, "dispraised it, because they understood it not."[8] He does not say why, but its unorthodox treatment of essentially foreign philosophical and mathematical ideas were likely reasons.

Dee's relationship with English academia had been deteriorating since he left Trinity College in 1548. The first sign of trouble had come in 1554, when he turned down a post to teach the "Mathematical Sciences" at Oxford. The *Monas* marked a decisive split. In his preface to the English edition of Euclid's *Elements* he pointedly identified the book's readership as "unlatined people, and not University scholars." He increasingly saw the latter as provincial, dogmatic, and mathematically illiterate.

This antagonism may have preserved his intellectual freedom, but it came at a high price. An independent mind needs independent means, but, thanks to his father's catastrophic fall from grace during Mary's reign, that luxury was denied him. Without the support of an academic stipend, he had to look elsewhere to make a living.

There was really only one alternative: the court, which was filled with the very people he had so roundly condemned for becoming "ensnared by the enticements of this world or burning with a desire for riches."

*   *   *

IN HIS POEM "The Lie," Sir Walter Raleigh famously described the court as a place that "glows and shines like rotting wood." Its theatricals were spectacular, often entertaining, but always deadly serious. The stakes were very high: wealth, status, power or poverty, oblivion, annihilation. In the Presence Chamber of the queen's palaces, where the courtiers gathered each day to catch Elizabeth's attention and, it was hoped, her favors, the selective pressures were intense and remorseless. It was survival of the quickest, smartest, sharpest, prettiest, wittiest.

Everything revolved around Elizabeth. For courtiers such as the poet Sir John Davies, she was at the center of the universe, almost literally, and they railed against the newfangled Copernicanism espoused by Dee and his like, for fear it might knock her and their whole world off balance. In a poem inspired by the sight of the queen dancing, Davies wrote:

Only the earth doth stand for ever still,
Her rocks remove not nor her mountains meet;
(Although some wits enricht with learning's skill
Say heav'n stands firm and that the earth doth fleet
And swiftly turneth under their feet):
Yet, though the earth is ever steadfast seen,
On her broad breast hath dancing ever been.[9]

Those who fell out of Elizabeth's orbit found themselves banished into utter darkness, without money, influence, or prospects. Following some unrecorded slight or insult, the poet and diplomat Sir Edward Dyer, Dee's pupil and close, if sometimes troublesome, friend, was banished for years, and driven to the edge of destitution. He eventually won his way back by staging a spectacular pageant featuring himself dressed as a minstrel, singing to the queen from the branches of an oak tree of his "tragical complaint."[10] Elizabeth was charmed, and patted a place for him by her side.

Dee believed he had a special place next to Elizabeth as well. To an extent, he did. He was one of very few commoners to be honored with personal visits. Twice, they coincided with personal tragedies. The first time she arrived with the entire Privy Council in tow just four hours after the death of his second wife. On the second occasion, Dee had just laid his beloved mother to rest. Both times, Elizabeth refused his befuddled entreaties to come into his house, and offered consolations. Both times Dee anxiously struggled to overcome the awkwardness of the situation by trying to entertain her as she waited outside. During the earlier visit, he brought out the magical mirror given to him by Sir William Pickering, which "to her Majestie's great contentment and delight" he demonstrated to her.[11]

He was frequently called upon to come to court to talk to her about the matters on her mind, some of which were quite intimate, such as the prospects for her proposed marriage to the duke of Anjou. He had become, one commentator noticed, "hyr philosopher."[12]

He reciprocated such attentions with a strong, almost overpowering devotion—something she engendered in many of her courtiers, who often translated their dependence upon her into expressions of rapturous love. He devised a special symbol, a capital letter *E* topped with a crown, which he used to refer to her in his diaries. He minutely noted every favor she granted, and refused to blame her for the many that were denied.

In January 1568, he gave copies of a new edition of his *Propaedeumata* to William Cecil and the earl of Pembroke to present to her. Three days later Dee heard back from Pembroke of her "gracious accepting and well liking of the said book."[13]

On 16 February, he was invited to see her at Westminster Palace. He approached her in the palace gallery, Elizabeth's preferred location for informal, unscheduled, and confidential meetings, as she could pick out from the scattering of courtiers hovering nervously around any that she wished to talk to. Today it was her philosopher's turn, and their conversation quickly moved on from a discussion of the *Propaedeumata*'s astronomical findings to something more sensational and enigmatic. He revealed to her "the great secret for my sake to be disclosed unto her Majesty by Nicolaus Grudius Nicolai, sometime one of the Secretaries to the Emperor Charles the Fifth."[14] He never let on what this secret was, and little is known about Grudius, a Belgian poet. Dee noted his death in 1569 in one of his books, and described him as a "friend." They also shared the same publisher in Antwerp, Willem Silvius.[15] The assumption is that Grudius's secret related to alchemy, a recurring interest among European monarchs desperate to find easier ways of enriching coffers regularly depleted by wars.

It was the promise of such mystical revelations that undoubtedly drew Elizabeth to Dee, and her appetite for them that drew him to her.

Elizabeth had a profound sense of the forces of the cosmos acting upon her, and regarded her monarchical powers as in some way magical. For example, she was an enthusiastic practitioner of the "royal touch." According to this rite, which had origins reaching back at least to the reign of Henry II, a monarch would touch the neck of a sufferer of epilepsy or scrofula, a painful and disfiguring inflammation of the lymph glands, who would thereby be cured.

Elizabeth's touch appeared to be so effective, it was often cited as vindication of her claim to the throne, and proof that the Pope's attempt to excommunicate her had been vetoed by God.

> *Not all the water in the rough rude sea*
> *Can wash the balm off from an anointed king,*

as Shakespeare put it.[16]

Dee apparently understood better than anyone how the magical balm worked. He could help Elizabeth make the most of it, become an adept at the magical practice of monarchy.

However, as he was to discover, even these powers were not enough to levitate him above the necessities of life.

⚜

ABOUT eight miles upstream of London on the meandering course of the River Thames lies the village of Mortlake. According to dubious tradition, the name means "dead lake." No such lake exists in the village now, nor in recorded history, though in the distant past one may have gathered on the bend of the River Thames, like water on the elbow, a dark and still pool fouled with the rotting remains of plague or war victims. A less picturesque explanation, suggested by Daniel Lysons in his 1792 survey of London, is that the name comes from the Saxon "Mortlage," meaning a compulsory law.[1]

The village that Lysons reached in the late eighteenth century was much like it had been in the sixteenth, a small, quiet community that had enjoyed only gentle expansion over the centuries, serving the endless stream of river and road traffic that passed through every day, delivering goods and travelers between London and the towns and palaces farther upstream. It was about 2,000 acres in size, part of the manor of Wimbledon, and comprised a modest church, a cluster of houses mostly concentrated along the Thames towpath, and a few asparagus fields.

Even without its dead lake, Lysons found that Mortlake had, like so many English villages, its share of local legends. One was recorded by Raphael Holinshed, a contemporary of Dee's and a source for Shakespeare's history plays, who wrote of a monstrous fish that had been caught there in 1240. Another of the legends mentioned by Lysons was that the village had once held the extraordinary library and laboratory of the great conjurer John Dee.

In 1672, Elias Ashmole, planning a biography of Dee (never written), visited Mortlake to interview the village's oldest inhabi-

tant, the eighty-year-old Goodwife Faldo, the last surviving link
with the time Dee lived there.

Her memories were vivid. He was "very handsome," tall and
slender with a fair complexion, smartly dressed in an "artists' gown"
with hanging sleeves, and sporting a long "picked" (pointed) beard
that in his latter years turned snowy white. Faldo recalled how
children would run screaming from his door because he was
"accounted a conjuror," how he would act as a "great Peacemaker"
among squabbling adults, how neighbors would come to him with
the most trifling domestic problems.

Faldo remembered an incident concerning a basket of precious
plate that had been sent to London to be polished in preparation for
a wedding. Once the job was done, the basket was delivered to a
prearranged spot on the banks of the Thames, where it was to be
collected by the boatman Robert Bryan. Bryan took the wrong basket, and the owner found that his gleaming pewter had been substituted by a pile of beef tripe. By means that Faldo could not fathom,
Dee had directed the hapless boatman to a woman who lived in
nearby Wandsworth. It turned out the tripe was hers, and she told
Bryan he would find the plate still sitting by the river, as she had
found it too heavy to carry home.

This ambiguous image of the cunning wizard and wise seer was
enhanced by Dee's impressive connections with mysterious foreigners and powerful courtiers. Many such figures came through Mortlake, en route between the queen's palaces at Westminster, Greenwich,
Richmond, Nonsuch, and Hampton Court. Faldo recalled Dee's frequent visits to nearby Barn Elms, the home of Sir Francis Walsingham
and later the earl of Essex, Queen Elizabeth's most rebellious favorite
and the husband of Walsingham's daughter Frances. Dee had also
taken Faldo and her mother to Richmond Palace, so they could watch
a royal dinner with the king of Denmark.

When she was just six years old, Faldo and her mother had even
been invited into Dee's home, where in a darkened room he showed
her the image of a solar eclipse projected through a pinhole.[2]
Despite the reactions of the other children in the village, Faldo
seemed quite unafraid of entering this strange world of ancient

manuscripts, intricate devices, and chemical smells, happily skipping into the labyrinthine corridors of what by then had become one of the most extraordinary residences in Europe.

*   *   *

DEE HAD MOVED to Mortlake out of necessity rather than choice. Despite the queen's welcome on his return from the Continent in 1564, he found life in England far from convivial. The marchioness of Northampton, whom he had gallantly escorted back from Antwerp, had secured a promise that he would get the deanery of Gloucester when it fell vacant, which was imminently expected. It was just the sort of post he needed, promising to provide him with the secure and relatively undemanding living he craved to continue his philosophical work. However, in April 1565 the marchioness succumbed to breast cancer, and so did his claim to the deanery. Such offices were sensitively entangled with growing antagonisms at court, the battles between the likes of Robert Dudley, just promoted to earl of Leicester and the leader of the militant Protestant faction, and the duke of Norfolk, the nation's most senior peer and a focus of Catholic sympathies. Dee's religious loyalties were not delineated clearly enough to arouse the support of either side, so he was swept aside in favor of John Man, a radical Protestant who later became bishop.

Dee did not help the situation by being so hopeless at cultivating aristocratic patrons. He attended court irregularly, and then only to see the queen. Robert Dudley knew Dee when the philosopher was appointed to the household of his father the duke of Northumberland in 1553, and was an excellent prospect as a generous benefactor, yet Dee did not dedicate a single work to him. Rather, he preferred to save his eulogies, in his "Mathematicall Praeface," for Robert's brother John, earl of Warwick, who had died in 1554.

He seemed to put as much effort into befriending the queen's servants as her courtiers, welcoming both her Italian dwarf, Tomasina, and a "Mr Fosku" of the queen's wardrobe to Mortlake.

His hopes that the queen herself might offer him a post as court philosopher were wildly optimistic. There was certainly a demand for philosophical advice of all sorts: astrological, alchemical, theological, even medical. When a wax effigy of Elizabeth stuck with pig bristles was found under a tree in Lincoln's Inn Fields, when a "blazing star" appeared in the sky, when the queen fell sick with a mysterious illness, it was Dee who was called upon to advise. Even on strategic matters, such as the maintenance of a navy or the management of trade, he could expect an eager audience. However, when the court summoned him, it was as a diligent subject rather than a paid professional. Only the sophisticated, lavish royal households of Continental monarchs could afford a professional court philosopher. In England, they were considered an unnecessary luxury. There were ladies-in-waiting, gentlemen-of-the-wardrobe, even grooms-of-the-stool, but no masters of philosophy.

So, with no prospects of office and little of income, Dee had done what so many in his situation do: he went to live with his mother.

Following the death of his father, Roland, Dee's mother, Jane, had settled herself in an "ancient messuage [dwelling] of outhowses, orchard and garden" opposite Mortlake church, overlooking the Thames.[3] This rather ramshackle residence was probably built in the previous century, and boasted no more than a hall, a scullery, two or three bedrooms, and a few cramped chambers when Dee moved in some time in the mid-1560s. He arrived with a new wife, one Katherine Constable, the widow of a London grocer.[4] Nothing more is known about Katherine. Dee apparently had no children by her, at least none that survived, and she died some time before 1575.[5]

His new home now became the focus of his ambitions. He had accumulated a huge collection of books and manuscripts during his trips abroad including titles that few in England had seen let alone studied, works such as Johannes de Burgo's *Treatise on Magic*, a strange document written in Spanish using the Hebrew alphabet, which he found in Louvain; the *Secretum secretorum* attributed to Aristotle on the nature of immortality, bought in Padua; volumes on the Cabala and Plutarch sent from Rome; commentaries on the great Greek geometricians Euclid and Appollonius; the *Liber experiementorum*, book of experiments, attributed to the Spanish mystic and philosopher Ramon Lull, found like the *Steganographia* in Antwerp. These had been added to a list already several hundred entries long, which included two copies of Copernicus's *De revolutionibus*, Boethius's *Consolations of Philosophy*, Norton's *Ordinal of Alchemy*, and a study of the *Tetrabiblios* by Ptolemy, the standard classical work on astrology, acquired from the library of the king of France.[6] In intellectual as well as material terms, such a concentration of rare and controversial texts was highly combustible, and Dee needed somewhere safe to store it.

He set about transforming his mother's cottage into one of the largest libraries in Europe, encrusting the house with extensions and buying up neighboring buildings and tenements to fit everything in.

The main addition was an "Externa bibliotheca," or chief and open library, a reading room where scholars and copyists could consult the main body of the collection. The works crammed into the shelves covered an immense range of subjects, including not just magic and mathematics, but, to list just a sample, the Armenian church, botany, chastity, demonology, dreams, earthquakes, Etruria, falconry, games, gymnastics, horticulture, Islam, logic, marriage, mythology, the nobility, oils, pharmacology, rhetoric, saints, surveying, tides, veterinary science, weather, woman, and zoology.[7]

Despite the multiplicity of subjects and number of volumes, the library was arranged according to no recognizable bibliographic scheme. Works were as likely to be arranged according to their size as their author or subject. Nevertheless, Dee became celebrated for his ability to pluck from among the bending shelves chapter and verse on any subject. William Bourne was a former innkeeper and gunner who became a successful writer on navigation. He visited Mortlake sometime before 1580, and happened to mention to Dee that there seemed to be very little information about the number of ships the emperor of China might have under his command. Dee "opened a book and showed me a note that . . . the number was 15,000." Expressing his disbelief that the emperor could call upon such a force, Dee instantly located another volume containing supporting evidence. It revealed that when the emperor sent his daughter on a sea journey he provided fourteen ships to act as her escort, indicating that at the very least he was generously provisioned. Bourne was so impressed by this display of bibliographic skill, he mentioned it in his navigational primer, *Regiment for the Sea*.[8]

As well as books, the Externa bibliotheca also contained Dee's collection of scientific instruments, including the celestial and terrestrial globes given to him by Mercator, which Dee had decorated with records of his own observations and discoveries, a five-foot-long quadrant, a ten-foot-long cross-staff, a sea compass, and a "watch-clock," or portable timepiece, accurate to the second.[9]

Several rooms or "appendices" led off from the Externa bibliotheca, housing Dee's collection of official papers and title deeds (stored in a "great case or frame of boxes"), a variety of marvels and rarities that he picked up during his travels, and his laboratories. Goodwife Faldo remembered five or six stills bubbling away in these buildings, distilling mysterious potions from eggshells and horse dung.

The room that she did not see, and which Dee did not mention in any of his published writings, was what he might otherwise have called his "Interna bibliotheca" or private study. Only a select few were ever invited to enter this room, and only he was allowed to enter the adjoining private chapel or "oratory," where he presumably shelved the Bibles and devotional texts so conspicuously lacking from the catalogs of the Externa bibliotheca. It was here that Dee stored his magical equipment, such as the strange mirror given to him by Sir William Pickering, his confidential writings on spiritual transactions, and books like Cornelius Agrippa's *De occulta philosophia*, which he kept open on the study desk for easy reference.

The cost of creating this labyrinthine academy-cum-laboratory, which was to occupy him for at least a decade, soon stretched beyond the modest £80 he continued to receive each year from his rectory at Long Leadenham. To supplement his income, he started to provide services of various sorts: tuition, astrological readings, dream interpretations, medical consultations, even forensic advice.[10] His diaries are littered with examples: interpreting a dream for Harry Price, advising on the deformed fingers of the London minister John Halton, assessing the guilt of a "melancholic" young man "very ingenious in many handiworks" suspected of burglary, trying to find the cause of the suicidal tendencies of a local woman called Isabel Lister.

He also accepted government research work. The most substantial commission came in 1570 from Christopher Hatton and Robert Dudley via Edward Dyer. In January of that year, the assassination of the earl of Moray, the Protestant Regent of Scotland, had opened up the "postern-gate of England" to Catholic insurgence in support of Mary Stewart, Queen of Scots, currently imprisoned in England, and the focus of innumerable plots to overthrow Elizabeth. Then, on 2 June, a bull issued by Pope Pius V entitled *Regnans in excelsis* was nailed to the door of the bishop of London's palace, declaring a holy war against Elizabeth. It was against the background of these unnerving events that Dyer asked Dee to write a synopsis of the state of the nation.

The resulting paper, entitled *Brytannicae Reipublicae Synposis*, a synopsis of the British republic, has been described as "one of the most important contemporary analyses of Elizabethan England," providing a snapshot of the nation's economy, political institutions, and defenses.[11] Organized in the form of a large flowchart, it was aimed at showing the true state of the nation, identifying a variety of problems, including those that continued to beset the economy, which Dee attributed to urban decay, low standards in the textile industry, the debasement of currency, and unemployment. By calling Britain a republic, Dee was certainly not recommending the end of monarchical government, but he was emphasizing the notion of the state being a commonwealth. In his other writings, he attacked privateers and the "enclosers of commons," and promoted the doctrine that every man was born to promote public prosperity rather than private gain.[12]

No record survives of the government's response to the *Synopsis*, nor of the fee Dee was paid for writing it. He felt obliged to refuse payment for other official work.[13] Even if he had been paid, it would not have been enough to cover his growing expenses. Nor would his astrological consultations, which were often sought by nobles, who were notoriously mean and expected such services to be offered for free.

In 1571, Dee received a "passport with my two servants and our geldings" to depart on a trip to the Duchy of Lorraine to buy laboratory equipment. He returned with "one great cart" laden with flasks and vessels made of clay, metal, and glass. He clearly intended to use them to develop a growing interest in alchemy, a discipline that he considered to be "the lord of all sciences and the end of all speculation."[14]

There was growing government interest in alchemy during this period. The historian Strype records that, in 1574, "a great project had been carrying on now for two or three years, of Alchymy, William Medley, being the great undertaker, to turn iron into copper. Sir Thomas Smith, Secretary of State, had by some Experiments made before him, a great Opinion of it. And for the better carrying it on and bearing the Expences it was thought fit to be done by a Corporation: into which by Smith's Encouragement, the Lord Burghley, and the Earl of Leicester entered themselves with others: each member laying down an £100 to go on with it."[15]

Whether Dee was a member of this enterprise is unrecorded. Dee was certainly known to Smith. There is a record in his diary, encoded in Greek text, of Smith lending him £10 at a time of particular penury.[16] Dee was also close to another of the project's backers, Sir Edward Dyer.

Even if he had been involved, it would not have been the main focus of his alchemical work. He considered the benefit of alchemy to be not the perfection of metals, but of the soul and even the body. Since the 1560s, he had been collecting the works of Theophrastus Philippus Aureolus Bombastus von Hohenheim (c. 1493–1542). Not content with that name, Theophrastus gave himself another: Paracelsus or "surpassing Celsus," to show his superiority to the great Latin medical historian. Paracelsus was a prolific German philosopher and physician who, like Dee, had been deeply influenced by the works of Trithemius. He also shared a dislike of academics, whom he considered having as much wisdom as his shoe buckle. He had developed an elaborate theory that saw alchemy as the means of exploring the interactions of celestial and physical forces through the medium of the human body. Despite its occult character, this theory would prove important to the development of modern medicine, as it emphasized the importance of chemistry in understanding living processes.

Studies of Dee's alchemical notes show signs that Paracelsus's ideas influenced his laboratory work. For example, the scholar Urszula Szulakowska has speculated that a series of experiments undertaken in 1581 involving vitriol, saltpeter, and marcasite may have been inspired by Paracelsus's own recipes for medicines that treated bone fractures and gangrene.[17]

If health was the primary focus of Dee's alchemy, his experiments did not prove to be particularly effective. At around this time his work was interrupted by the onset of a crippling illness. He does not identify the symptoms; however, it is possible that, like many who dabbled in alchemy and metallurgy at the time, he was poisoned by some of the chemicals he was handling.

His condition became so serious that the queen sent her own physicians, Drs. Apslow and Balthorp, to attend him at Mortlake. During his convalescence, they were joined by the sister of the earl of Leicester, Lady Sidney, who was one of Elizabeth's most trusted ladies-of-the-bedchamber, "to discern how my health bettered." As Lady Sidney sat at Dee's bedside dabbing his brow, she regaled him with "very pithy speeches," and fed him "divers rarities . . . to encrease my health and strength: the most dutiful and thankful memory whereof shall never die."[18]

For the next few years he seems to have given up foreign travel completely. Indeed, there is little sign of activity during this period, except for a burst of astronomical work with his pupil, the brilliant Thomas Digges.

By 1574, his financial situation had become desperate, and he decided to take action. On 3 October, he sat down at his desk at Mortlake, selected several sheets of the smoothest parchment, sharpened a quill into the finest nib, mixed the thickest lampblack into the darkest ink, and, in his neatest secretarial hand, penned a desperate plea for help to Elizabeth's chief minister, William Cecil, now Lord Burghley.[19]

Cecil received many such letters, and no doubt forwarded most of them to the fireplace. But this one he kept, and we are thankful that it has survived. In it, Dee painted a picture of penury totally at odds with the opulence of the document. He described the "incredible toil of body and mind" he had endured in his quest to serve his country by accumulating "the best Learning and knowledge." "This Land never bred any man" whose efforts had been greater than his, he wrote. And "the same zeal remaineth (yea rather greater is grown)," but he no longer had the means, the "hability," to fulfill it. He needed money "which (as God knoweth) findeth not me, and my poor family's necessary meat, drink and fuel; for a frugal and philosophical Diet." The "little exhibition which I enjoy" was simply not enough, and he would not have even that were it not for Cecil's previous interventions on his behalf.

The solution? Just £200 or £300 per annum. This was a small sum by the standards of court patronage. Nobles regularly received thousands of pounds from the queen's coffers. Sir Edward Dyer managed to secure a royal loan of £3,000 (never repaid). But Dee was not in Dyer's league, and knew it.

So, no sooner had he asked for the money than he suggested a cost-free way of providing it. It was related to the discovery of gold not through alchemy, but by locating buried treasure.

٭ ٭ ٭

TREASURE WAS A particular preoccupation of the Tudor era:

> Yea, all the wealth that our forefathers hid
> Within the massy entrails of the earth . . .

as Marlowe put it in *Dr. Faustus*. Before the age of banking, burial was a common method of safe deposit, and the countryside was assumed to be heaving with hoards of jewelry and coins.

We now tend to think of the Elizabethan age as one of prosperity and splendor, but it was in fact "narrow and needy," as one historian put it.[20] It was a time of beggars and cutpurses, scams and speculation, debt and inflation, a roiling economic climate intensified by the enclosure of the commons, urbanization, plagues, and, in the early

1570s, a series of famines that reduced many to a diet of acorns, saw-dust, and grass soaked in milk or animal blood.[21] Reflecting the general level of hardship, in 1572 Parliament had passed the Usury Act, making it illegal to charge more than 10 percent interest on a loan.

From the peasant classes upwards, money was so tight and income so precarious that the discovery of a hidden cache was for many the only hope left to them. Expectations were raised by widely circulated rumors that the fortunes of newly enriched families were dug up by a gardener's spade or farmer's plowshare. It was also believed that there was a distinct pattern to the distribution of buried treasure. The ruins of abbeys and castles were thought to be particularly rich terrain, especially since the dissolution of the monasteries. Corrupt priests who had for years fattened themselves on tithes and monopolies were popularly believed to have committed their ill-gotten gains to the protection of consecrated ground before they were chased off into the countryside. For the same reason wayside crosses and even ancient burial mounds were frequently to be found uprooted or pillaged, so much so that "hill-digger" became a term of abuse similar in meaning to "gold digger" now.[22]

These riches, however, remained infuriatingly elusive. In an age before metal detectors and mechanical diggers, even narrowing the search area to the precincts of a ruin still meant daunting excavations. The only realistic hope of discovery was to find a map, become adept at spotting anomalies in surface features and vegetation, or resort to more occult detection systems.

After a lifetime searching through the nation's monuments and libraries, Dee may well have turned up a treasure map or two. If so, it was likely to be in code, but that, too, was something he knew about. Dee ends his letter to Cecil with a request for a recommendation to the Keeper of the Records at Wigmore Castle, to gain permission to examine the archives there. "My fantasy is, I can get from them at my leisure, matter for chronicle or pedigree, by way of recreation," he wrote, in a tone that may have struck Cecil as suspiciously innocuous.

Dee also had some expertise in surveying and geology. He had collected an extensive set of books on mining, including the key contemporary works: *De re metallica*, by the German "father of minerology" Georgius Agricola (1494–1555) and *De la pyrotechnie* by the Italian armorer Vannoccio Biringuccio (1480–c. 1539).[23] These were full of practical information about identifying promising mining sites, assaying (purifying) metals from ore, sinking shafts, and digging tunnels. They no doubt proved useful when Dee came to run some mines of his own, leased to him by Sir Lionel Duckett, the member of Parliament and Lord Mayor of London. They were in Devonshire, on land under the control of Sir Walter Raleigh, and it was probably through his friendship with Raleigh that Dee became involved in the enterprise.

However, geographical surveying was not enough. To see what lay hidden beneath the soil, other skills were called for.

For Dee, as for most at the time, the earth and the stars were inextricably linked. For example, he thought that the appearance of a new star in 1572 signified "the finding of some great Treasure," and noted the discovery two years later of a gold mine. The idea of there being correspondences between the celestial and the terrestrial was one of the principles underlying alchemy. The same astrological sign was used for both the planet and the metal Mercury, for example, as both were thought to share the same "mercurial" characteristics. Similarly, Venus was copper and the Moon was silver. The Sun, of course, was gold, and it was believed that where one was most plentiful, so would be the other, as the heat of the Sun promoted the formation of gold seams in the soil. For this reason, the biggest concentrations of gold ore were assumed to lie in the tropics, a view apparently abundantly confirmed by the fabulous hoards brought back from Central America by the Spanish.

So, just as there may be ways of picking up astral forces using mirrors and lenses, Dee believed that there might be similar tools for picking up the emanations of buried treasure. The best known of these was the divining or "Mosaical" rod.[24] There was some skepticism about the use of such rods, as they were easily abused by fraudsters. "The greater part of Cozeners, when they are themselves very poor and most miserable of all men, profess themselves able to find out Treasure" using rods, wrote Giovanni Battista

Porta in his authoritative 1558 survey *Magia naturalis* (natural magic). Nevertheless "some metal Masters ... report that these forked rods are a great help to them in finding out of mines," and Dee undoubtedly fell into this category.[25]

Thus it was, he explained to Cecil, that he had become the focus of reports about strange terrestrial emanations and particularly of dreams hinting at the location of buried hoards, and wanted permission to act upon them:

> Of late, I have been sued unto by diverse sorts of peoples, of which some by vehement, iterated dreams, some by vision (as they have thought), others by speech forced to their imagination by night, have been informed of certain places where Treasure doth lie hid; which all, for fear of Keepers (as the phrase commonly nameth them) or for mistrust of truth in the places assigned and some for some other causes, have forborn to deal further, unless I should encourage them or counsel them how to proceed. Wherein I have always been contented to hear the histories, fantasies or illusions to me reported but never entermeddled according to the desire of much.[26]

He had "never entermeddled" because it would have been illegal to do so. To begin with, had he uncovered anything, it would under the ancient law of Treasure Trove automatically become the property of the queen. But to have admitted to acting upon such reports might also lay him open to the charge of engaging in magical divination, which was prohibited not just by government statute, but by divine law. "There shall not be found among you any that burns his son or his daughter as an offering, any one who practices divination, a soothsayer, or an augur, or a sorcerer, or a charmer, or a medium, or a wizard, or a necromancer," sayeth Deuteronomy. This scriptural prohibition was supported by an Act of 1563 that made the discovery of treasure or recovery of stolen goods by magical means an offense. A first conviction was punishable by a year's imprisonment and four appearances in the pillory, a second by death.

Dee believed that his proposal to search for treasure was, like his study of the stars, exempt from such prohibitions because it was essentially scientific. It was based on a coherent body of knowledge. He did not have some sort of magical power unavailable to others, but an understanding of the forces of nature, and therefore an ability to manipulate and exploit them. Thus in his letter to Cecil he cited several textural authorities for the idea of divination that demonstrated that it could be done in the "manner of Philosophers and Mathematicians."

Having carefully circumscribed the methods he would use, Dee set out the basis of his proposed deal. All he was asking was that, in return for half of the spoils, he be granted a license to search for treasure on the queen's behalf. This was not, he assured Cecil, the equivalent of being granted a mining monopoly. "The value of a mine is matter for King's Treasure," Dee conceded, "but a pot of two or three hundred [coins] hid in the ground, wall, or tree, is but the price of a good book, or instrument for perspective astronomy, or some feat of importance"—the very things he needed to pursue his scientific studies on the Crown's behalf.

The rewards, he promised, would certainly be enough to make it worth Cecil's while to grant such a license, for "if (besides all books, dreams, visions, reports . . . by any other natural means . . . or by attraction and repulsion), the places may be descryed or discovered where gold, silver or better matter doth lie hid within a certain distance, [think] how great a commodity should it be for the Queen's Majestie and the commonwealth of this Kingdom."

Despite such enticements, however, Cecil did not go for Dee's scheme, probably because he dared not give Dee what would become a de facto monopoly over treasure trove. Instead, Dee would find himself being drawn into a much more ambitious treasure hunt, one in which the prize was not just "a pot of two or three hundred," but the wealth of the Orient, the vast expanses of the Russian Empire, and the unexplored wonders of the New World.

PART FOUR
THE UNDISCOVERED LIMIT

✤

But let that man with better sense advise
That of the world least part to us is read:
And daily how through hardy enterprise,
Many great Regions are discovered,
Which to late age were never mentioned.
Who ever heard of th'Indian *Peru*?
Or who in venturous vessel measured
The *Amazon* huge river now found true?
Or fruitfullest *Virginia* who did ever view?

EDMUND SPENSER,
The Faerie Queen

XII

✤

ON 10 May 1553, as Edward VI's reign waned, three ships under the command of Sir Hugh Willoughby set off from Greenwich and headed out into the North Sea. The expedition's pilot was Richard Chancellor, a navigator and mathematician. The aim of this daring expedition was to find a navigable route along the northern coast of Russia to China, or "Cathay," as it was then called.

Willoughby's ship was lost in a great storm in the North Sea, but Chancellor "held on his course towards that unknown part of the world," aided by the latest charts and celestial readings, exceptionally accurate by the standards of the day.

English knowledge of navigation in the 1550s was primitive. Not a single map would be published or globe constructed in England for another two decades.[1] In the minds of most English mariners, the world was still shaped according to principles going back to the ancient Greeks. Only one book, a tract written in 1511, had so far been printed in English that even mentioned America.[2] Up-to-date information on the geography of the New World or, indeed, the Old one, was confined to the Continent, where it was jealously guarded and rarely released.

There was, however, one local source, a young English scholar who had spent some time studying at such centers, and who had unique access to such leading cartographers as Mercator and Gerard Frisius: John Dee.

Chancellor went to see Dee sometime in the early 1550s, taking with him Willoughby's audacious plans for a "new and strange navigation" of the northern seas. He also brought a set of scientific instruments of his own design, including a treasured "excellent, strong, and fair quadrant of five foot semidiameter."[3] The two became close friends, Dee later describing Chancellor as "incomparable" and "well-beloved." Together, they prepared charts for the voyage, presumably based on maps Dee had copied during his stay with Mercator and Gerard Frisius in Louvain, and used the quadrant to compile detailed tables of solar and celestial positions.

It was upon these maps and measurements that Chancellor now relied as he sailed northeast, off the edge of the charted world and into a strange, alien one "where he found no night at all, but a continual light and brightness of the sun shining clearly upon the huge and mighty sea."

Eventually, he came across a bay, and a small fishing boat. Its crew was so amazed by the "strange greatness" of Chancellor's ship, they tried to flee. Using "signs and gestures," Chancellor reassured the fishermen that he had come in peace. Despite the lack of a common language, he was able to establish a rapport with them, and asked them to inform their leader of his arrival in their country, whichever country it might be.

He had to wait a long time for a response, during which the realm of "continual light and brightness" became a place of perpetual dark. Eventually he was summoned, and departed on an expedition to the interior of the country. He had to endure a journey of 1,500 miles in conditions of "extreme and horrible" cold, much of it on sled. Eventually, his party reached their destination: a city "as great as the City of London." It was Moscow, and the king who welcomed them was Ivan the Terrible.[4]

Chancellor's encounter with Ivan, the first tsar of the Russian Empire, was to lead to the creation of new and strategically vital trade routes between England and Russia that bypassed the hostile dominions of the Catholic Holy Roman Empire. The bay where Chancellor had made landfall became the principal seaport for this trade, later known as St. Nicholas and more recently Archangel. The Muscovy Company was founded in London to manage these new links, and was given a royal monopoly over the business that arose from them.

Chancellor's trip, under Dee's guidance, also opened up in the imaginations of a new generation of English adventurers the feeling that the northern latitudes might yield further treasures, that the frozen seas, though less enticing and more dangerous than the southern, might provide England with the bounty that had so enriched the Spaniards and the Portuguese.

However, Chancellor was lost with his ship in the North Sea while on another expedition, and the Muscovy Company had proved reluctant to back any further ventures. Since its blanket monopoly extended to the exploration as well as exploitation of the northern latitudes, this policy effectively brought England's age of discovery to a premature halt.[5] It was on this matter that the adventurer Martin Frobisher approached the Privy Council in 1574.

According to one government paper, Martin Frobisher had "such a monstrous mind, that a whole kingdom could not contain it."[6] A portrait of him seems to support this judgment. He strikes an arrogant pose, frowning, his nostrils dilated, his eyes glancing to one side, as though delivering a silent warning to some impudent scoundrel who has interrupted the sitting.

Frobisher was recklessly ambitious, aiming for the title of England's Columbus. He faced stiff competition. Two years earlier, Francis Drake had stolen a lead by embarking on a privateering voyage to America that had already yielded a vast treasure of plunder and the first sight by an Englishman of the Pacific Ocean, to which Drake would return in five years' time during his circumnavigation of the globe. Frobisher now proposed a great mission of discovery into the uncharted seas of the northern latitudes. He had taken part in the expeditions to the Gold Coast of West Africa in the 1550s, which had returned with rich ores and black slaves, with tales of the giant "oliphant" and its strange "snout . . . that it is to him in the stead of a hand," and with the ships' keels "marvellously overgrown with certain shells of such bigness that a man might pit his thumb in the mouths of them."[7] His appetite whetted by such marvels, he was now ready to embark on a voyage of his own.

Frobisher's proposal to the Privy Council was a magnificently daring one. Spain had established for itself dominance of the southern seas, and reaped vast rewards as a result. Thanks to the Muscovy

Company's apathy, England had failed to do the same with the northern seas. A new mission was called for, a Protestant adventure that would rival the Catholic quest, as well as enrich the queen's treasury. And to launch this mission Frobisher proposed the most daring enterprise of all: to search for the sea route supposed to pass along the northern coast of America to Cathay—the fabled Northwest Passage.

* * *

IN THE LATE 1560s, Humphrey Gilbert, an MP and soldier knighted in 1570 by the queen for his military service in Ireland and the Low Countries, had started work on a treatise that examined whether or not the Northwest Passage existed. His argument was, in the manner of the time, based not just on current geographical information, which was still scanty, but on ancient authority.

The most important authority of all on geography (as on many subjects) was Ptolemy, whose map of the world divided the globe into three continents, Europe, Asia, and Africa, all joined together by land. However, this view had been challenged by Plato, who wrote of the existence of another landmass, a huge island larger than Asia Minor and Libya combined. According to Egyptian priests, it was situated beyond the Pillars of Hercules, the ancient name for the Straits of Gibraltar, which was then taken to be a gateway into the immeasurable unknown. That island was called Atlantis.

According to the Egyptians, Atlantis had been swallowed up by the ocean that shared its name—the Atlantic[8]—following a series of earthquakes. Gilbert, however, thought it had survived, and was the continent the Spanish had called America. This would explain such fabled discoveries as the coins of Augustus Caesar found in the mines of South America and Red Indians swept up on the coast of the Baltic. It also meant that this "New World" had already been discovered by explorers in antiquity, which meant their descendants had equal, if not better, claims to exploiting and ultimately colonizing it.

If it was an island, then obviously it was surrounded by water, which meant there must be a way around its northern shore: the fabled Northwest Passage. Via this route navigators would soon come upon Cathay, the home of the Kublai Khan. The fabulous wealth of the Khan's court was described by the great thirteenth-century Venetian traveler Marco Polo, and would later inspire Coleridge's famous lines "In Xanadu did Kubla Khan / A stately pleasure-dome decree." By the fifteenth century, upheavals in the Mongolian and Ottoman Empires had made the old land route east to Cathay increasingly difficult, so explorers had tried to find another way around. That was why Columbus set sail to the west in 1492, hoping to reach Cathay by circumnavigating the globe.

The central idea of Gilbert's thesis, that Columbus's new world was Atlantis, was supported, perhaps inspired, by John Dee, whose name was used in the dedicatory epistle to Gilbert's treatise to endorse the scheme: "a great learned man (even M[r]. DEE) doth seem very well to like of this Discovery, and doth much commend the author."[9] Around this time, Dee was also studying an account published in Italian of Christopher Columbus's travels written by Columbus's son. As the annotations show, Dee clearly thought the work might yield some of the secrets of Columbus's extraordinary success, marking the passages dealing with the adventurer's methods for keeping records, dealing with natives, and exploiting the discoveries of precious ores.[10]

Naturally, then, when news emerged of Frobisher's plan to put Gilbert's ideas to the test and find the Northwest Passage to China, Dee was an obvious source of the navigational knowledge that the adventurers would need.

However, Frobisher soon encountered an obstacle between him and his objective every bit as obstructive as America: the Muscovy Company. The company's directors, most of them rich and comfortable city merchants, were making healthy profits developing the trade links with Russia. They did not want to risk such a bounty by embarking on a hazardous venture in the opposite direction. Even the backing of the Privy Council was insufficient to make them yield.

Showing the sort of determination that would prove vital in his coming adventures, Frobisher refused to be put off. He returned to court, and this time got a letter of support from the queen herself. When he presented this to the company, it capitulated, granting him a license in February 1575. But in return Frobisher had to accept the appointment of one of the company's own men, the prosperous merchant Michael Lok, as the mission's treasurer.

Lok turned out to be an enthusiastic supporter of the idea. Twenty years earlier his trading business had taken him from Flanders to Spain, where he beheld for himself "the marvellous great trade" of the Spanish and Portuguese. He had watched the ships arriving along the Lisbon quayside disgorging "jewels, spices and other rich merchandise" from the East and West Indies.

He threw everything, including his own fortune, into getting Frobisher's venture off the ground. He founded the "Company of Kathai," and set about looking for backers to provide the frightening amounts of money needed. The final list of shareholders was a formidable one and included the most important people in the country: William Cecil, the Lord Treasurer, and the earls of Sussex, Warwick, and Leicester subscribed £50 each, Francis Walsingham, the queen's new principal secretary of state, and his future son-in-law the poet Philip Sidney each subscribed £25. The total came to £875, a sum approaching at least a million in today's terms.[11]

With so much money and lordly dignity at stake, risks had to be minimized, so the Muscovy Company asked one of its members, Sir Lionel Duckett, who had leased out his tin mine to Dee, to ask the philosopher to "examine and instruct" the expedition's leaders. Time was short, so, in May 1576, Dee brought his books and maps to Muscovy House, the company's headquarters in Seething Lane, in the shadow of the Tower of London, where he was to stay in the weeks leading up to the departure date.[12]

Lok, perhaps feeling protective of a scheme he had now adopted as his own, later claimed that Dee had originally approached him, offering to provide "such instructions and advice as by his learning he could give." Whether or not this was so, Lok developed a "great good opinion" of the "learned man," and on 20 May, with just a month to go before the ships were due to set sail, he invited Dee to his house. There he was to meet Frobisher, Stephen Borough, one of the Moscow Company's chief pilots and an old pupil of Dee's, and Christopher Hall, master of the *Gabriel*, a diminutive twenty-five-ton bark that was to be Frobisher's flagship (a quarter the size of Drake's *Golden Hind*; the other two ships in the fleet were even smaller: a fifteen-ton bark called the *Michael*, to be captained by Matthew Kindersley, and a ten-ton "pinnace" or scouting ship).

At the meeting, Lok was desperate to demonstrate to Dee that he was no dilettante in the world of navigation, and laid before the philosopher "my books, authors, my cards, and instruments, and my notes thereof made in writing, as I had made them of many years study before." Dee was duly impressed, and offered in return his own books and maps, which Lok declared he "did very well like."[13]

Reassured that Dee was not about to take over, Lok now enthusiastically embraced the philosopher as a fully fledged member of his company. Dee's fortune and reputation were, like his, to rest on its result.

Dee's role was to instruct Frobisher and Hall in the "rules of Geometry and Cosmography" and in the use of navigational instruments. Dee may also have told Frobisher what he had learned from Columbus's experiences, as the captain would adopt remarkably similar standards of record keeping, dealing with natives, and exploiting deposits of promising ores.

Lok had spent a lot of money equipping the expedition with the latest maps and equipment, which included a "very great chart of navigation" (cost: £5), a case containing several small iron "instruments for geometry" (£10 6s 8d), an armillary, a brass clock, and a "great globe of metal" made by Humphrey Cole, London's leading instrument maker and assistant to the assay master at the Royal Mint.[14] If such assets were not to be squandered, the sailors evidently had to be taught how to use them properly.

Unfortunately, there was not enough time. Unlike Richard Chancellor, Frobisher and Hall were ignorant of mathematics and were in any case probably distracted by practical matters they considered to be of more pressing interest, such as organizing crews and victuals for a voyage that appeared as perilous then as a mission to Mars would be considered today.[15] There was also a feeling among the saltier tars that arithmetic and geometry—essential to any scientific system of navigation—were for landlubbers. William

Borough, brother of the pilot Stephen, lambasted "the best learned in those sciences Mathematical, without convenient practise at sea."[16] He does not mention Dee by name, but it is possible he was thinking of him. There was certainly no love lost between the two, and they would exchange angry words during a later encounter at Muscovy House.[17]

Dee did what he could, and on 7 June, his pupils left their lessons and took to their ships. After an early mishap during which the pinnace crashed into another craft at Deptford and lost its bowsprit, the tiny fleet of three vessels and its crew of just thirty-four men assembled on the Thames next to Greenwich Palace and, to attract the queen's attention, let off a volley of guns. "Her majesty beholding the same, commended it, and bade us farewell, with shaking her hand at us out of the window," Christopher Hall recorded in his log. That evening, they were boarded by Secretary John Wolley, one of the commissioners who would interview Dee at Mortlake in 1592. Wolley lectured the crew to "be obedient, and diligent to their Captain," and wished them well.

The fleet then set sail for Gravesend, where Hall, perhaps to practice some of the techniques he had just been taught by his master, Dee, tried to measure his ship's position and the variation of the compass, carefully noting the results in his log. By 24 June, they had sailed up the east coast of Britain, and had reached Fair Isle, a tiny island to the north of Scotland, where the weather started to deteriorate. By 26 June, conditions had improved, a "fair gale" from the south blowing them west northwest. Here Hall attempted to take another measurement of latitude, his first in open seas. It was not an easy procedure, as it entailed standing on the rolling deck, holding up the unwieldy measuring instrument (a cross-staff), and trying to gauge the angle between the pitching horizon and the blinding noonday sun. Despite these problems, he seemed to achieve a reasonably accurate result, which he once again carefully recorded in his log.

Then another minor disaster struck. One of the ships, the *Michael*, developed a leak, and the fleet was forced to stop in the Bay of Saint Tronians in the Shetland Isles. While repairs were being made, Frobisher sent a letter to "the worshipful and our approved good friend M. Dee." In it, Frobisher dutifully reported Hall's latitude measurement (59°46'—accurate to within a few nautical miles), and reassured their master that "we do remember you, and hold ourselves bound to you as your poor disciples."[18]

The following day they set off at a fast clip into the north Atlantic. They were entering a realm about which virtually nothing was known. One influential geographical textbook owned by Dee described a region in the far north called "Thule" where "there was no longer either land properly so-called, or sea, or air, but a kind of substance concreted from all these elements, resembling sea-lungs." Dee later wondered whether this was a description of the world of "mountains of ice" that Frobisher was now entering.[19]

Finally, land was sighted. Hall took his measurements and Frobisher declared it to be "Frieseland," a landmass believed to exist in the mid-Atlantic. This identification would cause confusion for generations of navigators to come, whose maps would mark this island as lying to the south of Greenland. In fact they were farther north than they realized, and had encountered Greenland itself.

Their first sight of the land was a series of sharp peaks, like church steeples, covered in snow. These were to be the first geographical features to which they would give a name, and they chose to call them "Dee's Pinnacles" in honor of their teacher. They launched a boat in an attempt to land, but were repulsed by the ice.

Having failed to make landfall, they decided to keep going, heading farther west into waters now well off the edges of their navigation charts. Then a great storm blew up and in the huge seas the tiny pinnace and its crew, reduced to three men, was lost. It was never seen again. The *Gabriel*, with Frobisher and Hall aboard, also lost contact with the other main bark, the *Michael*, which was forced to turn back.

The *Gabriel* sailed on, but the storm intensified. Two days later, a huge wave crashed over the ship and tipped her over. The weight of the soaked rigging and the foresail kept her down, and she began to sink. "All the men in the ship had lost their Courage, and did despair of life"[20]—all except Frobisher. Showing "valiant courage," he clambered onto the side of the prostrate ship, and crawled to the bow, where he somehow managed to free up some of the rigging.

As the vessel started to right herself, the other crew members hacked away at the mizzen mast at the stern to lighten the ship further, and would have taken the main mast down too had not Frobisher stopped them.

Somehow they managed to recover control of the stricken *Gabriel*. The storm melted away and they once more found themselves in the frozen stillness of the arctic waters. With a mast missing and every corner of the ship soaked with freezing saltwater, and without the company of the other two ships, they sailed on.

Two days later, they sighted land again. It was the New World, Atlantis. However, where Columbus had been greeted with soft sands and lush forests, Frobisher and his crew confronted a soaring, impenetrable wall of ice. The great white precipice ran along the shoreline for mile after mile, rising out of dark waters so deep it was impossible to anchor. They also now found themselves being swept along by a powerful current, bringing with it great fleets of pack ice that threatened to smash the ship's fragile wooden hull.

"Meta Incognita." That was the name Frobisher gave to this terrifying terrain—the Unknown Limit. Some maps still mark the area surrounding Baffin Island in northeastern Canada with that name.

They spent nearly a fortnight probing the coastline until, on 11 August, they saw a small, barren island a half mile in circumference "one league from the main."[21] They decided to despatch a group of four men led by Hall to investigate it. With the *Gabriel* having to keep a safe distance off shore, the landing party was forced to row across ten miles of open seas to reach the island.

When they eventually got there, the conscientious Hall immediately started to measure the tidal flows, while the other crew members set off for the center of the island. It was little more than a barren rock, and there were no signs of life. The only thing of interest they encountered was a black stone "as great as a halfpenny loaf," spotted by Robert Garrard.[22] They carried it down to the shore and showed it to Hall. There is no record of the particular quality of this rock that aroused the landing party's interest, and subsequent events would prevent Garrard from leaving his own account. Perhaps it had a sparkling patina, or some colored vein could be glimpsed in the pits of its fractured surface.

There was no time to make a detailed inspection. They were dangerously distant from the mother ship, and Hall was anxious to return before they became enveloped in the thick arctic fog. They heaved the stone into the boat, and took it back to the ship, where Hall presented it to Frobisher. Frobisher was unimpressed by the gift, and put it to one side. He knew it could not be of much value, because according to scientific orthodoxy precious metals only formed in the sorts of sunny climes discovered by the Spanish farther south, in the tropics of Central America.

The following day they found what they had been searching for, a wide inlet in the coastline. Frobisher became convinced that the current running up the inlet showed it to be a strait, open at the other end—the entrance, perhaps, to the Northwest Passage.

They started to navigate up the inlet, through the scattering of small islands on its northern side. The temperature had dropped, and at one point the entire ship was encased in a quarter inch of ice. They were also apparently running low on supplies. So, on 19 August, they decided to weigh anchor and investigate the surrounding territory. They rowed to one of the islands, and made their first contact with the native population.

At first, relations were cordial, but within days took on a more hostile aspect. Frobisher and Hall visited the village where these people lived, and one of their number came back to the *Gabriel*. Frobisher gave him a bell and a knife, in payment for acting as a pilot for their coming journey up the strait. However, apparently distrustful of the man, Frobisher sent five of his crew (one of them Robert Garrard, the man who had found the stone on the island) to maroon the man on a rock rather than return him to the village.

The crew of the *Gabriel* waited all night for the party's return, but it did not appear. The following morning Frobisher took the *Gabriel* close to shore, where he "shot off a fauconet, and sounded our trumpet" to see if his men would appear.[23] There was no response.

The next day, he returned to the same place, where this time he was greeted by a fleet of kayaks. The *Gabriel*'s crew managed to entice one of the boats to the ship by dangling a bell over the side, whereupon its occupant was seized with a boat hook and dragged onboard to be held as a hostage. The other locals then took off "in great haste, howling like wolves or other beasts."[24]

Frobisher waited four days to see if his men would reappear, but they did not. On 26 August, he set off for home, taking the unfortunate captive with him.

* * *

FROBISHER'S BATTERED SHIP finally arrived in London on 9 October 1576. The last report of its progress had come months before from the returning crew of the *Michael*, who had watched it disappear into the storm that had forced them back and destroyed the pinnace. The appearance of the *Gabriel* and its captain thus was "joyfully received with the great admiration of the people."

Frobisher came ashore with a trophy to present to the gathered crowds: the kidnapped Inuit. This "strange man" caused "such a wonder unto the whole city and to the rest of the realm that heard of it as seemed never to have happened the like great matter to any man's knowledge." They gaped at his broad face, his "very fat and full" body, his short legs, "small and out of proportion," his little eyes and little black beard, his complexion, which seemed to those who saw him like that of a Moor or Tartar—where it was assumed his race must have originally hailed and somehow transferred to the northern shores of Atlantis. It was also noted that his countenance was "sullen or churlish, but sharp."[25]

Interest in the uprooted Inuit soon cooled, and there is no record of what happened to him. Perhaps he ended up serving in the household of one of the adventurers, or pined to death in such alien surroundings. Excitement quickly transferred to another of Frobisher's trophies, one he had not initially considered to be of any importance: the stone.

On 13 October, Michael Lok, the expedition's backer and treasurer, came on board the *Gabriel* to meet its captain. Frobisher dug out the stone found by Garrard and handed it to Lok. Lok, who considered himself something of an expert on metallurgy as he did navigation, became very excited by it.

Frobisher's stone was received like a sample of moon rock. According to George Best, later Frobisher's captain, it was one of the adventurer's wives who first hinted at the fabulous wealth it might contain. She "by chance" threw it on the fire "so long, that at the length being taken forth, and quenched in a little vinegar, it glistered with a bright marquesset of gold."[26]

Samples were sent to the leading metallurgists or "assayers" in the country. Three, including William Williams, the assay master at the Tower of London, and a "gold refiner" called Wheeler could find nothing of interest, but an Italian alchemist called John Baptista Agnello "made three several proofs and showed Lok gold."[27] Lok presented this glistening grain to the queen, and at once the entire court was overcome with gold fever.

Possibly working on the court's behalf, Sir William Winter, Sir John Berkley, and others secretly gathered at a house in Lambeth to check Agnello's results, and apparently confirmed them. They immediately called for a new mission to be organized back to Meta Incognita, but in the utmost secrecy, "least foreign princes set foot therein."

A sense of excitement swept through the City. "Frobisher . . . has given it as his decided opinion, that the island is so productive in metals, as to seem very far to surpass the country of Peru, at least as it now is. There are also six other islands near to this, which seem very little inferior," the great Renaissance poet and courtier Philip Sidney wrote to Hubert Languet.[28] A new mission was set up, immeasurably more ambitious than the last, with subscribers, including the queen herself, breaking down Lok's door in their efforts to get him to accept their credit (though very rarely their cash).

Dee was among the investors, promising £25 toward the venture. It is unclear whether his main interest was now in the prospect of discovering gold or the Northwest Passage. He would probably have suspicions about the ore's yield, as he subscribed to the alchemical notion that gold was bound to be sparse in such cold climes.

For the new venture, the *Gabriel* and *Michael* were to be joined
by a new and more substantial flagship, the 180-ton *Aid*, a medium-
class naval vessel from the queen's own fleet.[29] It was a measure of
the national prestige and hopes now attached to the venture that the
queen had made such a vessel available.

Crewing and equipping the expedition was enormously expensive. The indefatigable Lok needed to find a total of £4,400, only
half of which he had managed to raise by the time the fleet was
ready to set sail.

The ships left Blackwall on the River Thames on 26 May 1577,
with a crew of 140, including 90 sailors, gunners, and carpenters, 30
miners and metallurgists (the latter expressly commanded "not to
discover the secret of the riches" they found until it was returned
home), and a handful of convicts plucked from the London jails,
such as "John Robertes, *alias* Beggar," a highway robber.[30] At least
some of these "condemned persons" were apparently to be left in
Frieseland with weapons, victuals, and instructions on "how they
may by their good behaviour win the good will of the people of that
land and Country"—one of the earliest recorded examples of a policy of transportation that would later populate so many corners of
the British Empire.[31]

The fleet spent six weeks in the arctic seas, where "in the place of
odoriferous and fragrant smells of sweet gums and pleasant notes
of musical birds which other countries in more temperate zones do
yield, we tasted Boreal blasts mixed with snow and hail," as one of
the crew caustically noted.[32] They finally reached "Frobisher's
Strait," as it was now called, on 16 July.

It was blocked by ice. A few days later the ice dispersed and the
ships sailed up the "strait" before finding a natural harbor, where
they moored. Frobisher called it "Jackman's Sound" "after our
master's mate" and claimed the surrounding land for God and the
queen—arguably England's first documented act of colonial conquest in America, as during the first trip Frobisher apparently saw
no point in enacting such a ceremony. They then "marched through
the Country, with Ensign displayed, so far as was thought needful

and now and then heaped up stones on high mountains, and other places in token of possession."[33]

However, they could not find any more of the black stone they had discovered during the first trip. They continued their searches for days, during which the only notable find was a "dead fish floating, which had in his nose a horn . . . of length two yards lacking two inches, being broken in the top." It was a narwhal, which they identified as the "sea Unicorn."

Soon after, a rich seam of Frobisher's ore was discovered on the island where it had originally been found, and the miners immediately set about their business. Tons of the black rock were laboriously transported to the ships, and stored as ballast, partly to disguise its value in case the fleet was intercepted by pirates.

The remainder of the expedition was spent in a series of skirmishes with the locals, who this time proved themselves to be more aggressive toward the invaders. The fleet, dispersed by storms, finally made its way back to England, with the *Aid* reaching Milford Haven on the western extremity of Wales on 17 September 1577.

Frobisher immediately rode to the court, where he "affirmed with great oaths" that he had found "rich ore . . . precious stones, diamonds, and rubies." He also presented the unicorn's horn to the queen as a personal gift, much to the irritation of Lok, who considered it to be the property of the Muscovy Company.

The ore—over 140 tons of it—was locked up in Bristol Castle, with a sample being taken to the Tower of London for testing. There it was secured with four locks, with the Tower's warden, the "workmaster" of the Royal Mint, Frobisher and Lok each being given a key.

Jonas Schutz, a German metallurgist,[34] was appointed to determine the true value of the stone. He had been on the expedition, but was taken ill following its return. Finally, on 25 November, writing from the home of a friend in Smithfield, he informed Sir Francis Walsingham, the court's representative, that he was ready to "finish the proof."

He performed a series of trials at the Royal Mint's metalworks on Tower Hill and reported back within days. Despite his efforts, all he had managed to extract from the ore was just a grain or two of gold. The tons of material Frobisher had brought from the opposite side of the world, now securely stored in Bristol and London, were apparently worthless.

Frobisher was furious. He went to Tower Hill, where he found Jonas, stripped of his clothes, bent over a furnace, sick "almost to death" with the toxic fumes rising up from his crucibles. There he "reviled him, and drew his dagger on him for not having finished his works."

Frobisher now unilaterally appointed another man to test the ore, a Dr. Burcott. Nobody seemed to know very much about him—not even his proper name (in the records of the Privy Council, he is identified as both Dr. Burchard Kraurych and Dr. Burcott). Nevertheless, within days of his appointment he had a result, Frobisher triumphantly delivering to Francis Walsingham a sample of silver and gold as proof of the ore's value.

On 6 March 1578, John Dee was invited to go to Tower Hill, where he was to act as an expert witness for a final and definitive trial of the ore.

Jonas worked away at two hundredweight of the stone delivered from Muscovy House, grinding it down, heating it up, producing great clouds of acrid smoke and, eventually, a tiny quantity of precious metal: five shillings' worth of silver and three shillings' worth of gold. If the rest of the ore yielded similar quantities, that would mean it was worth £28 per ton. To some it was a disappointment. "Frobisher's gold is now melted and does not turn out so valuable as he at first boasted," Philip Sidney wrote to his friend Languet the following month.[35]

But Frobisher claimed that the ore could be mined and transported back to England for less than £8 a ton. And Jonas pledged that, if the samples were like the ones he had tried that day, he could probably extract the metals from them for around £10 a ton. It did not require Dee's mathematical expertise to work out that even with the ore producing such modest yields, there were still big profits to be made.

Just to egg the pudding, Frobisher also claimed that the French were even now equipping twelve ships to sail to Meta Incognita and take possession of the land. So if he did not get back there fast, they might find both the ore and the country taken.

And so, on 25 May, another expedition departed, this time with a fleet of fifteen ships, hastily equipped and manned by shoemakers, tailors, musicians, gardeners, anyone Frobisher could find—and also, it has recently been discovered, a highly placed Spanish spy. Through his ambassador to the English court Don Bernadino de Mendoza, King Philip of Spain had been monitoring Frobisher's enterprise at least since the launch of the second expedition. Mendoza had even managed to smuggle a sample of Frobisher's "minerals" back to Spain. From the detailed report later submitted to Mendoza, it is clear that the spy was one of the assayers taken on the expedition, perhaps even Frobisher's chief assayer, Robert Denham.[36]

The fleet returned the following September having lost a ship and several crew members, and found an astonishing 1,150 tons of the black rock. As the Spanish spy noted, they had also discovered other glistening souvenirs, such as "a stone like white sapphire, though not as hard, and another like ruby, but with a depth of colour inferior to jacinth."[37]

Despite such apparent bounty, poor Michael Lok was sunk. Two months later, he totted up the totals and arrived at a provisional result of over £20,000, well over the initial budget, and roughly equivalent to 10 percent of the entire Royal Exchequer.[38] Buried in the midst of that vast total was over £2,000 of his own money, including £100 he had invested on behalf of John Dee, perhaps as payment for consulting services.

Lok also found himself the target of increasingly hostile attacks by Frobisher, presumably launched to deflect any blame for the overspend that might otherwise be aimed at the captain of the enterprise. Lok was, Frobisher fulminated, a fraud, a cozener, "no venturer at all in the voyages, a bankrupt knave." On the latter point at least Frobisher was not far from the truth. Lok was declared bankrupt, and the Cathay Company he had founded went into receivership under Thomas Allen, a scientist whose name was closely coupled with Dee's (often by their enemies). Lok ended up in Fleet Prison, where he passed his time issuing desperate petitions for help.

Meanwhile, efforts continued to extract gold from the mountain of ore that had been brought back, which was stored at Dartford. They proved fruitless. One of the final attempts was made by William Williams, the assay master at the Tower of London, who had tested Frobisher's original sample. After weeks of hot work, he sent the results of his efforts to Walsingham. Embedded in the sealing wax was a pinhead of silver.[39]

XIII

❧

ON 22 November 1577, Dee set off for Windsor Castle, where the court was in residence. He opted to make the fifteen-mile journey by horse rather than boat, perhaps because of the strange tidal movements he had noted in the river two days earlier. In his satchel, he carried a document that he had been working on for some time, and upon which rested his latest and most ambitious bid to be recognized as the court's official philosopher and cosmographer.

He arrived at the castle to find the court in a fluster. It had been an eventful year: Walsingham's spies had exposed yet another plot to unseat Elizabeth, this one masterminded by Don John of Austria; a bad outbreak of plague during the summer had confined the queen to Greenwich and prevented her from making her usual progress around her kingdom; and Sir Francis Drake was making final preparations for his epic voyage around the globe, a risky venture into the Spanish main that the queen herself was backing to the tune of 1,000 marks. Within the past few days a heavenly sign had appeared that had intensified the histrionic mood. It was a comet or "blazing star," which, Dee observed, had "bred great fear and doubt in many of the Court."

It was possibly in the midst of the hubbub that Dee's eye first fell upon the woman he would marry: Jane Fromonds, lady-in-waiting to Lady Howard of Effingham, wife of the Lord Admiral who later commanded the fleet that defeated the Armada. Jane came from Cheam, a village six miles south of Mortlake and within sight of the extravagant Tudor turrets and cupolas of Elizabeth's magnificent summer palace, Nonsuch.

She would be his third wife. His second marriage had been

blessed by the queen herself, but his wife, whose name remains unknown, had died in 1575 just a few months after the wedding. Jane was then just twenty-two years old, and Dee fifty. Despite the age difference, they would develop a strong bond that endured epic travels and testing travails.

Dee finally got to see the queen on 25 November. He does not record what they talked about, but it was likely to be the significance of the comet, which, as we shall see, he considered to be a sign not of imminent catastrophe for Elizabeth, but part of a much greater cosmic realignment.

They met again on 28 November. Drake was in the midst of preparations for his voyage around the world, and, catching the mood of adventure sweeping through court, Dee laid before the queen an astounding proposal. England, he said, should challenge Spain's imperial claim to the New World.

England was at this time a relatively poor European nation, on the political as well as geographical margins of the Continent. The court was riddled with debt, its dazzling displays just a disguise for the sparseness, poverty, and fragility of everyday life. Militarily, the country was weak. Following an abortive intervention in France to gain Le Havre, naval policy had been reduced to little more than licensed piracy against Spanish merchant shipping. So Dee's proposal to challenge the might of imperial Spain must have seemed ambitious, if not ridiculous.

Following Columbus's discovery of South America in 1492, Pope Alexander VI had issued a bull proposing a division of the New World between Portugal and Spain along an imaginary north-south line that ran 370 leagues west of the Azores. This gave Portugal control over established routes to the West Indies, and Spain possession of any discoveries made in North America and the area of South America west of modern Brazil.[1] The bull had been formalized by the Treaty of Tordesillas in 1494, and it was on this basis that the two nations had established their domination not just of America, but the Atlantic, a position that had so far barely been dented by the English mariners' adventures into the northern oceans.

Pages from Dee's private diary, a copy of the *Ephemerides Novae* by Ioannes Stadius for the month of November 1577. The tables show the positions and astrological conjunctions of the Sun, Moon, and planets for each day of the month. The scribbles in the margins, which collectively make up Dee's personal diary, are his notes on events that took place during the month.

For example, for 3 November (marked with a cross and entered at the bottom of the page above), he has written "William Rogers of Mortlack, abowt 7 of the clock in the morning, cut his own throte, by the fiend [deletion] his instigation." For 22 November, he has written "I rid to Windsor, to the Q. Maiestie" beneath a sketch of a crown. His sketch of the comet that appeared that month is at the top of the page. *Bodleian Library, University of Oxford. MS. Ashmole 487*

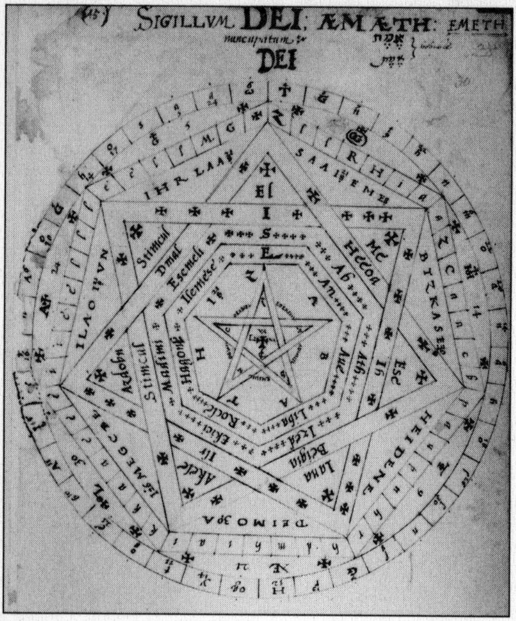

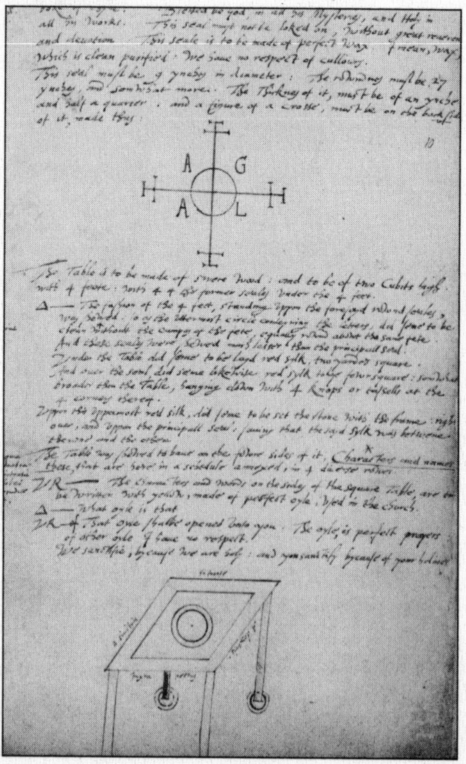

At the right, Dee's transcript for his first angelic action with Edward "Talbot" (Kelley), which took place on 10 March 1582. The triangle that appears in the left-hand margin was the device Dee used to refer to himself (the symbol for delta, the fourth letter of the Greek alphabet). "UR" is the angel Uriel. The diagram above shows the device to be imprinted on the back of the Sigillum Dei; the diagram on the right shows how the seal was to be positioned on the table of practice, and the placing of four smaller seals beneath the table's feet. In the text, Uriel is telling Dee how the seals and table are to be made. *The British Library, MS Sloane 3188f.10*

Dee's birth chart, one of three to be found among his papers. The central square shows the date and location of his birth (13 July 1527, 4:02 P.M., at a latitude of 51 degrees and 32 minutes north of the equator). The surrounding triangular segments represent the astrological houses, and the symbols and numbers the positions of the star signs and planets in degrees and minutes. *Bodleian Library, University of Oxford. MS. Ashmole 1788, fol. 137r*

A sixteenth-century sailor navigating by reference to the Sun. Few English mariners of the time had the experience of ocean sailing, and had to be taught unfamiliar methods of celestial and solar navigation by Dee (engraving by P. Galle after Stradanus). *Mary Evans Picture Library*

(LOWER LEFT): The frontispiece of Dee's *Monas Hieroglyphica* or The hieroglyphic monad (1564). The hieroglyph itself is shown in the center of the page, combining several astrological symbols into one, which Dee believed represented the unity of the cosmos. *The British Library g718.g.6*

(LOWER RIGHT): The frontispiece of Dee's *General and Rare Memorials* (1577), his work on navigation. The highly allegorical image depicts Queen Elizabeth at the helm of Britain's imperial destiny. *The British Library 48.h.18*

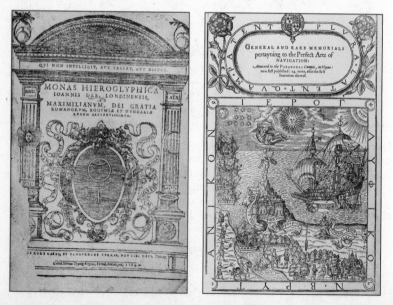

(LEFT): Gerardus Mercator (DeBrij, 1648), sixteenth-century Europe's greatest cartographer and Dee's close friend. *Mary Evans Picture Library*
(RIGHT): Sir Francis Walsingham (John de Critz the Elder, 1585), Elizabeth's chief spymaster. *National Portrait Gallery, London*

(LOWER LEFT): Queen Elizabeth (Marcus Gheeraerts the Younger, c.1592). *National Portrait Gallery, London*
(LOWER RIGHT): Sir Philip Sidney (unknown artist), who half-jokingly described Dee as his "unknown God." *National Portrait Gallery, London*

Gemma Frisius, Mercator's tutor, at his desk (from *Arithmeticae practicae methodus facilis per Gemma Frisium medicum ac mathematicum*, Antwerp, 1540). *Museum of the History of Science, Oxford*

(RIGHT): Sir Martin Frobisher, adventurer. *Bodleian Library, University of Oxford*

(ABOVE): Sir Humphrey Gilbert's 1576 world map drawn up to demonstrate the existence of a Northwest Passage around America, which provided a navigable route from Europe via the Strait of Anian to the Moluccas Islands, Japan, and China ("Cataia"). *The British Library C.32.b.29*

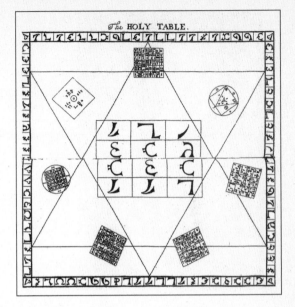

The design for Dee's table of practice, upon which the crystal ball or "shew stone" was to be placed. The strange characters written in the word squares and around the edge were letters from the "Enochian" alphabet communicated to Dee by the angels.

One of a series of lurid illustrations that appeared in John Foxe's *Acts and Monuments*, showing the death by burning of Protestant heretics during Queen Mary's reign. *British Library c.37.h.2*

William Cecil, 1st Baron Burghley,
Elizabeth's Lord Treasurer
(unknown artist). *National
Portrait Gallery, London*

Depiction of a Copernican universe by Dee's pupil Thomas Digges in his
Prognostication Everlasting (1576). The image, drawn "according to the most
ancient doctrine of the Pythagoreans," was also one of the first truly modern
pictures of the cosmos, as it not only showed the earth orbiting around the
Sun, but described the stars as extending "infinitely up." *The British Library
C.54.d.15*

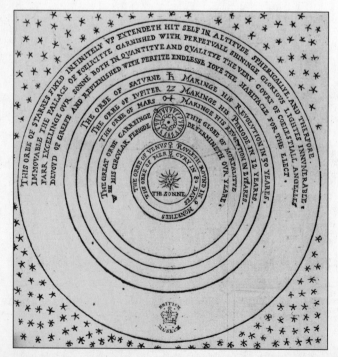

Dee now proposed to the queen that England should contest Pope Alexander's division of the globe. He justified this on the basis that several lands declared under the Treaty of Tordesillas to be the possessions of the Iberian nations, such as Frieseland, had already been colonized by the English. Much of the information for this claim came not just from the books in his library but from a detailed letter received from Mercator earlier that year, in which the great cartographer related the story of King Arthur's incursion into the northern "indrawing" seas around the Pole in the year 530. Mercator cited sources showing that some of the 4,000 members of the expedition who were lost had survived, the proof being that eight of their descendants appeared at the king of Norway's court in 1364.[2]

Dee had been working on this idea for some time, and proposed featuring it in a series of new works aimed at shifting English foreign policy into a new, adventurous, expansionist mode. One of these works was planned as his magnum opus, a four-volume survey of the idea of a "Brytish Impire" entitled *General and rare memorials pertayning to the Perfect Arte of Navigation*. The influence of this extraordinary work is hard to judge, because, despite its subject matter, it has been ignored by most Tudor histories, presumably because Dee's magical ideas do not fit in with modern conceptions of the scientific basis of discovery. What can be said is that it was the first authoritative statement of the idea of a British Empire, and it was delivered to the queen during the period when that Empire was about to make its first appearance on the geopolitical scene.

*   *   *

MEMORIALS WAS A typical Dee production: practical, political, scholarly, and mystical. Its title page combined all these elements in an elaborate allegory that has been called a "British hieroglyphic."[3] It features Elizabeth at the helm of the ship of imperial monarchy, watched over by St. Michael, and drawn by the figure of "Lady Occasion" ("Lady Opportunity," in more modern terms) to a fortified citadel overlooking conquered lands. And above Elizabeth hang the Sun, Moon, stars, and a glowing sphere bearing the tetragammaton, a potent cabalistic formula, all of which shine down their blessings on the enterprise.

The first volume of the *Memorials* was about building and financing a substantial navy, the "Master Key" of the whole scheme, providing the security England needed to pursue her imperial ambitions.[4] Since the end of Henry VIII's reign, England had boasted one of the few standing fleets of military ships in Europe. However, the fleet was small, around thirty-four ships at the time Elizabeth ascended to the throne, of which twelve were considered "of no continuance and not worth repair." By comparison, Spain, at the height of her powers, boasted over 200 ships.[5] Dee proposed that the disparity should be corrected by creating a "Petty Navy Royal" of sixty "tall ships" weighing between 160 and 200 tons and twenty smaller barks between 20 and 50 tons "very strong and Warlike," crewed by 6,660 men "liberally waged."[6] The money for this would come not from the queen's own coffers, but through taxation, on the grounds that it would ultimately be the nation's wealth rather than just hers that would benefit from the investment.

The second volume was to be a series of navigational tables giving longitudes and latitudes calculated using Dee's invention, the "Paradoxical Compass." It was to be bigger than the English Bible, which then set the standard in terms of book size, and printed on large sheets or "quires" of paper. It proved too elaborate to publish, and the manuscript is now lost.[7] The contents of the third volume were secret—so secret that, Dee pledged, it "should be utterly suppressed or delivered to Vulcan's custody." Whether or not he cast the work into Vulcan's fires, or whether he kept it, remains unknown. Like the second volume, it is now lost.

The fourth volume, *Of Famous and Rich Discoveries*, has survived, though unfortunately Vulcan briefly got his hands on it. A badly burned copy is to be found in the British Library,[8] and a list of the contents of the missing parts (the first five chapters) is summarized by Samuel Purchas.[9]

The other work Dee was writing at this time was a manuscript aimed exclusively at the queen. It was much smaller, but in many respects more potent. Entitled *Brytanici Imperii Limites*, it summarized Dee's contention that British claims to foreign lands extended well beyond the borders of the British Isles. As well as the voyages of King Arthur, he cited mariners such as Madoc, the Welsh prince said to have crossed the Atlantic in 1170, which proved that "a great part of the sea coasts of Atlantis (otherwise called *America*) next unto us, and of all the isles near unto the same, from *Florida* northerly, and chiefly of all the islands Septentrional [i.e., northerly], great and small, the Title Royal and supreme government is due."[10]

Dee left Windsor a week and a half after his arrival, having attended the knighting of Christopher Hatton, to whom Dee dedicated his *General and rare memorials*. The following August, he reported to the queen again, this time in Norwich, where she was in the middle of her summer progress around the realm. He showed her the latest version of his *Brytanici Imperii Limites*, together with a map (now lost), which marked the extent of the domains to which he felt she could lay claim.

News of Dee's daring proposals spread. Despite the failure of Frobisher's ore to yield its riches, interest in exploration intensified, and Mortlake quickly became a clearinghouse for the latest information about new discoveries. The mapmaker Abraham Ortelius, who had recently been made the Spanish geographer royal, dropped by; Alexander Simon, "the Ninevite," outlined plans for an overland journey to Persia; the lawyer Richard Hakluyt, whose cousin and namesake would publish the chronicles of the age of discovery, discussed the claim that King Arthur had conquered Frieseland; Simão Fernandez came with maps made after a trip to Norumbega, the area of America that would become New York and New England.[11]

Just as the navigators came with news, so privateers gathered in search of opportunities. The most frequent visitors were Adrian Gilbert and John Davies. They were an odd couple. Dee found them awkward and argumentative and frequently fell out with them. The historian John Aubrey described Gilbert as "the greatest buffoon in England," and Dee did not think much better of him.[12] Davies was no buffoon, but neither was he an angel, later being arrested on the orders of the Privy Council for using a mission organized by the earl of Cumberland to launch an unprovoked attack on a friendly trading vessel owned by Florentine and Venetian merchants.

Nevertheless, they were to be tolerated. Adrian was a key figure in an important seafaring dynasty; his brother was Sir Humphrey, the man who started the search for the Northwest Passage, and his half-brother Walter Raleigh. Together with Dee, Adrian and Davies set up the "Fellowship of New Navigations Atlanticall and Septentionall [i.e., northerly]," and in 1583 succeeded in getting royal backing to "discover and settle the northerly parts of Atlantis, called Novus Orbis"—in other words, to colonize North America.

This plan was first mooted on 28 August 1580, when Dee was visited by Sir Humphrey Gilbert himself. Two weeks later, their discussions culminated with Gilbert's agreement that, should he succeed in taking possession of the northern parts of the New World, Dee would get the "royalties of discoveries all to the north above the parallel of the 50 degree of latitude"—in other words, most of Canada and all of Alaska.

Gilbert, however, was having difficulties finding the backing he needed to launch the venture, and in a desperate attempt to raise more money had teamed up with Sir George Peckham and Sir Thomas Gerard, two Catholics whose sympathies had led to their estates being, as the Spanish ambassador put it in an alarmed report to King Philip of Spain, "ruined."[13] In 1582, Peckham visited Dee to discuss the plan. He was particularly concerned to learn Dee's grounds for challenging the Treaty of Tordesillas. He did not want to embark on a venture that would anger the Pope, and needed to know whether the treaty applied to the "whole world's discoveries," including the north. In return for reassurances that it did not, he promised Dee 5,000 acres of Norumbega. Dee was promised a further 5,000 acres from Peckham's partner, Sir Thomas Gerard.[14]

Dee's involvement with these schemes helped define the sense of mission, almost of national destiny, that drove the adventurers across the Atlantic. "It is no small comfort unto an English Gentleman," wrote the diplomat Charles Merbery, "finding him self in a far country, when he may boldly shew his face, and his forehead

unto any foreign Nation: sit side by side with the proudest
Spaniard: cheek by cheek with the stoutest German: foot to foot
with the forewardest Frenchman: knowing that this most Royal
Prince (her Majesty's highness) is no whit subject, nor inferior unto
any of theirs. But that she may also (if she please) challenge the superiority both over some of them, and over many other kings, and
Princes more. As *master Dee hath very learnedly of late . . . shewed
unto her Majesty, that she may justly call her self LADY, and
EMPERESS of all the North Islands.*"[15]

Elizabeth became increasingly enthusiastic about this idea, and
was anxious to be kept informed of its development. Dee, however,
was being distracted by other matters. At the beginning of 1580 he
started to conduct a series of alchemical experiments with his assistant, Roger Cook, whose flourishing if somewhat turbulent career
would later bring him into the employment of Henry, the "Wizard
Earl" of Northumberland and Rudolf II, the Holy Roman Emperor.
There is also evidence that Dee was trying to contact the spirit world,
occasionally with Adrian Gilbert. It was perhaps in connection with
rumors about these activities that Dee found himself the target of a
campaign of defamation launched by one Vincent Murphyn, the
son of a royal cook, who had been forging letters in Dee's name.[16]

Such distractions drew Dee away from court. Elizabeth started
to notice his absence, and wanted to know what he was up to. So,
on 17 September 1580 she decided she should go to Mortlake and
see for herself.

❊   ❊   ❊

DEE WAS HARD at work in his library when her coach drew up on
the main road from Richmond. Alerted by a member of the household, he went to the door to find her standing in resplendent isolation in the field beyond his garden. "She beckoned her hand for
me," he wrote in his diary. "I came to her coach side: she very
speedily pulled off her glove and gave me her hand to kiss: and to be
short, willed me to resort to her Court."[17]

He duly did as he was commanded, two weeks later delivering
"my two rolls of the Queen's Majesty's title," the finished version

of his *Brytanici Imperii Limites*, as she strolled through her gardens at Richmond Palace. She was excited by what she saw, and following lunch invited him to her inner sanctum, the Privy Chamber, where they were joined by William Cecil, Lord Burghley and, as Lord Treasurer, Elizabeth's chief minister. Here Dee got an abrupt shock. Cecil, who was by nature conservative, did not approve of Dee's ideas. He did not want to upset the Spanish, or lay claim to North American lands of doubtful value. Where hotter bloods such as Robert Dudley and Philip Sidney were seduced by Dee's vision of a new empire, Cecil was alarmed by it.

Dee stayed on at Richmond for two further days, spending most of the time in Cecil's chambers arguing his case. The discussion was civil, but when Dee returned once more he found that Cecil would not speak to him. "I doubt much of some new grief conceived," he later recorded in his diary.[18] From the frontispiece of *General and Rare Memorials*, through his maps of "Atlantis" and the opportunities described in the *Brytanici Imperii Limites*, he had summoned up this fantastic vision of a new world order that might ultimately reunite Christendom, build a new Jerusalem, and at the moment that Elizabeth hovered on the brink of embracing it, Cecil had wandered in, raised a doubt, and swept it all away.

The stars, whose positions were tabulated next to his diary entries, now began to conspire against Dee. He returned home from court to find his mother seriously ill. She died on 10 October at four in the morning, a "godly end."[19] Later that day the queen called by, and offered Dee her condolences. She also reassured him that Cecil had not taken against him, and she would study his proposals further. Indeed, Cecil would send Dee a haunch of venison as a peace offering a few days later. But as Dee well knew, a joint of meat did not denote a change in policy. He would retain a suspicion and a fear of Elizabeth's indomitable grandee that he could never overcome, and he remained at a distance from court that would never close.

Of course, much that he had described in the writings he presented to the queen would in one form or another happen. The navy would become the "master key" of English military strength,

England would challenge the Spanish—to spectacular effect in its defeat of the Armada in 1588—North America would be colonized, a British Empire would emerge, and the expeditions that Dee had in the last few years been helping to plan would lay its foundations. But he would have no part in this future, not even in the adventures of the "Fellowship of New Navigations Atlanticall and Septentionall" that he had set up with Adrian Gilbert and John Davies. His place in the fellowship was taken by a younger navigator, the man who would soon attempt to found England's first true colony in the Americas: Sir Walter Raleigh.

The reason Dee withdrew from such geopolitical issues, and ultimately from courtly affairs, may partly be related to Cecil's rejection. But there was another reason. It is hinted at in a doodle in the top margin of the page of his diary in which he describes his visit to Windsor in November 1577. There he has drawn the curved trajectory of the celestial phenomenon that had caused such a stir at court and across the country that winter, the arrival of the "blazing star."

PART FIVE
THE FIERY
TRIGON

✤

Prince: Saturn and Venus this year in conjunction!
What says th'almanac to that?
Poins: And look whether the fiery Trigon, his man
be not lisping to his master's old tables, his
note-book, his counsel-keeper.

WILLIAM SHAKESPEARE,
2 Henry IV

XIV

⚜

A T about nine in the evening on Thursday, 8 March 1582, Dee watched the sky over Mortlake turn the color of blood.[1] He had never seen anything like it before. A strange glow formed and spread out, as though the clouds themselves had caught fire.

Earlier that day, a Mr. Clerkson had turned up. Clerkson seems to have been acting as an agent for scholars and itinerant "skryers" or spirit mediums, introducing them to prospective patrons. A week before, he had arrived at Mortlake with a Thomas Robinson—"Magnus," Dee had called him, suggesting that he was some sort of noble or learned figure, though apparently neither noble nor learned enough to figure again in Dee's diary.[2] This time Mr. Clerkson had turned up with someone new, a "friend" who called himself Edward Talbot.

Talbot is a mysterious figure, every bit as elusive as the spirits he would soon release into Dee's life. If he did not exist—and that seems to be the only fact about him beyond dispute—it would be only too easy to invent him. When he was first introduced to Dee, even his name was an invention. He was really Edward Kelley. Kelley had possibly decided to call himself Talbot because it was the name of an ancient Lancastrian dynasty, and he may have thought that the lineage would impress Dee (or Clerkson, or his previous employer, who was perhaps Thomas Allen, the mathematician and receiver for Lok's bankrupt Cathay Company[3]).

According to a birth chart drawn up by Dee, Kelley was born in Worcester on 1 August 1555, which would make him twenty-six years old at the time of this first encounter. An interpretation of the

chart made a century later by the antiquarian and mystic Elias Ashmole certainly indicates that there was something extraordinary
about the young man. He was, the stars suggested, "of clear understanding, quick apprehension, an excellent wit, and a great propen-
sity to philosophical studies." The position of Jupiter promised great
fame, but, being ill-aspected, portended misfortune and ultimate disaster. Mars's position indicated he was rash, boastful, presumptuous,
stubbornly weak, histrionic, deranged, and treacherous.[4]

This vivid astrological portrait (written, of course, retrospectively and clearly colored by the incidents of Kelley's life) is supported by the only independent documentation concerning his
origins, the parish registers of Worcester. These show that an
Edward Kelley, son of Patrick, was christened on 2 August 1555
(i.e., the day after his birth) at St. Swithin's, Worcester. It seems very
likely that this is the man who turned up at Dee's door that March
day, as both Edwards had a brother called Thomas (christened
1564) and a sister (identified as Elizabeth in the parish records).[5]

Thereafter, we are lost in legends. If these are to be believed,
the man Dee met was by any standards a remarkable figure, just the
sort of strange creature one might expect to meet the day after the
sky caught fire. He was a cripple, "Il Zoppo," as one papal official
once contemptuously described him, who went around with a
walking staff and due to his disability—or was it his diabolical
nature?—had difficulties kneeling.[6] He wore a cowl, giving him the
appearance of a monk, to conceal his ears.[7] At least one ear was certainly "diminished," according to a curious observer.[8] The unanswered question was why. It was commonly supposed that it had
been lopped for "coining" (forging or adulterating coins). There
were reports that at one stage in his eventful career he was a notary
in London, and specialized in forging title deeds—the sorts of deeds
that Dee himself collected as part of his scheme first proposed to
Queen Mary to preserve national "monuments," and which he now
kept in the "appendix" to his library at Mortlake.[9] Kelley was
reputedly found guilty of forgery, in which case his face might have
been scarred by the stones that had been hurled at him while he lan-
guished in the stocks.

He was also accused of being a "necromancer," a dabbler in dead bodies. According to one story, Kelley and a Paul Waring one night entered a park at Walton-le-Dale, near Preston in Lancashire, where they "invocated some one of the Infernal Regiment, to know certain passages in the life, as also what might be known by the Devil's foresight, of the manner and time of the death of a Noble young Gentleman, as then in Wardship."

These "Black Ceremonies of that Night being ended," Kelley then asked a local, one of the noble young gentleman's servants, to direct him and his companion to the freshest corpse in the adjoining church-yard. He was shown the grave of a pauper, interred that day. "He and the said Waring entreated this foresaid servant to go with them to the grave of the man so lately interred, which he did; and withal, did help them dig up the carcass . . . whom by their incantations, they made him (or rather some evil Spirit through his Organs) to speak, who delivered strange Predictions concerning the said Gentleman."[10] The source of this deliciously diabolical tale was apparently the servant who had directed Kelley to the pauper's grave, although neither the servant nor the gentleman he served has ever been identified.

This story linked Kelley with another colorful Lancashire character, the self-styled "Baron of Walton," Thomas Langton, who in 1593 was accused of harboring Catholic spies. According to one account, Kelley was hauled up before Langton, who as local squire had to decide what to do with him. Langton shared Kelley's interest in the occult, and used his influence as a friend of Lord Strange, the son of Lancashire's Lord Lieutenant, to engineer Kelley's release.[11]

Yet another legend suggests the reason why Kelley turned up at the house of Dr. Dee that March morning. Elias Ashmole heard a tale about Kelley from the alchemist William Backhouse. Ashmole described himself as being Backhouse's "Son," in other words, the inheritor of his alchemical knowledge. Backhouse lived at Swallow-field in Berkshire, at a house packed with "all manner of Inventions and Rarities."[12]

Knowing of Ashmole's interest in Dee and Kelley, Backhouse told his "son" that Kelley had once "Cheated a Lady of certain jewels"—a hint, perhaps, that among his many other powers were those of the con man. Having acquired his booty, Kelley evidently made his escape from the cheated lady's house, but found himself being chased by an unidentified "Pursevant."

Kelley had arrived at Dee's under an assumed name with the intention of lying low. However, the cover failed to fool the Pursevant, who, according to Backhouse, eventually caught up with his quarry at Mortlake and confronted him. Exercising the same powers that had enabled him to dupe the lady in the first place, Kelley somehow managed to persuade this man that he would recompense the lady for his crime, whereupon the Pursevant agreed to go away.

The truth of this story, which only too conveniently confirms Kelley's reputation as a swindler, is impossible to establish, as Backhouse, through Ashmole, is the only source. Dee makes no direct reference to the episode in his own diary, though he does include an entry three months after their meeting that "I have confirmed that Talbot was a cosener," in other words, a fraud. Beside these words Kelley indignantly (and, given it was Dee's private diary, impertinently) scribbled "a horrible and slanderous lie."[13]

According to Backhouse, one of the reasons Kelley decided to follow Dee to the Continent eighteen months after they first met was that he was still being stalked by the implacable Pursevant. However, the tactic failed, and the outraged gentleman, hearing reports of Kelley's subsequent fame in Bohemia, traveled out there to confront him again. This time he was rewarded with one of Kelley's now celebrated alchemical "projections." Using a tiny scattering of magic "powder," Kelley produced £2000 worth of gold, which, together with a sample of the powder, he handed over to the now placated Pursevant. The gentleman took the booty home and used it to buy up large areas of Warwickshire, and to turn a flint he found in the grounds of his expanding estates into a huge diamond.

Disentangling the truth from such a tapestry of tales has proved impossible. Dee, however, knew little or nothing about the reputation of the man who turned up at his home with Mr. Clerkson.[14] Indeed, as he opened his front door, his initial impression might have been that Clerkson had picked up yet another desperate itinerant "skryer" looking for work.

Thanks to a combination of factors—a series of famines in the early 1570s, the destabilizing influx of gold and silver from the New World, urbanization, religious turmoil—the Elizabethan highways had become crowded with itinerants. This was something Dee himself had commented on in one of his reports for the government. Such people would have been a common sight, tramping past his door on their way to what they supposed to be the gilded cobbles of London's streets, but where they were more likely to encounter poverty or plague.

Skryers like Talbot were usually drawn from the ranks of these dispossessed souls. As church records show, they were a particularly common sight during the late sixteenth century. Almost every parish, and apparently several aristocratic households, boasted a "cunning man," who for the price of a beer or a bed would summon spirits and tell fortunes. They were a strange fraternity of young men, literate but generally lowborn, often outcasts or fugitives forced to live on the fringes of society. Like actors or artists in the modern era, they were expected to be odd, as it was their distinctive sensibility that enabled them to pick up occult emanations. Hence even the most respected patrons would tolerate their eccentric, "melancholic," even criminal behavior.[15]

"Talbot" was apparently just such a creature. However, there was something more. He was unusually well educated for a man of his status, and strangely determined to get a place in Dee's household. Indeed, there is every indication that at some level the mysterious man who turned up at Mortlake on that March afternoon of 1582 had been expected.

XV

·※·

J UST as the skies lit up the day before Kelley's arrival, so they
had a decade earlier, on the evening of 11 November 1572. Dee
saw it happen, though left no contemporary record of the sighting. Hundreds of miles away, in Denmark, Tycho Brahe, an admirer
of Dee's and one of the world's greatest astronomers, saw it too, and
left a detailed account.[1] These two men, and in the coming months
many others scattered across Europe, from Prague to Paris, were all
held in rapt attention by what they saw at a single point in the sky: a
new star.

Brahe was living in an abbey near Helsingborg, which his Protestant uncle, Steen Bille, had taken over with orders to purge it of
"ungodly life." Bille had allowed Brahe to build a small laboratory
in one of the abbey's outhouses, where the young scientist had been
able to continue with his studies for two years undisturbed—just
the conditions Dee so desperately sought, but was still denied.
Brahe did not discuss the experiments he conducted there, but he is
likely to have been dabbling in alchemy, which would remain an
interest throughout his career.

On the November evening in question, on his way from the laboratory to the abbey buildings for supper, he glanced up at Cassiopeia, a constellation that forms the shape of a squashed W, with
two bright stars called Schedar and Caph making up the last
upward stroke of the letter.

As he looked at the constellation, Brahe noticed a point of bright
light suspended over the second V of the constellation. It was con-
siderably brighter than Schedar and Caph, the equal, even, of the
planet Venus at maximum brilliance—the brightest object, after the
Moon, in the night sky.

Brahe could not believe his eyes. He asked his servants if they could see anything. They confirmed that they could. So could a group of passing peasants. Something was definitely there, a cosmic beacon flickering in the midst of the Milky Way.

Brahe went back to his laboratory to fetch an observing instrument he had just built. It was an enormous sextant, the height of a man, with arms five and a half feet long. It was made of well-seasoned walnut wood rather than iron to make it lighter, but several servants were still needed to manhandle it into position. As soon as it was set up, Brahe began a series of observations to establish the apparition's exact position—an important measurement, for to discover what sort of entity it might be, he needed to know whether or not it moved in relation to the fixed stars, like a comet, or remained stationary.

The star remained clearly visible throughout the winter, revolving slowly in transit with its companion constellation around the nearby Pole Star. In the first few weeks of its appearance, it shone so brightly it could be seen in daylight hours. Its gleam was said even to penetrate thin cloud cover.

At some point during this period, Dee started making measurements of the star too. He was joined by his brilliant protégé, Thomas Digges. Digges's father, Leonard, had died when Thomas was fourteen, and sometime after, the boy had evidently adopted Dee as a surrogate parent.

Leonard had been a scientist, and Thomas had made it his vocation to continue with his father's work. In 1571, the year before the appearance of the strange light in Cassiopeia, Thomas had completed a book started by Leonard entitled *Pantometria*. In this work Thomas described how it was possible to put frames in lenses in a way that made distant objects seem close—to build a telescope or "perspective glass," as it was then known.[2]

The history of modern science tends to be portrayed as a series of brilliant ideas that formed more or less spontaneously in the capacious minds of individual men of genius. Usually, however, developments emerge in a far more haphazard fashion, their full significance remaining historically invisible for decades or even centuries. So it was with the telescope and its use as an astronomical instrument. Roger Bacon, the medieval English Fransciscan who Dee held up to be the ideal philosopher, had toyed with the idea of using lenses to "make the sun, moon and stars apparently descend to here below" as early as the mid-thirteenth century.[3]

During the late sixteenth century, research into the idea intensified, arousing government interest. In 1580, William Cecil, Elizabeth's chief minister, commissioned a report on the possible uses of mirrors and glasses. It identified England as having two leading figures in the field: John Dee and Thomas Digges.

Whether Dee and Digges actually built or used a telescope, however, remains undocumented. It is possible they simply could not afford to pay for one to be constructed, or if they did, could not get lenses of sufficient quality to see anything useful. In the early 1600s, Thomas Hariot, who visited Dee at Mortlake and like Dee was a close associate of Sir Walter Raleigh's, certainly owned a telescope, and used it to observe sunspots and the moons of Jupiter at the same time as Galileo.

It is unlikely that Brahe, Dee, and Digges used a telescope to observe Cassiopeia, even if they had access to one. Their primary instruments were cross-staffs and, in Digges's case at least, a six-foot ruler (probably hanging from the branch of a tree), from which he would observe from a fixed vantage point the alignment of the new star with those around it, to see if it was moving.

In 1573, as the object they had been watching began to fade, Dee and Digges both rushed out publications featuring their findings, which booksellers would often bind together as a single work. Brahe, who may have corresponded with Dee on the subject and openly praised the English astronomer's scientific skills, also released his findings. They sent tremors through the courts of Europe. This apparition, they showed, was a new star.

There was some dispute as to the last occasion a new star had appeared in the heavens.[4] Certainly there had not been one for centuries. There was the star observed by Hipparchus, the Nicaean astronomer, which appeared in 125 B.C. and was, it had been noted, followed by "great commotions" among the Jews. The only other heavenly body to appear that was clearly documented as being a star was, in Christendom at least, the most auspicious astronomical phenomenon ever to be recorded: the Star of Bethlehem.

Another possibility was that the apparition was a comet or meteor with a tail too small to be seen with the naked eye. Such an explanation had placated troubling appearances of this kind of phenomenon before. But this was no comet. The work done by Brahe, Dee, Digges, and others provided abundant evidence that it was simply too far away to be within the "sublunar" realm of air and fire between the earth's surface and the sphere carrying the Moon— the only region, according to the accepted cosmology, where such entities could exist.

The idea of a new star split political opinion across Europe. Valesius of Covarruvias, physician to Philip II of Spain, reassured his powerful patron that it must be an existing star that had become visible because the air or condensation on one of the spheres carrying the planets had cleared.[5] In Italy, the veteran mathematician Girolamo Cardano, whose own philosophical speculations had led to a number of brushes with the papal authorities, agreed, proposing that it might even be a reappearance of the Star of Bethlehem.

These desperate explanations, however, were dismissed by most astronomers. Thaddeus Hagecius (Hajek), later physician to Holy Roman Emperor Rudolf II as well as Dee's associate and landlord, came to the same conclusion as his future tenant, as did the powerful Landgrave (or prince) of Hesse in Germany, William IV, Europe's most scientifically minded ruler, who wrote a paper on the subject.

The issue was not simply a matter of academic debate. It went to the heart of the existing cosmological and, by implication, theological and political order, and did so at a time when, across Europe, that same order was facing innumerable destabilizing challenges from elsewhere. If this was a new star, it meant that the great outer orb of the universe, unchanged since the moment of Creation, which in its very pattern ordained the arrangement of earthly powers, had somehow changed, sprung a leak, and let through a flash of divine radiation. Indeed, when all the implications were worked through, the new star threatened to undermine the entire basis of current cosmology. This created the perfect environment, Digges observed, for alternatives to be seriously considered, one in particular that, like the new star itself, would soon expand from a barely detectable glimmer to a sparkling beacon of change: the theory advanced by the Polish scholar Nicholas Copernicus of the heliocentric universe.

Copernicus was not primarily an astronomer, being more interested in studying books than stars. It was in one of these books that he noted the work of a Greek astronomer Aristarchus, who suggested in the third century B.C. that the Sun rather than the earth was at the center of the universe. Copernicus began to develop this idea, seeing if it fitted in mathematically with the known positions of the planets over time. Aristarchus, Copernicus also noted, had faced charges of impiety for such speculations, which perhaps explains the Pole's initial reticence in publishing his views on the subject. Nevertheless, reports of his ideas circulated in 1540 by George Rheticus had failed to provoke the anticipated cries of outrage, so he decided to write a book setting them out in full: *De revolutionibus orbium coelestium* (On the revolutions of the heavenly bodies). It finally appeared in 1543, the year of his death.

The universe described in *De revolutionibus*, with the Sun in the center, and the earth demoted to a mere satellite, was presented as a mathematical model of the universe, rather than a picture of physical reality. Indeed, gazing up at the stars from sixteenth-century Poland, England, Denmark, or anywhere else on the globe's surface, there was nothing anyone could point to that decisively proved Copernicus's model to be either true or false. Furthermore, as a physical theory, it had a number of problems, such as explaining why, if the earth was in a state of constant and rapid revolution, anything remained stuck to it.

A greater problem was that Copernicanism did not merely involve a slight adjustment in the human point of view of the stars and the planets. It left the Aristotelian basis of natural philosophy in tatters. For example, with the old geocentric model, gravity was explained on the basis that all objects tend toward the center of the universe. Shift the earth from the center and an entirely new theory of gravity would be needed—a theory that would be forthcoming the following century, when Isaac Newton published his tract *De Motu* (On motion), the precursor of his magnum opus *Principia Mathematica*.

So, in the absence of conclusive evidence to prove Copernicanism, it is perhaps surprising that so many astronomers believed in it. However, the system had its attractions, too. One was its elegance. It did not require the many elaborate orbital mechanisms such as "epicycles" and "deferents" that Ptolemy had been forced to invent to fit his own theory in with the way the planets moved.

However, the main attraction, at least for some astronomers, and almost certainly for Dee, was philosophical as much as mathematical. On the page of *De revolutionibus* where Copernicus depicted his new universe, he decorated it with what appears to be a paean to sun worship.

In modern eyes, *De revolutionibus* is represented as a work that wiped away an old worldview. But for its author, it represented quite the reverse: a return to an ancient, simple idea, one that Copernicus's detractors considered pagan, and his supporters argued would bring philosophy and mathematics back into alignment. The work is full of allusions that were clearly inspired by the Renaissance fascination with recovering the ancient theology—the "*prisci theologi*"—believed to predate the Babel of competing doctrines that had been let loose by the Reformation. Copernicus even invoked Hermes Trismegistus, the "Thrice Great" prophet identified with the Egyptian god Thoth and considered by many Renaissance theologians as of equal status to Moses.[6] Trismegistus, Copernicus observed, had regarded the Sun as the "visible God." To confirm the truth of Copernicus's cosmos would represent not a great leap forward into the unknown so much as a step back to an earlier, more authentic understanding of the universe.

Now, with the appearance of this new star, there was a chance of settling the matter once and for all. Some Copernicans were convinced it was providential, a heaven-sent sign from God to support their case. This was the view of Thomas Digges, as he explained in a letter to William Cecil, pleading with the Lord Treasurer to support the sort of astronomical work he and Dee had undertaken:

> I cannot here set a limit to again urging, exhorting and admonishing all students of *Celestial Wisdom*, with respect to how great and how hoped-for an opportunity has been offered to Earthdwellers of examining whether the *Monstrous System* of Celestial globes . . . has been fully corrected and amended by that divine *Copernicus* of more than human talent, or whether there still remains something else to be further considered. This, I have considered, cannot be done otherwise than through most careful observations, now of this *Most Rare Star*, now of the rest of the wandering stars and through various changes in their appearances, and all done in the various regions of this dark and obscure *Terrestrial Star*, where, wandering as strangers, we lead, in a short space of time, a life harassed by varied fortunes.[7]

Digges's outspoken support for Copernicus was brave. The theory's Hermetic and therefore pagan resonances brought it dangerously close to heresy, as Galileo would later discover when his telescopic observations finally settled the matter. This explains why Dee was more circumspect. He was still regularly assailed by accusations of necromancy and sorcery, so in his published astronomical works he was careful to be noncommittal on the matter of heliocentricity. Nevertheless, he was undoubtedly a Copernican. In 1557 he and John Field, the man who was his cellmate when he was arrested during Queen Mary's reign, published a table of star positions. It was among the first ever to use calculations based on the Copernican system.[8] He would be naturally attracted to the theory, because it fitted so closely with his own mission to recover the *prisci theologi*.

Dee also, like Digges, clearly regarded the new star as an important piece of evidence in support of Copernicanism. In fact, the two of them thought it suggested an even more radical theory. The most significant feature of the star was not just that it appeared, but that its level of brightness changed. How could this be explained, given that stars were supposed to be stuck to the celestial sphere, illuminated by the heavenly light beyond? Dee came up with an extraordinary suggestion: that the star was moving in space. This implied that it was not attached to a sphere, and that there was space into which it could recede beyond the celestial sphere, traditionally regarded as the preserve of heaven itself. Young Digges, reflecting his more radical and open Copernicanism, took this idea further, suggesting that, as it orbited the Sun, it was the earth that was moving away from and toward the star. The problem with Digges's argument was that the star disappeared completely in March of 1574, and was never seen again.

Nevertheless, in 1576, Digges published a treatise in which he set out the idea that the universe was made up of continuous space in which the heavenly bodies were suspended like particles in a limitless body of water.[9] It appeared as an appendix to a new edition of his father's work, which perhaps explains why this most radical of theories appeared almost without comment, and has remained more or less unnoticed by historians of science ever since.

Such astronomical speculations had enormous astrological implications. The new star was a clear sign that the heavens were in a state of turmoil, which would inevitably have an impact on Earth. It portended terrifying changes, not just to cosmological theories, but the future of humanity. As William Covell later stated, it destroyed the belief that the cosmos was orderly and stable, and able to run on its own without the intervening hand of God: "All the world marked [the new star] . . . all the astronomers admired it, and remain yet astonished. The wise of the world who in a deep irreligious policy thought all things to be eternal, now began to worship a Creator."[10]

There was a specific astrological reason why it challenged the "deep irreligious policy" of cosmic stability. Dee noticed it, as did Tycho Brahe. In the year 1583, an extraordinary event was due to take place in the heavens, the transition to the "Fiery Trigon."

*   *   *

THE TRIANGLE IS a powerful form, rich with mathematical miracles. It gives us trigonometry, triangulation, the Trinity. Dee used it as a personal hieroglyph, as it is the symbol for delta, the Greek letter *D*. An equilateral triangle, one in which the length of all three sides and the angle of all three corners are the same, is the perfect triangular shape, and the one that produces the astrological trigon.

The signs make up the zodiac like twelve segments making up the rim of a cartwheel. This reveals certain spatial relations among the signs that astrologers regard as significant. One of the most obvious is polarity, where signs are on opposite sides of the wheel. Opposite signs are thought to denote opposite qualities. Then there is "quadruplicity." This can be imagined by placing a square within the wheel, with a sign at each corner. There are three such quadruplicities, each one associated with a particular set of qualities, identified as "cardinal," "fixed," and "mutable." The most powerful configuration of all is represented by an equilateral triangle within the wheel. This arranges signs into four groups, each associated with a particular element: earth, air, water, and fire. These are the trigons.

Every twenty years, Saturn and Jupiter, then understood to be the two outer planets, line up with each other, thereby falling into a "conjunction" or "Grand Copulation," as John Harvey called it. Each time they do so, it is in a different sign. However, for around ten of these conjunctions, the different signs in which they align all happen to be members of the same trigon. Then, after about 200 years, they align within a sign that is a member of a different trigon. For astrologers, this signified a 200-year cycle, with each 200-year period being an epoch ruled by the trigon, and therefore its associated element, in which Saturn and Jupiter conjoined.

In 1583, just such an epoch was about to come to an end and be succeeded by another, with a conjunction predicted to occur on 28 April of that year in the last phase of Pisces, the final sign of the watery trigon. This in astrological terms was momentous enough. But the event was of even greater significance, because the conjunction also marked the moment when the cycle had worked through all the combinations of signs of the zodiac and was about to return to the primary one, the "fiery" trigon.[11]

This cycle, the greatest of them all, took around 960 years to complete, and as astrologers noted, previous transitions had marked the onset of momentous times: the birth of the eras of Enoch, Noah,

Moses, the ten tribes of Israel, the Roman Empire, Jesus Christ, and the Holy Roman Empire. As if that were not enough, there were further factors that added to the significance of the conjunction. It would be the seventh since the beginning of history, and seven was a number of particular numerological power. Also, Ptolemy himself had shown that each conjunction within a trigon was associated with a particular part of the world, and the occurrence within the coming sign of Aries he linked to Britain and Germany.[12]

"[The] watery Trigon shall perish, and be turned into fire," wrote Richard Harvey in an essay on the conjunction. "I am astrologically induced to conjecture, that we are most like to have a new world, by some sudden, violent, & wonderful strange alteration, which even heretofore hath always happened. At the ending of one Trigon, & beginning of an other."[13]

The appearance of the new star, or "nova," as it came to be called, in the constellation Cassiopeia was taken as a herald of this epochal event, a divine signal to the world's astrologers that the global order was about to be transformed. For Tycho Brahe, the meaning was clear: it meant the end of the Roman Catholic Church's supremacy.[14] For the Czech astrologer Cyprian Leowitz, whose work Dee had heavily annotated, it meant a period of momentous change, focused upon his native Bohemia. "Undoubtedly new worlds will follow," he wrote, "which will be inaugurated by sudden and violent changes."[15]

The nova also seemed to fulfill a widely circulated prophecy attributed to the ancient sibyl Tiburtina, which had been discovered in 1520 inscribed on a marble slab buried in a Swiss mountain. "A Star shall arise in Europe over the Iberians, towards the great House of the North, whose Beams shall unexpectedly enlighten the whole World," she had foretold, which would be followed by "direful and bloody Comets, and flashings of Fire seen in the Heavens." The "Firmament of Heaven shall be dissolved, and the Planets be opposed in contrary courses, the Speares shall justle one amongst another, and the fixed Stars move faster than the Planets."[16]

Looking back from the following century, John Strype observed: "All Europe stood at gaze, vehemently expecting more strange and terrible alterations than ever happened since the world began."[17] In the midst of the Reformation, on the cusp of the Thirty Years' War, one of the most terrible conflicts ever to grip the Continent, and at the birth of the scientific revolution, such expectations could barely be called exaggerated.

* * *

AS TIBURTINA HAD predicted, after the Nova disappeared in 1574, the heavenly upheavals continued with the appearance of a comet or "blazing star" in 1577. The sight of it sent terror across Europe. A German correspondent writing to the Bishop of Ely noted that it meant "we can promise nothing to fall happy out of the world." He observed other signs of God's displeasure that accompanied the apparition, such as a series of "monstrous" births, including a "horrid monster" born to a doctor's wife in Novar with seven heads and arms and eagles' talons for feet, and in Piedmont a "dumb" maid producing a hermaphrodite with four horns and hands and feet like those of a goose.[18]

Such hysterical anxieties seemed to seize the entire English court. The comet's appearance coincided with Dee's discussions with Elizabeth at Windsor about the exploration of the New World, and he noted how it had reduced the court to a state of "great fear and doubt."

He was asked by Elizabeth to elucidate on its meaning.[19] He left no record of the advice he gave, but he evidently dismissed the traditional portents of plagues and famines. Indeed, he apparently encouraged Elizabeth not to fear it, advice that she followed. When her courtiers told her to look away, she gazed directly at it through a window, saying "Iacta est alea"—meaning that the die was cast. This may well have been an allusion to Dee's interpretation of its significance, for he believed that these were portents not of Elizabeth's destruction, but of her elevation, the fulfillment of a destiny greater than even she might have imagined.

He drew a sketch of the comet in his diary, arcing through the sky. It had appeared five years, almost to the day, after the nova, on the evening of 10 November, just above the Tropic of Capricorn. Within three days it had moved above the head of Sagittarius, glowing with a clear, white light. It was surrounded by a discolored mane, and had a long tail curved like a Turkish sword.[20]

Again, astronomers across Europe rushed to get their instruments to measure the comet's position and distance.[21] Again, it seemed impossibly far away. Since comets were supposed to be atmospheric phenomena, closer to Earth even than the Moon, this conclusion further confounded received astronomical theory, and gave astronomers a growing feeling that they were lost in a universe infinitely larger than anyone had imagined.

A series of pamphlets also appeared discussing the comet's astrological significance. Its scimitar shape fueled fears of invasion by Ottoman hordes. Its appearance in the seventh astrological house, relating to marriage, stoked anxieties about church disunity and the failure of the Holy Roman Emperor Rudolf II and Queen Elizabeth to marry. It had appeared in the west, suggesting that the direction of its influence might be in that direction, toward the New World, but, as Brahe noted, its tail pointed to the northeast, where it would "spew its venom" over the Muscovites and the Tartars.[22]

The portents continued coming. At 6:10 P.M. on 6 April 1580, as Dee recorded in his diary, an earthquake shook the whole country for two minutes. Its epicenter was London, where the shocks were so intense that bells across the city spontaneously tolled. Along the south coast, there were reports of the sea foaming, ships swaying, and cliffs collapsing.[23] On 10 October 1580, another blazing star appeared in Pisces, Dee noting its disappearance a month later. And on Thursday, 8 March 1582, the day "Talbot" had first appeared at Dee's house, the skies over Mortlake had been filled with the "flashings of Fire" anticipated by Tiburtina.

As these events happened high in the heavens and deep in the earth, others were taking place at ground level that seemed to be part of the same destabilizing trend. In 1579, Jean de Simier, master-of-the-wardrobe and "chief darling" of the French prince Francis de Valois, duke of Anjou, arrived in England with a bag of jewels to tempt Elizabeth into reviving marriage negotiations with his lord. A union had first been mooted eight years before, but Elizabeth had procrastinated, claiming her suitor was too young, too small, and too ugly. Elizabeth now seemed to have overcome her aversion, and welcomed Anjou's advances.

Elizabeth's marital status had been a highly sensitive and deeply significant issue since her accession. Her vaunted virginity emphasized the divine aspects of her rule, turning her almost into a regal abstraction. The great magician Merlin himself had prophesied, "Then shall a Royal Virgin reign, which shall stretch her white rod over the Belgic shore and the great Castile smite so sore withal that it shall make him shake and fall."[24] She was that Royal Virgin and the "great Castile" her Catholic enemy Philip of Spain. However, virginity also meant she could not produce an heir, a prospect that many saw as a violation of the natural order and a denial of her dynastic duties.

Now she had to make her choice. The duke of Anjou's suit represented, as everyone realized, her last realistic chance of marriage. She was in her mid-forties, at the very limit of, if not beyond, her childbearing years. If she did not marry now, she never would. The French ambassador was optimistic that the union would be fruitful, observing that Elizabeth had been born under a fertile constellation. The duke himself was keen, and so increasingly was the queen. In August of 1579, he secretly stole into the country to meet Elizabeth for himself, the first of many visits, each of them discreetly noted in Dee's diary. "A passport granted to Monsieur," he noted on 17 June 1579, showing he was privy to the most secret details of the duke's movements. "Monsieur came secretly to the Court &c. from Calais," he wrote on 16 August.

And so, as the earth moved beneath them and a blazing star burned overhead, Elizabeth and Anjou embarked on a surprisingly amorous courtship, exchanging gifts and rhyming couplets. However, the prospect of their union stirred Protestant unrest both within the court and across the country. Pamphlets appeared attacking the match, claiming that she was surrendering the throne to a pox-ridden Catholic foreigner.

Unsure what to do, Elizabeth consulted Dee. His prognostications were gloomy. When the queen called by at Mortlake one day, on her way to visit Dee's neighbor Francis Walsingham, she invited him to walk next to her horse and give his assessment of Anjou's prospects. Dee replied with the Greek word "biothanatos," meaning a violent death.[25]

A year later, Anjou did die, not violently, but of typhoid, and the marriage issue was brought to a close.

Dee's choice of the term *biothanatos* in the context of such great dynastic developments was significant. He had noted the word's use in a book called *Astronomica* by the Roman poet Marcus Manilius, which he had bought in Louvain in 1550. In the same work, he made two further marginal notes. One reads, "The finding of the Gold Mine 1574 and 1576 after the strange star in Cassiopeia appearing." The other, added later, reads, "I did conjecture the . . . star in Cassiopeia appearing anno 1572 to signify the finding of some great treasure of the philosopher's stone. . . . This I told to Mr. Ed[ward] Dyer at the same time. How truly it fell out in anno 1582, Martij [March] 10 it may appear in time to come [to an astonished world]."[26]

Indeed, the star's appearance was so momentous he dated one of his works, a defense against the "malicious and wilful enemies" who accused him of being "*the arch conjurer*, of this whole kingdom," 4 July in the year 5 "*Anno Stellae*," in the year of the star.[27] In other words, he thought the appearance of the nova significant enough to equate with, even succeed the more conventional method of dating, *Anno Domini*, in the year of our Lord, which coincided with the last appearance of a new star in the heavens.

The date 10 March 1582 was two days after Mr. Clerkson had first appeared at Dee's door with his friend Edward Talbot, and the day that this captivating stranger revealed to Dee the real reason for his coming to Mortlake.

XVI

❧

AT 11:15 A.M. on Saturday, 10 March 1582, Edward "Talbot" reappeared at Dee's door. The evening before, he and Mr. Clerkson had stayed to dinner. They were joined by Jane, Dee's wife now of four years, and Kelley had for the first time an opportunity to study at close quarters a woman who would become an object of obsessive interest in years to come.

Their conversation turned to Barnabas Saul. Barnabas, a former priest, had been part of Dee's household for at least five months, but had disappeared the previous day, just as Mr. Clerkson had come to Mortlake to introduce Kelley to Dee.

Now the reason for his disappearance became clear. These two knew Saul, and knew that he was not to be trusted. He had been telling tales about Dee behind his back, Kelley and Clerkson chimed; he had "cosened" (duped or deceived) his master. For Dee, such revelations were very unwelcome but probably not all that surprising. Saul had a particularly sensitive role in his household. He had been Dee's skryer.

*   *   *

THERE IS NO record of when Dee started using skryers or spirit mediums, but there are hints that show he was engaged in spiritual activities of a sort as far back as 1568, and probably before. In the margin of a table of star positions, he scribbled a note, dated 22 May 1568, that he had learned the exact time and date of John Davies's birth "by magic" at Mortlake with the help of one William Emery, possibly the father of a William Emery who later came to work for Dee.[1]

Davies, the adventurer and pirate, was himself experimenting with magical practices at around this time. There is a manuscript by Dr. John Caius, the founder of Caius College, Cambridge, that details a series of attempts to contact the spirit world undertaken in 1567 involving Davies and one "H.G.," probably the explorer Humphrey Gilbert.[2]

Other than these inklings, there is no documentary evidence of Dee's involvement in any such practices until 1579. However, the growing background noise of rumors and "slanders" linking him to magical activity show that, from the outside at least, Mortlake was now identified as a center of magical activity, a reputation that would have been stoked up by the constant traffic of mysterious foreigners and furtive itinerants passing through its front door. Such rumors rarely coalesced into outright accusations or indictable slanders. The case already mentioned of Vincent Murphyn, the son of a royal cook who forged letters in Dee's name, was a very rare example of a source of such rumors being flushed out, allowing Dee his day in court and public vindication. Usually he was wrestling with whispers. He found this so frustrating that in 1577 he published a "Necessary Advertisement" against the "divers untrue and infamous reports" that accused him of being a "*Conjurer*, or caller of divels: but *a great doer* therein, yea, *the great conjurer:* and so, (as some would say) *the arche conjurer*, of this whole kingdom."[3]

Despite such protestations, Dee was undoubtedly dabbling in magic at this time, but of a sort that he considered fundamentally different from the activity caricatured by those who accused him of being an "arch conjuror." The first explicit (if disguised) reference in Dee's diary is in the entry for 22 June 1579. It records the arrival at Mortlake of, among others, one Richard Hickman and his nephew Bartholomew. They had come with the commendations of Sir Christopher Hatton, the powerful courtier and favorite of Queen Elizabeth, whose knighting Dee had attended two years earlier during his visit to Windsor. The entry ends with a line of Greek, which translates as "The crystal-gazers did their work."[4]

The fact that these men were sent to Dee by Hatton shows that interest in spiritual communication went right to the top of government. This aspect of Elizabethan political life remains largely undocumented and unexamined. Like Dee's Greek diary entry, any references to spiritualism in the historical record of the time are heavily disguised, or used to discredit those associated with it. Nevertheless, the list of names associated with such activities is an impressive one. Besides Christopher Hatton, it apparently includes the earls of Leicester (Robert Dudley), Pembroke (Henry Herbert), and Northumberland (Henry Percy). A letter Dee later wrote to Sir Francis Walsingham shows that even he, Elizabeth's most practical of politicians, probably knew of the spiritual activities that Dee had undertaken and was apparently comfortable with them.[5]

No courtier would publicly admit to such interests, not because it would make him seem gullible—the existence of spirits was as clear as the existence of God—but because it would suggest that he was trying to tap into a reservoir of power that was not his to control. It is unsurprising, then, that Dee was so discreet about his own spiritual activities, and those of his powerful friends.

Dee drew a very clear distinction between what he was doing and what the common "Conjurer, or caller of divels" did.[6] He was engaged in a form of science, the "other (as it were) OPTICAL Science," he circumspectly called it.[7] This "other" science was the chief form of "Archemastry," Dee's term for experimental observation. Thus, for him, crystal gazing, properly and devoutly conducted, had the same validity as star gazing. It was a way of beholding the universe in all its glory, and understanding its manifold and mysterious workings.

There were differences between looking at the heavens directly and through a dark glass. Dee could not himself see visions in crystals. This could be done only through a medium or skryer. Barnabas Saul was a typical example of the breed—typical in, among other things, having obscure origins. He appears in Dee's diary out of nowhere, claiming to have discovered two chests of books at Oundle in Northamptonshire. Dee did not believe him, but did believe he had some sort of occult sensitivity, so retained him. Saul was given a bedroom over the main hall in the house, where he reported being "strangely troubled by a spiritual creature."[8]

The first recorded séance or to use Dee's preferred term "action" with Saul took place on 22 December 1581, when Dee asked him to look into a "great crystalline globe." Saul reported seeing a spirit he identified as Anael. According to various sources, Anael was one of the seven angels of Creation and described by Dee as "the Angel or Intelligence now ruling over the whole world."[9] Dee was skeptical that this spirit was Anael himself, and asked Saul to confirm that he was who he said he was, whereupon another spirit appeared, "very beautiful with apparel yellow, glittering, like gold." His head emitted "beams like star beams, blazing, and spreading from it: his eyes fiery."[10] This spirit, whom Dee identified as the real Anael, wrote a series of Hebrew letters upon the crystal in "transparent gold," whereupon there appeared a "bright star" that ascended and descended, and then "a great number of dead men's skulls" and a "white dog with a long head."

Dee, who had several crystals for skrying, set another, his "stone in the frame," beside the one in which Anael had appeared, and asked the angel: "Is any angel assigned to this stone?" Anael said that there was, Michael. The answer excited Dee, as Michael was one of the two angels identified by name in the main body of the Scriptures.[11] But Anael told Dee that Michael would not appear until after Christmas. "Then thou must prepare thyself to prayer and fasting," Anael told Dee. "In the name of God, be secret." The angel then left, after announcing himself to be "ANNAEL," spelling his name out through Saul. Dee was puzzled by this. He considered the names of angels to be extremely significant, as the letters had cabalistic power, and Anael was by tradition spelled with one "n."[12]

Perhaps this aroused doubts in Dee's mind about Saul's honesty as a skryer. Such doubts were to be reinforced in the New Year when Saul was charged with committing a crime. Dee left no record of the offense, and when the case was heard at Westminster Hall on 12 February 1582, Saul was acquitted due to lack of evidence. However, on 6 March, Saul admitted to Dee that he "neither heard or saw any spiritual creature any more." When Edward "Talbot" first came two days later, Saul disappeared.

And here now were "Talbot" and Clerkson, sitting at the dinner table, confirming Dee's worst fears about his previous skryer. Saul had engaged in "naughty dealing" against Dee, they said. He was weary of his master, he claimed, and accused Dee of trying to steal Talbot from Clerkson.[13] Talbot/Kelley "told me (before my wife and Mr Clerkson) that a spiritual creature told him that Barnabas had cosened both Mr Clerkson and me &c. The injuries which this Barnabas had done me divers ways were very great," Dee noted in his diary.[14]

After supper, Kelley had another, private word with Dee about spirits. He would, he confided, "do what he could to further my knowledge in magic ... with fairies."[15] Dee was appalled by this offer. Dee did not want to communicate with such pagan entities as "fairies." The very suggestion was "a monstrous and horrible lie," he wrote.

It is a measure of how quickly and intimately Kelley would manage to insinuate himself into Dee's household that, within a few months, he had somehow got hold of Dee's diary and scribbled out these comments, adding, "You that read this underwritten assure yourself that it is a shameful lie, for Talbot neither studied for any such thing: nor showed himself dishonest in anything." When Dee found these annotations, he added his own: "This is Mr Talbot, or that learned man, his own writing in my book, very unduly as he came by it."[16]

Talbot and Clerkson left that evening, and Talbot returned alone the following morning. He was "willing and desirous to see or show something in spiritual practice," he announced. Dee warned the precocious twenty-six-year-old that he was not interested in "vulgarly accounted magic ... but confessed myself long time to have been desirous to have help in my philosophical studies through the company and information of the blessed angels of God." In other words, Dee was engaged not in circus magic, but a momentous philosophical enterprise, and thought Talbot might be able to help.

Talbot apparently reassured Dee that he understood the seriousness of the venture, and upon this frail understanding, Dee agreed to try out his skrying skills. He led Kelley through to his study and placed upon the desk the "stone in the frame" in which Saul had promised the archangel Michael would appear. Kelley fell to his knees (apparently not at this moment suffering from the lameness that was said to prevent him doing so), and with the glinting crystal before him, began to pray for the power to see into it.

Dee withdrew into his adjoining "oratory," a small private chapel. He, too, now began to pray, as he would before every angelic action, making "motions" to God and asking that his "good creatures" appear "for the furthering of this Action." Within a quarter of an hour he heard a voice. It came from the study.

PART SIX
BRIGHT
SQUADRONS

✤

And is there care in heaven? And is there love
In heavenly spirits to these creatures base,
That may compassion of their evils move?
There is: else much more wretched were the case
Of men than beasts. But oh th' exceeding grace
Of highest God that loves his creatures so
And all his work with mercy doth embrace,
That blessed angels he sends to and fro
To serve to wicked men, to serve his wicked foe.

How oft do they their silver bowers leave
To come to succour us that succour want;
How oft do they with golden pinions cleave
The flitting skies like flying pursuivant
Against foul fiends to aid us militant.
They for us fight, they watch and duly ward
And their bright squadrons round about us plant;
And all for love and nothing for reward.
Oh, why should heavenly love to men have such regard?

EDMUND SPENSER,
Faerie Queen

꙳

THE study was quiet, sealed behind a pair of double doors from the hubbub of a busy household and Dee's two young children, Arthur, aged two, and his infant daughter, Katherine. The room was furnished with a desk, several chairs, including a "Saracen" upholstered in green silk,[1] and a cedar-wood chest. There was a fireplace, and a chimney breast inside of which Dee hid secret manuscripts, sealed in a "capcase," a traveling bag.[2] The floor was covered with mats and haphazard piles of books. All was illuminated by a large window facing west.

In one corner stood his precious "great perspective glass." The queen herself had posed before this mirror, when she visited Dee soon after the death of his second wife. It had once stood in the home of Sir William Pickering, who had presumably bequeathed it to his old friend and mentor when he died in 1575. Anyone who "foined" or lunged at it with a dagger or sword found their reflection, "with like hand, sword or dagger" lunging back at them, an effect so unsettling that many had claimed that it must have magical powers. Dee used it to demonstrate how such effects could all be explained by the mathematics of perspective.

Dee seems unlikely to have used this mirror for any sort of occult practice, though he did use another, a "speculum" made of polished "obsidian," a dense, dark, vitreous form of volcanic lava.[3] He also had at least two crystal balls, and it was in one of these that "Talbot" now claimed to see a vision of an angel, a good creature whom he identified as Uriel.

Uriel is mentioned several times in the "Pseudepigrapha," a collection of ancient writings that, like the Apocrypha, had once appeared as part of the Bible. According to one of the books in the

Pseudepigrapha, the "Life of Adam and Eve," it is Uriel who with the archangel Michael buried Adam's body following the Fall. Another book, the "Book of Enoch," identifies Uriel as the angel who warned Noah of the Flood.[4] But perhaps of most interest to Dee was Uriel's role in revealing the astrological secrets of the "heavenly luminaries" (meaning the stars and planets) to Enoch. Enoch was the seventh patriarch of Genesis (in other words, seven generations down from Adam) and the father of Methuselah. He lived a third as long as his famously durable son (365 years) and prophesied the Day of Judgment when God would "convict all the ungodly of all their deeds of ungodliness which they have committed in an ungodly way."[5]

Enoch also had a more contemporary significance for Dee. In 1553, a French scholar called Guillaume Postel had published a book called *De Originibus* in which he related a meeting with a priest from Ethiopia. This priest told Postel of a Book of Enoch, which had been for centuries lost to Europe but was known to the Ethiopians. It contained Enoch's own record of the language God had taught to Adam, which he had used to name all the beasts and the birds.

This Adamic language was one that since ancient times had been rumored to exist, but was long lost to the world. It was of enormous significance, as it had come straight from the mouth of God, and had yet to be corrupted by the Fall.[6] Whoever rediscovered that language would rediscover the key to divine knowledge.

Dee owned a copy of *De Originibus*, which has survived.[7] The sections concerning the Ethiopian priest's testimony were particularly heavily annotated by Dee.

Dee had been expecting a minor spirit from the great hierarchy of the heavens, and here he had before him an archangel, one who apparently had a direct line to Enoch and perhaps the Adamic language Enoch had recorded. His reaction was immediately to ask Uriel about the "Book of Soyga."

*   *   *

THE BOOK OF Soyga was particularly precious to Dee. His only mention of it before now was in a diary entry made earlier that year, where he reports having the volume fumigated to protect it from mildew.[8]

In 1583, the book went missing from Dee's library, but he managed to recover it a decade later. Following Dee's death, it passed into the collection of the duke of Lauderdale, but then this slippery text went missing once more. It was finally rediscovered in 1994 by the Dee scholar Deborah Harkness, who found it in both the Bodleian and British Libraries, but cataloged under an alternative title mentioned by Dee, *Aldaraia*.[9] Both copies are anonymous sixteenth-century manuscript versions of a (presumably) lost original. It seems likely that the British Library copy was the one owned by Dee, the very work that was now in his study and the focus of his intense curiosity.

The book is full of lists and tables. There are lists of spirit names, of astrological conjunctions, of spells and invocations—the very sort of cabalistic codes that had filled Trithemius's *Steganographia*.

Dee's first question to Uriel, communicated via Talbot, was an anxious inquiry about the status of this work. "Is my Book of Soyga of any excellency?" he asked.

"That book was revealed to Adam in paradise by the good Angels of God," Uriel replied.

A revelation, and not just to Adam. Dee must have now dared to think that this book was of divine importance—perhaps a copy of the Book of Enoch mentioned by the Ethiopian priest to Postel. Perhaps its tables and lists were a coded version of the very language Adam had been given by God.

"Will you give me any instructions, how I may read those tables of Soyga?" Dee asked Uriel.

"I can," Uriel replies, tantalizingly. "But only Michael can interpret that book."

Dee was desperate, but had probably expected the reply, as it was Michael he had previously attempted to contact in this stone through Saul. "What may I, or must I do, to have the sight and presence of Michael, that blessed angel?" Dee asked. "Summon and invoke our presence with sincerity and humility," Uriel replied, with what to Dee must have been maddening serenity.

"Michael is the angel who lights your way. And these things are revealed in virtue and truth, not by force."

At that point, the conversation was interrupted by Talbot reporting the appearance of a new vision in the stone, a triangular talisman engraved in gold. Worn on the chest, Uriel promised, this device would protect its bearer "at every place and time and occasion."[10]

There, the session ended. Dee spent the afternoon musing on what he had experienced. It was evidently a kind of communion that was very different from any he had experienced with his previous skryers. There was something compelling, convincing about the spirit this Talbot had summoned that morning.

At five o'clock in the afternoon, the two of them were in Dee's study again. After saying their prayers, Talbot managed to summon Uriel back to the stone. Dee pressed to know more about the Book of Soyga. "Peace," Uriel replied, "you must use Michael." "I know of no means or order to use in the invocating of Michael," Dee replied.

Uriel was obligingly specific in reply. He and Talbot must recite certain psalms, which will deliver them before the "seat and Majesty of God." They did as instructed, and a "rich chair" appeared briefly in the stone. "There must be conjunction of minds in prayer, betwixt you two, to God continually," Uriel added. "It is the will of God that you should jointly have the knowledge of his angels together. You had attained unto the sight of Michael but for the imperfection of Saul. Be of good comfort." In other words, Dee's failure to discover the secret of Soyga in the past had been Saul's fault. If he now stuck with Talbot, all would be imminently revealed.

There followed a detailed specification of some of the equipment Dee would need to reach the "rich chair," the "seat of perfection, from the which things shall be showed unto thee." He was to make a table, constructed out of "sweet wood," two "cubits" square (i.e., between three and four feet, a cubit being the length of a forearm) and two cubits tall. Each leg of the table was to stand on a "Sigillum Dei," a divine seal, made of pure, colorless wax, nine inches in diameter and one and one eighth of an inch thick. On the back of the seal was to be inscribed a motif that appeared in the stone: a cross with a circle at the point of intersection and surrounded by the letters AGLA.[11]

Just such a table as Uriel had described appeared in the crystal ball, as though the space Uriel occupied was a model of Dee's own study, but now furnished in the manner Uriel had instructed.

Uriel then suddenly changed the subject. Dee's house was haunted by an evil spirit. "He is here now," said Uriel. His name was Lundrumguffa, and he had been in the house for some time. It was he who had "maimed" Dee in the shoulder (Dee had reported in his diary a year before suffering pain in his right shoulder and elbow so extreme that he could not lift his arm more than an inch for a period of two weeks). He now sought the destruction of Dee's wife and daughter, and would try to kill the "accursed" Saul. Dee must get rid of him, exorcise him, using "brimstone" (sulfur).

Dee once again complained of not knowing how to carry out Uriel's instructions. He had tried using brimstone once before, when Saul had summoned a demon called "Maherion." The strategy had failed, with Maherion making many further appearances, despite Dee's repeatedly commanding Saul not to dabble with such spirits. "The cursed will come to the cursed," Uriel replied, clearly indicating that Saul, rather than the brimstone, was the cause of the problem.

"Brimstone is the means," Uriel concluded. "When shall I do this?" Dee asked. "Tomorrow at the time of prayers," Uriel replied, and was gone.

Thus Dee's first action with Edward Kelley came to an end. The experience was quite different from any he had had before. Where Saul could only manage middle-ranking angels, Talbot had conjured an archangel, one who understood what Dee wanted, and dangled before him the chance of achieving it.

Talbot may have stayed the night at Mortlake, as the following day they were at it again, presumably after Dee had ignited samples of brimstone to smoke out Lundrumguffa. They started at 3 P.M. As Talbot stared into the stone, he beheld a magnificent creature, wearing a long purple robe spangled with gold, and a gilded garland around his head. His eyes were "sparkling." Dee showed him the notes he had made the previous day on the design of the table he had been instructed to build, to check that they were accurate.

"They are perfect, there is no question," the magnificent spirit replied.

"Are you Uriel?" Dee asked.

Talbot reported the appearance of another creature in the crystal. He threw the spangling and sparkling spirit to the floor and started to beat him with a whip and tear at his clothes. The spirit was revealed to be a hairy, ugly monster: Lundrumguffa, the wicked spirit that haunted Mortlake, and its assailant was Uriel, who "drew the wicked spirit away by the legs and threw him into a great pit, and washed his hands . . . with the sweat of his own head." "Lo," said Uriel, "thus the wicked are scourged," and he left.

Shortly after he reappeared, this time with a creature even more magnificent than the disguised Lundrumguffa, with a sword and his head glistening like the sun. He sat down in the "seat of perfection," the "rich chair" that had been revealed the previous day, and was surrounded by a host of angels. This, Dee realized, must be Michael himself.

Michael made the following pronouncement to Dee:

> Go forward: God hath blessed thee.
> I will be thy Guide.
> Thou shalt attain unto thy seeking.
> The World begins with thy doings.
> Praise God.
> The Angels under my power, shall be at thy commandment.
> Lo, I will do thus much for thee.
> Lo, God will do thus much for thee.
> Thou shalt see me: and I will be seen of thee.
> And I will direct thy living and conversation.
> Those that sought thy life, are vanished away.
> Put up thy pen.

Dee did as he was instructed. He did not write anything further for three days. Then, during another séance, Talbot once more beheld Michael enter the stone, and sit upon the seat of perfection. This time, the archangel was accompanied by another, his face hidden by a black hood. Uriel, who was also present, went up to the hooded man and took off his cloak. He then robed him in silk, and placed laurels on his head. The man knelt down before Michael, who unsheathed his sword and dubbed the man. The man stood up and turned so that Talbot could see his face. It was Dee.

And so Dee beheld his own anointing by the great archangel Michael: a moment of rapture after so many of disillusionment, and confirmation that all he had been waiting for was about to occur.

✢

DEE treated his actions with the spirits with the utmost seriousness. In a list of instructions he drew up about how they should be conducted, he specified that for three days before each action, the participants should abstain from "Coitus & Gluttony," that on the day they should "wash hands, face, cut nails, shave the beard, wash all," and that just before a session commenced, invocations should be made "5 times to the East, as many to the West, so many to the South, & to the North." The spirits should be called only during certain phases of the Moon, under the influence of a "good planet . . . well placed" and "in the sunshine," when beams of sunlight would penetrate the west-facing window of the study and illuminate the crystal.[1]

The action that took place on 29 April 1582, a Sunday, broke at least one of these injunctions as it began at 8:15 in the evening. Michael appeared and announced that he was about to reveal an important message about the relationship between divine and earthly powers. "We show unto you the lower world: the Governors that work and rule under God." This was to be done by revealing the names of the forty-nine angels "whose names are here evident, excellent and glorious." Forty-nine is numerologically significant, being the square of seven, and the number of heavenly bodies in the cosmos (the Sun, Moon, Mercury, Venus, Mars, Jupiter, and Saturn). "Mark these Tables," he commanded. "Mark them. Record them. . . . This is *the first knowledge*."[2]

There then appeared one of the most elaborate tables yet—indeed a table of tables, seven in all, each of which was made up of seven rows and seven columns, each cell of which contained a number and a letter. One table related to "wit and wisdom," another to "the exaltation and government of princes," another to "counsel [i.e., royal advisers] and nobility," another to the "gain and trade of merchandise," another to the "quality of the earth and waters," another to the "motion of the air," and finally, set in the center, the table relating to divine government. This demonstrated that the angelic revelations about to be delivered were not about personal but political salvation, creating a new global order run according to godly principles.

Talbot spent nearly three hours reading out to Dee the contents of these tables, cell by cell, letter by letter, number by number, which Dee laboriously copied into his notebook. Then the skryer fell silent. He was, he later told Dee, being addressed by the angel Michael directly. The session finally came to an end at 11:30 P.M., after which Talbot revealed to Dee what Michael had commanded. "He said that I must betake myself to the world, and forsake the world. That is, *that I should marry*. Which thing to do, I have no natural inclination, neither with a safe conscience may I do it, *contrary to my vow and profession.*"

The last comment, which Dee underlined, is striking. It suggests that Talbot was or wanted Dee to believe that he was a Catholic priest, who had been ordered by no less an authority than an archangel to break his vow of celibacy. This is yet another pungent ingredient dropped into the cauldron of speculation and legend surrounding this enigmatic figure. Was he really a priest? Was this what Elias Ashmole was referring to when, a century later, he described Kelley as the "canon of Bridlington"?[3] And if so, was he really a Catholic?

If he was, his presence placed Dee's household in great peril. As one historian put it, during this period "the air of north-west Europe was, if not thick with the cries of the massacred and martyred, thick with the expectation of massacre and martyrdom."[4] In the coming months, religious conflict would intensify sharply, provoked by Elizabeth's revived marriage negotiations with the Catholic duke of Anjou, with which Dee was intimately if discreetly involved, and culminating with the uncovering of the "Throckmorton Plot," an attempt to secure the release of Mary, Queen of Scots, and overthrow Elizabeth's Protestant regime. Throckmorton had been foiled by the extremely powerful and sophisticated intelligence network set up by William Cecil and now run by Sir Francis Walsingham, whose home at Barn Elms was a short walk from Dee's house at Mortlake. Walsingham and Dee had several meetings during this period, mostly in connection with the exploration of the Northwest Passage. Another visitor was one of Walsingham's most mysterious and sinister associates, Charles Sledd. Sledd had been instrumental in uncovering the role of the English College in Rome as a training camp for the Catholic priests sent to spy on England. Whenever Sledd came to Mortlake, the outcome seemed to be unpleasant. On one occasion he suffered two nosebleeds, which seemed to spontaneously erupt the moment Dee talked to him about "virtue and godliness"—"Meaneth he well toward me?" Dee anxiously inquired of the spirits. On another occasion Sledd had a violent row with Talbot/Kelley.[5] Dee does not record the cause of the argument, but a suspicion on Kelley's part that Sledd had been sent to spy on him may well have had a part in the matter.

Sledd was by no means the only person to fall out with Talbot. The intense, turbulent young man soon started to cause problems much closer to home. On Friday, 4 May 1582, a few days after Michael had told Talbot to get married, the skryer was in a truculent mood. At first he would not even invoke the angelic "creatures" that had been their daily company in the past month, "utterly misliking and discrediting them." Dee eventually managed to persuade him to continue, but as a mark of protest he insisted on wearing his hat throughout the proceedings.

Two days later, Dee reported in a badly mutilated entry in his diary that his wife, Jane, had spent the entire evening and night, and the "next morning until 8" in a "marvellous" rage over Talbot. She was "melancholic and choleric for the cosening"—in other words, furious because Talbot had been deceiving her and her husband. This skryer was like all the rest, brought to Mortlake by Clerkson (who, along with his brother, was also apparently implicated) "as honest learned men," who then "used" Dee for their own ends.

Dee was, at the time, apparently at a loss to account for her behavior. A week later he reports that she "rode to Cheam," where her father lived.[6] By the end of the month, however, he too had come to understand Talbot's "wicked nature and his abominable lies."[7] In the following weeks, Talbot went away from Mortlake on several occasions, on at least one to track down some mysterious books once owned by the late William Stanley, the third Lord Mounteagle. The Stanleys were a fiercely independent Lancashire family that would act as a focus of Catholic rebellion for years to come.

Talbot returned to Mortlake on the 13 July. He and Dee had a falling out, but soon made up, parting "on friendly terms" after Talbot revealed that he had managed to trace Mounteagle's books. Three days later, Dee had a particularly hectic day, nursing his wife, who was suffering from stomach pains and vomiting "very much green stuff," as well as receiving Sir George Peckham to discuss the colonization of America and one William Pole, whom Dee knew through the earl of Pembroke. At the end, he tersely noted, "I have confirmed that Talbot was a cosener."

"Talbot" was never to be seen again.

XIX

❧

A FEW days after Dee "confirmed" Talbot's deception, Barnabas Saul, the skryer whom Talbot and Clerkson also accused of cosening, suddenly resurfaced with a peace offering: two "chests," probably chests of books supposedly found in Oundle, Northamptonshire, that Saul had mentioned two years earlier. Dee gave him short shrift, "chiding" him for "his manifold untrue reports. . . . He tarried not."[1]

That November of 1582 "Talbot" reappeared as Edward Kelley. Unlike Saul, Kelley was welcomed back with open arms, despite the change of identity. Dee marked the event by starting a new notebook to record actions eagerly anticipated, which he entitled *Mysteriorum Liber Post Reconciliationem Kellianam*, "The book of mysteries after the reconciliation with Kelley."

Many future apologists and commentators would find Dee's attachment to Kelley baffling. The fact that Kelley had come to Dee under a false name, that he had been accused of deception by Dee's own wife, that he had suspicious connections with the Catholic world and may well have been a recusant priest, that he was, as Dee later discovered, a fugitive accused of forgery and coining, that he was fractious, irascible, and unreliable—none of this seemed to dent Dee's trust in the man's skrying skills. At one point, he was so dependent on Kelley he confessed that his heart "did throb" at the thought of the skryer's absence.[2]

Kelley himself seemed to provide Dee with more than sufficient grounds to be suspicious of the visions he was delivering. On one occasion, Dee reported Kelley suffering "a great storm or temptation . . . of doubting and misliking our instructors and their doings."[3] On another, the skryer claimed that the spirits he had summoned were "all devils." He added that Dee's servant John "can well enough deliver you these letters, and so you need not me."[4] On such occasions, all Dee would do was calmly reassure Kelley that he should have more faith, that it was God's will that had brought them together. Truly, then, Dee seemed to fall under Kelley's spell.

However, for Dee, Kelley's value was not a matter of character. Indeed, the flaws in his nature were evidence of his strengths as a skryer. An effective medium needs to be like a child or even an animal: instinctive, volatile, highly sensitive to his surroundings, and unconstrained by intellect or experience. So a certain juvenile petulance must be expected. Furthermore, where it counted, Kelley delivered. The richness and sophistication of his visions, the combination of clear divine light and complex cabalistic formulas was not only captivating, but convincing.

During the winter of 1582 and spring of 1583, their actions proceeded, ranging across a vast range of subjects and concerns, some issues relating to Dee's other work for the government and in connection with voyages of discovery, some relating to the revelations the spirits themselves were promising to deliver. It set the somewhat haphazard pattern that would prevail for the coming years, with exciting progress in one area accompanied by frustrations in another.

*   *   *

THE FIRST ACTION *"Post Reconciliationem"* with Kelley took place on 21 November 1582. It confirmed Dee's belief that he had found the right medium for an important divine message. This time, Kelley summoned up a spirit called King Camara. Camara stood resplendent before Kelley, brandishing a rod of black and red to "measure us and our power," and said, "What is your desire?" Dee confessed to Camara that he was having difficulties understanding the complex tables the spirits had previously communicated, fearing that he had mistranscribed some of the words. "One thing is yet wanting," the king proclaimed. "A meet receptacle . . . a Stone . . . One there is, most excellent, hid in the secret of the depth &c., in the uttermost part of the Roman Possession. Lo, the mighty hand of God is upon thee. Thou shalt have it. Thou shalt have it. Thou shalt have it. Dost thou see? Look and stir not from thy place."

"I see it not," Dee confessed.

"It is sanctified," the king announced. "Thou shalt prevail with it, with kings, and with all creatures of the world: whose beauty (in virtue) shall be more worth than the kingdoms of the earth. Look, if thou seest: but stir not, for the angel of his power is present." At this point, Kelley turned toward the west window of the study, and saw resting on the mats by a pile of books an object "as big as an egg, most bright, clear and glorious."

Kelley saw an angel "of the height of a little child" that held the glistening jewel up to Dee, offering it to him.

"Go toward it, and take it up," Camara commanded. Dee did as he was told, and got within two feet of the place where this object was supposed to be. But he could see nothing. Then he saw a shadow on the ground "roundish and less than the palm of my hand. I put my hand down upon it, and I felt a thing cold and hard." It was a crystal. "Keep it sincerely," said Camara. "Let no mortal hand touch it, but thine own. Praise God."[5]

It was a new magical lens, through which Kelley would perceive the most compelling visions yet.

The next day, Kelley left Mortlake for London, and then for Blockley, a village about thirty-five miles northwest of Oxford. The entry in Dee's diary recording this apparently innocuous news is mutilated.[6] Two days later, Dee had a nightmare about being disembowelled. The frightening figure of the Lord Treasurer William Cecil, Baron Burghley looms sinisterly, entering Dee's house to riffle through his books and looking "sourly" upon him.[7]

Dee does not specify which books he feared Burghley might find, but they included his "Arabic" Book of Soyga, the one so promisingly described by the spirits during his first action with "Talbot" as containing the language of Adam. A few months later Dee discovered it had gone missing, and suspected that Burghley might have it, though a more likely suspect is Kelley, who may have wanted to study it privately in preparation for future angelic actions.[8]

Following Kelley's departure for Blockley, there is no record of any further actions for four months. Then on 22 March 1583, Kelley turned up at the door with one John Husey. Husey, Kelley told

Dee, came from Blockley, and together they had found a "certain monument of a book and a scroll" at nearby Northwick Hill, having been directed there by a "spiritual creature." Just before he died, Dee identified the book as one written by St. Dunstan, the patron saint of the City church around which he had played as a boy.[9]

The scroll was some sort of map, with ten locations cryptically identified by a collection of objects: feathers, pots, leaves, crosses. Each figure was accompanied by a short message written in an unfamiliar alphabet, and accompanying the whole was a block of text written using the same alphabet.

Later Kelley revealed to Dee that they had also discovered a red substance, variously described as a "powder," "earth," and a "congealed thing." It was later claimed to be a sample of the Philosopher's Stone or elixir, the cherished alchemical tincture that turned base metal into gold, and dead matter into living. Elias Ashmole wrote that the powder was so potent that one ounce was capable of producing 22,694 pounds of gold.[10]

In the coming years, many legends would accumulate around Kelley's curious finds. A century later, the story circulated that these "monuments" had been found buried among the ruins at Glastonbury Abbey. This tale was no doubt reinforced by the connection with St. Dunstan, a courtier to King Athelstan who was exiled following accusations of sorcery, and later made Abbot of Glastonbury, rebuilding the institution after its sacking by the Danes. Glastonbury was also, of course, thought to be the resting place of King Arthur and the birthplace of English Christianity, the sort of legendary locus that made the perfect setting for the discovery of such mysterious artefacts.

According to another tale, recorded by the French writer Nicolas Lenglet du Fresnoy, the powder and scroll had been found by grave robbers in the tomb of a Welsh bishop, and sold to Kelley for £1 by an innkeeper.[11]

Wherever they came from, the book, scroll, and red powder were to become central features of Kelley's continuing revelations. However, as always, the spiritual advice concerning them was obscure, deeply allegorical, and haphazardly delivered.

On 23 March 1583, the day after Kelley's return from Blockley, another action commenced, during which Dee and Kelley hoped to receive "some exposition of the scroll, written in strange characters." On this occasion, none was forthcoming. Instead there followed a vision of a tree, with a pool of water around its roots. The moisture was drawn up into the tree, causing it to swell and produce fruit, "great, fair and red." Raphael, appearing under the label Medicina Dei, started to eat the fruit from the tree.[12] "It lighteth the hearts of those that are chosen," he told Kelley, and said it would have the same effect for Dee.

The following day, Medicina Dei appeared again, lying prostrate face down, his head being licked by a lamb. The spirit suddenly rose and "wiped his face as though he had wept." "Man's memory is dull," he announced, and said he had a medicine from God that will heal it. This medicine was "understanding and reason." These had "elevated and lifted up the dignity and worthiness of man's memory," he said. "New worlds shall spring of these," he added. Then he produced a book with leaves of gold covered in text written with blood. He instructed Kelley to count the number of pages in the book: forty-eight. Dee then unraveled the scroll Kelley had found: "Will you of these characters and places of treasure hid (here portrayed by picture) say anything?"

"The thing there, which you desire of me, is no part of my charge," the spirit replied, and departed, putting his golden book "in his bosom as he goeth."

The spirit appeared again on 26 March. Dee immediately asked for more information about the "medicine" the spirit had mentioned before. "What liquor is more lively than the dew of truth, proceeding from the fountain most sweet and delectable?" the spirit replied. He then produced the golden book again, and opened it up. He pointed to a series of strange characters, and counted them from left to right, twenty-one in all. "Note what they are," he commanded. Dee copied them down. They were the letters of the celestial alphabet, his first sight of the written language handed by God to Adam, and lost in the turmoil of the Tower of Babel.

After he had finished copying down the characters, Dee asked the spirit about Adrian Gilbert, the adventurer and half-brother of Sir Walter Raleigh. The previous day, Gilbert had been invited to partake in an action. As they had all gathered in the study, a man had appeared from the direction of Dee's oratory and laid a "fiery ball" at Gilbert's feet. Dee wanted to know "whether it were any illusion, or the act of any seducer."

"No wicked power shall enter into this place," the spirit reassured.

"Must Adrian Gilbert be made privy of these mysteries?" Dee anxiously asked. The spirit did not directly answer, though Dee noted in the margin of his notebook that Gilbert "may be made privy, but he is not to be a Practicer." The spirit instead linked Dee and Kelley's own journey into "New Worlds" with those being undertaken by Gilbert and other adventurers. They were all part of the same enterprise. "The corners and straights of the earth shall be measured to the depth: and strange shall be the wonders that are creeping in to new worlds. Time shall be altered, with the difference of day and night. All things have grown almost to their fullness," the spirit said.

The reference to time would have had a special significance to Dee. For, in the midst of all the actions, and his involvement with the navigators of the New World, he was also working on an important but delicate government report on the matter of reforming the calendar.

*   *   *

THE PREVIOUS YEAR, a bull had been issued by Pope Gregory XIII commanding the Catholic world to remove ten days from October. This had been considered necessary because the calendar introduced by Julius Caesar in 45 B.C., and adopted by the Christian world at the Council of Nicaea in A.D. 325, was based on erroneous measurements of the solar and lunar cycles. As a result, holy and feast days had drifted out of alignment with the celestial events they were supposed to mark, notably the equinoxes (in spring and autumn, when the day and night are of equal length) and solstices (in summer and winter, when the day is longest and shortest). One result was that the principal Christian festival, Easter, was no longer occurring on the date it was supposed to, the first Sunday after the first full moon after the spring equinox.

Sir Francis Walsingham had acquired a copy of the papal bull, and asked Dee what he thought of it. Dee came up with an alternative plan, set out in a sixty-two-page illuminated treatise that he delivered to Lord Burghley on 26 February 1583.[13] The proposals backed by Pope Gregory, the basis of the Gregorian calendar already established across the Continent and in centuries to come across the entire globe, was based on calculations that reached back to the time of the Council of Nicea. Citing a range of authorities, including Copernicus, Dee argued that this was the wrong starting date: it should be the birth of Christ. This necessitated the removal of eleven rather than ten days to realign the calendar. Anticipating the criticism that this would put Britain out of kilter with most of the Continent, Dee argued that the difference resulted from "Gregorian negligence" rather than English "singularity or insufficiency." Indeed, it was the Gregorian calendar that was singular and insufficient, as it was based on an artificial foundation, the date of the Council of Nicaea, a political, not cosmic coordinate. His alternative was doctrinally neutral, oriented around a universal (as far as he and all Christians were concerned) moment: the birth of Christ. This, he proclaimed, was the true "Radix of Time."

Dee had another reason for proposing his alternative scheme, one that related directly to the angelic actions. An accurate calendar, based on astronomical observations and mathematical principles, is essential, as he put it, for "the consideration of Sacred Prophecies."[14] Without one, knowing when such millennial events as the coming of the "fiery Trigon" would actually occur would be impossible.

The Privy Council gave his proposals its support. Walsingham was impressed, and addressed encouraging letters "To my very loving friend Mr. Doctor Dee."[15] Even the sour-faced Cecil considered the paper to be "in the right line." "He proveth [his proposals] by a great number of good authorities," Cecil approvingly noted, "such as I think the Romanists cannot deny."[16]

Cecil also wanted a decision to be taken quickly, "for that it is requisite, for a secret matter, to be reformed before November." It is not known what this tantalizingly secret matter might have been. Dee knew of it, as he alludes to it in his paper, which shows that he was still given access to confidential matters being discussed by the Privy Council.[17]

Despite the backing of Walsingham and Cecil, the scheme soon foundered. It was blocked by the Archbishop of Canterbury Edmund Grindal, whose long-standing feud with Elizabeth had reached a new intensity. He wrote to Walsingham arguing that the very idea of reforming the calendar was Papist, and insisted that the matter should be discussed at a convocation of all Protestant churches across Europe, knowing full well that this would be impossible to arrange. By 28 March 1583, Maunday Thursday, Dee had given up on the scheme, complaining to one of the spirits that he was "grieved" to discover that the calendar was not to be reformed "in the best terms of verity." As a result of the decision, England remained outside the Gregorian system for a further 170 years, communications during that period customarily carrying two dates, one "OS" or Old Style, the other "NS" or New Style.[18]

Dee's preoccupation with the cosmic calendar took its toll on his own time. For years he had been agitating for the restoration of the rectorship of Upton-under-Severn, which had been taken from him following his arrest during Queen Mary's reign. If he secured it, the £80 annual income he made on the living from Long Leadenham would be instantly doubled. In 1576, Sir Christopher Hatton finally extracted the necessary letters from the queen. They now needed the approval of the Archbishop of Canterbury, which took a full six years to be granted. However, under the convoluted rules of Tudor bureaucracy, Dee's claim was invalid without the Great Seal. Dee was so preoccupied with drawing up his paper on reforming the calendar that he failed to make the necessary application, and the order expired, ending once and for all his hopes of getting Upton back.[19]

He also learned that Adrian Gilbert had just received his letters patent from the queen concerning the voyage to the New World he had been discussing with Dee. Without consulting the other members of the company, Gilbert had applied for and been awarded sole and exclusive rights on all royalties that the expedition might yield. Dee admitted to the spirits that his mind had become "afflicted" by such "unseemly doing[s]." Gilbert and he would have no further dealings.

"Thou shalt prevail against them," the spirit Medicina Dei consoled him on 28 March 1583. "Thy weapons are small, but thy conquest shall be great."[20]

Reassured by this angelic endorsement, Dee turned his attention to the business of the actions themselves. In the very first spiritual conference he had undertaken with Kelley, the spirits had told Dee to provide a special table, the "table of practice," as he now called it, which was to stand on a sheet of red silk two yards square, with each leg supported by a "Sigillum Dei" or sacred seal. Work had begun on making this spiritual equipment, but Dee was now concerned that it would not be portable, "because I think that some services to be done in God's purposes by me will require other places than this house." The spirit agreed, and gave Dee permission to make appropriate alterations.

The following day was Good Friday. As they prepared to begin another action, Kelley complained that he could smell burning. Then a sword was thrust out of the crystal that struck him in the head, "whereat he started, and said he felt a thing (immediately) creeping within his head, and in that pang became all in a sweat." The sensation continued for a quarter of an hour, and then disappeared.

On Easter day, 31 March 1583, Kelley reported feeling the same sensations in his head, and heard the sound of "musical harmony."

No further actions were reported until 6 April. Then Uriel, the spirit whom Dee had encountered during his first action with Kelley, reappeared, and announced that in just forty days "must the book of the secrets and key of this world be written." Uriel commanded that Kelley was to perform daily "the office committed to him," in other words, continue skrying until the job was done.

The sudden sense of pressure was intensified by an interruption. "Mistress Haward" or Lady Frances Howard had called by. She was a "Gentlewoman" of Elizabeth's Privy Chamber, a senior position, and had possibly come to see Jane. She had somehow discovered what Dee and Kelley were up to, perhaps even come into the study as they were in the middle of the action. The actions were supposed to take place in the utmost secrecy. Only outsiders approved by the spirits, such as Adrian Gilbert, were allowed to know what was going on. Dee was worried that her unintentional intrusion would bring upon her the angels' wrath. "Is it the will of God that for her great charity used toward many (as in procuring the Queen's Majesty's alms to many needy persons), the Lord intendeth to be merciful to her?" Dee anxiously asked. As usual, the response he got was cryptic: "Who is he that opened thy mouth, or hath told thee of things to come?" said Uriel. "What thou hast said is said."

There followed a prolonged session in which lines from the "book of the secrets" were dictated to Kelley: "Arney vah nol gadeth adney ox vals nath gemseh ah orza val gemáh, oh gedvá on zembáh nohhad vomfah olden. . . ."

On 9 April, a visitor arrived at Mortlake, a mysterious "Macedonian" carrying letters written by one "Sanford." Sanford may have been James Sandford, a writer and astrologer who had translated Agrippa's book of magic and had been promoting the idea of Elizabeth having a key role in the coming "new world" foretold by the coming of the fiery Trigon.[21] The following day, Kelley reported seeing a black shadow in the corner of the study, which announced itself to be the same Macedonian, now wearing a hat bearing a message showing that he was defiled and sinful. This was a rare instance where a real person other than Dee and Kelley themselves became insinuated in the actions.

Soon after, Dee had a breakthrough. He had been to court on some unspecified business and upon his return decided to spend a few private moments examining the scroll that Kelley had reported finding at Blockley. Looking at the strange text accompanying the map, he wondered if it might be an encoded passage of Latin. Several of the coded words had similar endings, a characteristic feature of inflected languages such as Latin.

After many attempts, he broke the code. The passage began "Tabula locorum," table of locations. It promised to reveal where "the objects and hidden treasures" of a Danish warrior king, Menabon, and of many other "famous men" based at military camps in southern Britain were to be found.[22] Dee also managed to decipher the labels accompanying the figures on the "Tabula locorum." The results were not particularly illuminating: "Huteos cros ... Gilds cros ... blankis Suters cros ... Marsars got cros ... Montegles arnid." Was the latter a reference to Lord Mounteagle, whose books Kelley had helped to recover, or to his estates in Lancashire? Dee recognized "Huteos cros." Kelley had said that the scroll had been found at "Huet's Cross" on Northwick Hill. Perhaps the other labels were similar locations elsewhere.

A few days later the queen visited Mortlake on her way from Richmond to Greenwich, arriving on horseback. Sir Walter Raleigh, who by now was a close ally of Dee's, had suggested she call. "Quod deferturm, non aufertur," she told Dee: that which is offered will not be taken away, referring to the various promises made to find him a secure position and living, presumably to compensate for the loss of income from Upton and Long Leadenham. She then offered him her hand to kiss.

The same day, Dee also met a new spirit. He was "very merry," dressed like a "vice" or fool in a play. At first Kelley assumed he was an "illuder," so Dee decided to "powder the pith" of his words—treat them with suspicion.

"Will you see my heart?" the spirit asked. He opened up his body to show that his heart was inscribed with the word "El." Dee asked this "El" if he knew anything about the now missing Book of Soyga.

"Soyga signifieth not Agyos," El replied. "*Soyga alca miketh.*"

"What language is that?" Dee asked.

"A language taught in Paradise to Adam."

"Be there any letters of that language yet extant among us mortal men?"

"That there be," said El. "Before the Flood, the spirit of God was not utterly obscured in man. Their memories were greater, their understanding more clear, and their traditions most unsearchable. Nothing remained of Enoch but might have been carried in a cart."

In twenty-eight days, the Book of Enoch, the legendary text written in the language taught in Paradise to Adam, would be Dee's, El promised. Meanwhile, he was to go and dig up the treasures identified in the map.

Dee was nervous about this idea. Digging for treasure without a royal license was "dangerous," he pointed out. His previous attempt to get Cecil to sanction such a scheme had failed.

"If thou hast a parcel or part out of every place of the earth, in any small quantity, thou mayest work by the creatures whose power it is to work in such causes," said El. In other words, if Dee and Kelley were to collect samples of earth from each of the locations, the spirits could then recover whatever lay buried there.

* * *

DEE WAS NOW in a state of confusion. The continuing spiritual dictation of the Adamic language had become overwhelming, its remorseless disclosure threatening to undermine Dee's attempts to transcribe it accurately. At the same time he had to grapple with the other occult revelations: the Book of Soyga, the strange alphabet, the Danish treasure. The nature, timetable, and purpose of his entire angelic mission seemed to be in chaos.

Over the following days, he and Kelley quarreled violently. Kelley had himself been in a disturbed state for some time. Three days before the action with El, the skryer had been set about by four spirits "like labouring men, having spades in their hands and their hair hanging about their ears." Dee had seen the wounds they had left, two bright red stigmata on Kelley's arms "as broad as groats." As they continued to attack Kelley, who cowered behind a stool, Dee tried to beat them off with a stick, flailing at the empty air until he was told they had disappeared.[23]

Now Dee reported that the skryer was once more assailed by "illuding spirits seeking his destruction." Kelley felt he was wasting his life. He was "a cumber to my house, and that he dwelled here as in a prison." He wanted to escape, to study, to get a job, earn a living. The day before, he told Dee, he had been attacked by someone called "little Ned" at the Black Raven Inn in Westminster, for having a part in a bargain Ned had struck with a surgeon called Lush, "now fallen into poverty." He wanted to get away from all this, to find peace, somewhere "where he might walk abroad without danger or to be cumbered or vexed with such slaunderous fellows."

He started to complain of suffering pains, of his belly and bowels swelling up and being "full of fire." These sensations, he confided to Dee, called to his mind the recent burning of an adulterous man and woman at St. Bride's Church in London. The reference was a telling one. A growing sexual tension had stalked Mortlake since Kelley's arrival.

Kelley was by now married to a Joanna Cooper, a union he had not wanted and now rejected. Even the spirits seemed to join in with the protests against his matrimonial state. "Cursed wives, and great devils, are sore companions," commented one, apparently referring to Kelley.[24]

The first mention of Joanna in Dee's diaries occurs in April 1583, in the second action involving El (or "Il" as he was now called). After the spiritual conference had ended, "E.K. rose up from the table and went to the west window, to read a letter which was even then brought him from his wife," Dee wrote. Kelley then withdrew to his chamber upstairs taking with him a little prayer book left by Adrian Gilbert, "intending to pray on it a certain prayer which he liked." Kelley did not reveal what was written in that letter, but a few weeks later he told Dee, "I cannot abide my wife, I love her not, nay I abhor her; and here in the house I am misliked, because I favour her no better."[25] The latter complaint was a clear reference to Jane Dee, who had obviously sided with Joanna.

Such tensions must have disturbed a household that had, until Kelley's arrival, been settled and happy. Dee doted on his wife and children, being unusually involved in domestic affairs for an Elizabethan father. His astrological interests encouraged him to note in detail the exact moment of many family events. A touching example of this occurred just a few weeks before Kelley first appeared. Dee was watching his eldest son Arthur playing with Mary, daughter of Sir William Herbert, a close neighbor and friend. The children, who were both three years old, decided to conduct "a show of a childish marriage" together, "calling each other husband and wife," and Dee noted how astrologically auspicious such a marriage would be.[26]

Kelley's show of a marriage was proving far less auspicious. One possible reason is that Kelley had been paid to marry Joanna, in order to legitimize children she had with an aristocratic lover. The scholar Susan Bassnett has shown that Joanna had at least two children by a previous relationship. One of them was Elizabeth Jane Weston, or "Westonia," who went on to make her name as a Latin poet in Bohemia. Westonia, later described as "probably the most highly gifted woman during Elizabeth's reign," insisted she was of noble birth, and there has even been speculation that there was some link between her natural father and Dee's friend, the courtier Sir Edward Dyer.[27]

Whether or not this was the cause of Kelley's hostility toward Joanna, her inclusion, and presumably that of her two infant children, in his life, and ultimately in the Dee household introduced a further element of instability into Mortlake's already volatile infusion of emotion, magic, and millenarianism.

Dee tried desperately to keep these explosive ingredients under control, and concentrate on the job in hand, namely finishing the holy book that the spirits had told him to complete within forty days.

On 26 April, following a series of arguments among Kelley, Jane Dee, and Adrian Gilbert, Dee thought he had finally managed to establish a "new pacification" between all parties. But the confusion and unrest continued. Over the following days, list upon list of strange words and names were communicated, culminating in an action on 5 May, when a new alphabet of "holy letters," the alphabet of Enoch's divine revelation, was communicated.

Dee also started to make arrangements for collecting together the "earths" at the ten locations identified on Kelley's scroll. It was decided Kelley would embark on a circulation of the sites himself on horseback, a trip that it was estimated would take ten to twelve days. Dee, however, could not find a suitable horse that was affordable. Kelley eventually managed to get hold of a "pretty dun mare" from a local, "Goodman Pentecost," for £3 in "angels," a gold coin stamped with a picture of the archangel Michael that was widely used at the time.

Dee was now worried that if Kelley went away they would break the forty-day deadline set for the completion of the angelic book. He was no longer even sure how many days they had used up, as there was no obvious moment that he could identify as the starting date.

He was also confused as to how he should deal with the material he had already received, and bombarded the spirits with questions, most of which were impatiently dismissed: What should he write the angelic book on, paper or parchment? Since the "holy language" was written from right to left, like Hebrew, should the book go from back to front? How should the diagrams be laid out? Whom should he hire to paint the top of the Table of Practice? "Can Master Lyne serve the turn well?"[28]

To add to the confusion, Kelley started suffering from strange visions outside the confines of the study. On 4 May, as he and Dee were having supper in the main hall, Kelley suddenly said he could see an ocean "and many ships thereon, and the cutting off the head of a woman, by a tall black man." What, Dee anxiously asked the spirits the following day, could this mean? "The one did signify the provision of foreign powers against the welfare of this land, which they shall shortly put in practice," Uriel replied. "The other, the death of the Queen of Scots. It is not long unto it." These were terrifying prophecies, which years later Dee noted were fulfilled in 1587 with the beheading of Mary and the "great preparation of ships against England by the King of Spain, the Pope and other princes called Catholic"—the Armada, which attacked the following year.[29]

In the midst of Kelley's visions, spirits continued to cast doubt on the proceedings. One said: "How pitiful a thing is it, when the wise are deluded" and added that "all that is done is lies." When Dee rebuked him, the spirit mocked him, and threatened to destroy his family. For the first time, Dee started to harbor misgivings about what he was doing. He would go to his oratory to seek guidance, to pray a "lamentable pang of prayer," or recite supplications such as Psalm 22, quoted by Jesus on the cross: "My God, my God, why hast thou forsaken me?"[30] Doubts assailed him just as the demons had assailed Kelley, and left him feeling "sorrowful." "I was in an exceeding great heaviness and sorrow of mind," he recorded, "and bewailed my case to God, and promised a greater care henceforward, of governing my tongue: and consenting to forbear to accompany with my own wife, carnally: otherwise than by heavenly leave and permission."

On 9 May, Kelley finally took his leave to recover the earths. He left for London by boat, where he was to buy a saddle, bridle, and "boot-hose." Dee watched him disappear down the Thames, and noted in his diary, "God be his guide, help and defence," then with a note of finality, "Amen."

And there the entire episode of Dee's action with the spirits and search for the divine language might have come to a premature end, but for the magnificent entrance at Mortlake of another colorful, charismatic, and not entirely trustworthy character.

PART SEVEN
THE PRINCE AND
THE JUGGLER

✣

[He] had read Dee's prefaces before
The Devil, and Euclid o'er and o'er,
And all th' intrigues 'twixt him and Kelley,
Lascus and th' Emperor, would tell ye.

SAMUEL BUTLER,
Hudibras

XX

✤

ON 15 June 1583 a fanfare of trumpets rippled across the
river, announcing the arrival of the royal barge. Beneath a
canopy of royal cloth, escorted by Lord Russell, Sir Philip
Sidney, and other noble members of the queen's court, sat a Polish
prince, Lord Albert Laski, basking in the trappings of a regally
anointed visit.[1] The water-borne cavalcade moored at Mortlake,
and Laski proceeded up the waterstairs at the back of Dee's house
to be presented to the philosopher by Sidney. He had come, as Dee
put it, "to do me honour, for which God be praised."

Laski had turned up unexpectedly in England two months earlier. The queen was concerned that he had fallen out with the
elected king of Poland and prince of Transylvania, Stephen Báthory,
in which case his arrival could spark a diplomatic incident. The
French ambassador Michel de Castelnau was convinced his mission
was to persuade the English to stop selling arms to Russia, a trade
that had prospered since the formation of the Moscow Company.
Laski unconvincingly claimed he was simply there to meet the
queen and enjoy the scenery.

Laski was a powerful and unpredictable figure in Polish politics.
He was the palatine of Sieradz, a central region of Poland west of
Łódź. In 1575, he was suspected of raising a private army to seize
the Polish throne, which had lain temptingly vacant for more than a
year following the flight of its previous occupant, the French prince
Henry de Valois. He was a committed but unorthodox Catholic,
with links to the world of alchemy and magic, and had sponsored
the first edition of a work by the German physician and mystic
Paracelsus. Dee had a particular interest in Paracelsus, now
regarded as one of the founding fathers of modern medicine, and

there was a comprehensive collection of Paracelsian works in the library at Mortlake.

Laski supported the sorts of universalist schemes that appealed so strongly to Dee. He was a backer of Jakob Basilikos, an adventurer who claimed to be the descendent of Levantine princes, and who wandered between the courts of Central Europe promoting the cause of the reunion of the Greek Orthodox and Catholic churches. Laski also had links with the "Family of Love." One of the movement's leading figures was Johannes à Lasko, a kinsman of Laski. Johannes was based at Emden, a town in East Frisia that had become the center of familism since the movement's founder, Henrick Niclaes, settled there.[2]

Despite the uncertainty about his intentions, Laski was welcomed in England with full princely honors. His homeland and neighboring Bohemia were in the middle of a bewildering array of religious and political tensions, between Protestant reform, Ottoman imperialism, and Catholic incumbency. England had few contacts and little influence in the region, and the queen's Lord Treasurer William Cecil and her spymaster Francis Walsingham saw a chance of getting an insider's view of the complex dynamics at play there. He was offered quarters at Winchester House in Southwark, where he found himself surrounded by exiled Italians, and the bear pits and brothels that lined the southern shore of the Thames. There he enjoyed the queen's hospitality under the watchful eye of his servant and escort, William Herle, a Welshman from a respectable family who had connections with the house of Northumberland and was also a government informer.

The Polish prince's combination of intellectual and physical attributes charmed his hosts. He was learned, fluent in several languages, amiable, and, though in his mid-fifties, of "good feature of body," as William Camden put it.[3] According to Holinshed, he also sported a very fine beard, which was of "such length and breadth, as that lying in his bed, and parting it with his hands, the same overspread all his breast and shoulders, himself greatly delighting therein, and reputing it an ornament." His ordinary attire was bright scarlet, but on special occasions, such as when he met the queen, he would wear robes of purple velvet "with other habiliments and furniture agreeable" including shoes "of a strange fashion, supposed of some not altogether unlike Chaucer's." Elizabeth reciprocated his gallant attentions with invitations to Greenwich and Nonsuch, where feasts and jousts were held to celebrate his visit.[4]

*   *   *

AT AROUND THE same time of Laski's visit, an Italian friar called Giordano Bruno arrived in London. Bruno was born at Nola, among the foothills of Vesuvius, in 1548, and, as Frances Yates put it, he "never lost traces of this volcanic and Neapolitan origin."[5] He entered the Dominican order in 1563 but left in 1576 following charges of heresy. Such charges would pursue him through Italy, into France and England, and ultimately to his death in Rome, where he was burned in 1600. His crime was to criticize the Catholic Church for using "punishment and pain" to force people into accepting its doctrines, where the Apostles had relied upon love.

While in Paris, Bruno had written two influential works rich with references to Hermes Trismegistus and Pythagoras and filled with striking magical motifs. In one, *De umbris idearum* (On the shadow of ideas), he imagined a world divided between the creatures of light and darkness, the latter, the witches, toads, basilisks, and owls, banished into their lairs by the brilliant sun of divine knowledge, the former, the cock, the phoenix, the swan, the lynx, and the lion taking possession of the world's sunlit surface.

Bruno's brilliance was noticed the moment he set foot on English soil, not least by Laski, who developed a fascination for the strange friar. The two probably first encountered each other at a tournament held at Greenwich in June. Soon after, Laski was offered the queen's barge for a trip up the Thames to Oxford. Bruno probably accompanied him, having been invited to engage in a series of lectures and disputations with the learned professors of the university.

On arrival, Laski beheld the magnificent spectacle of the Vesuvian Bruno erupting all over his academic hosts, spouting his ideas about the Sun being at the center of the universe and the stars glimmering in an infinite void. The professors were unimpressed. A don at Balliol College described the "Italian Didapper" as "stripping up

his sleeves like some juggler, and telling us much of *chentrum &
chirculus & circumferenchia* (after the pronunciation of his Country language) he undertook among very many other matters to set
foot the opinion of Copernicus, that the earth did go round, and the
heavens did stand still; whereas in truth it was his own head which
rather did run round, & his brains did not stand still."[6]

The feeling was mutual. "The leader of the Academy on that
grave occasion came to a halt fifteen times over fifteen syllogisms,
like a chicken in the stubble," Bruno pithily observed.[7]

The combination of the snobbishness and chauvinism Bruno
found (and in truth, provoked) reflected Dee's own experience of
the academic world. This was not the place to resurrect ancient wisdom or conjure up new ideas. And so Laski left, with Sir Philip Sidney and presumably Bruno in tow, staying overnight at Bisham
before arriving with trumpets at Mortlake.

*   *   *

LASKI'S GRAND ENTRANCE into Dee's house has elements of the-
atricality, a staged meeting designed to demonstrate to the accompanying courtiers that this was just another item in Laski's tour of
England's intellectual attractions, a chance for the two men to
admire the impressiveness of each other's accomplishments and
beards. However, this was by no means their first encounter. Laski's
name had first been brought to Dee's attention on 18 March 1583,
when a Mr. North, having just returned from a trip to Poland, had
come to see Dee following an audience with the queen, and presented "salutations" from the "palatine." They first met two
months later, a fortnight after Laski's arrival in England, when a
private audience was arranged at the Greenwich Palace chambers of
Robert Dudley, the earl of Leicester.

Was this the true purpose of Laski's visit, to make contact with
Dee? Suspicions must have been aroused further on 19 May, when
Laski's minder, William Herle, went to Winchester House to check
on his charge. He discovered that Laski had slipped out in the company of two discreet "gentlemen" and gone upriver to Mortlake to
visit Dee.[8]

Dee reported the visit in his diary. Kelley was still absent, collecting the earths from the sites identified in his scroll. But Laski was already fully aware of the spiritual conferences, and now wanted to participate. In particular, he wanted to see if the spirits could answer three questions: how long Stephen Báthory, the king of Poland, could be expected to live, whether or not Laski was to be his successor, and whether or not Laski would "gain possession of the kingdom of Moldavia."[9]

Kelley returned with the soil samples on 23 May, three weeks before Laski's public progress to Mortlake. What happened to them is unclear, for as soon as the spiritual conferences recommenced, Dee focused entirely on Laski. He laid before the angels the questions Laski had posed about his dynastic fortunes. An answer was delivered by Raphael: "Many witches and enchanters, yea many devils have risen up against this stranger," he said. "But I will grant him his desire."

The following Tuesday, a more explicit endorsement of Laski was delivered, its messenger being a new spirit, one who would later have a powerful and ultimately catastrophic influence over Dee. A pretty girl "of seven or nine years of age, attired on her head with her hair rolled up before and hanging down very long behind, with a gown of changeable green and red, and with a train" appeared from Dee's oratory. "She seemed to play up and down, child-like, and seemed to go in and out behind my books, lying on heaps: and as she should ever go between them, the books seemed to give place sufficiently, distinguishing one heap from the other, while she passed between them."[10] She skipped past the "great perspective glass" in the corner of the room, but, Kelley noted, there was no reflection of her in the mirror.

"Am not I a fine maiden?" the spirit asked flirtatiously. "Give me leave to play in your house."

Dee asked her name. "I am a poor little maiden, Madimi. I am the last but one of my mother's children. I have little baby-children at home." Madimi was a spiritual name that would have been known to Dee. It features in Agrippa's book of magic, a text that he kept ready for consultation in his study.

"Where is your home?" Dee asked.

"I dare not tell you where I dwell, I shall be beaten," Madimi replied.

"You shall not be beaten for telling the truth to them that love the truth," Dee reassured. "To the eternal truth all creatures must be obedient."

"I warrant you I will be obedient. My sisters say they must all come and dwell with you."

While Dee considered the possibility of this angelic ménage, Madimi produced a pocketbook. She opened it and pointed at a picture of a man, and asked Dee if he thought the man "pretty."

"What is his name?" Dee asked. "Edward," she replied. "Look you, he hath a crown upon his head. . . . This was a jolly man when he was King of England."

"How long since is it that he was King of England?" Dee asked.

"Do you ask me such a question? I am but a little maiden. Lo, here is his father, Richard Plantagenet, and his father also." In other words, he was Edward IV, who in 1461 seized the throne from the House of Lancaster for the House of York in the Wars of the Roses. Madimi continued to leaf through her pocketbook, on each page revealing an earlier generation of this family, back through forefathers described as grim, wicked, hairy, "writhen," passing across the lands they possessed, Bewdley, Mortimers Clybery, Wild Wenlock, Ludlow.

After an interruption for supper, Madimi continued with her genealogical catalog, until she came to one William Lacy. The pocketbook showed him going into France, and from there into Denmark, and from there into Poland, where he married and had children. The purpose of this elaborate pedigree was suddenly revealed: it was to show some link between the English royal family and Laski. But as soon as Dee asked Madimi to explain further, she stopped.

No further actions were recorded until the following Monday, 3 June, when Dee and Kelley were visited by another spirit, Murifri, who was dressed in the russet garb of a yokel, "all in red apparel, red hose close to his legs, a red jacket, red buttoned cap on his head, yea, and red shoes."[11] Where Madimi had been playful, he was morose. "Hell itself is weary of Earth," he said. "The son of Darkness cometh now to challenge his right: and seeing all prepared and provided, desires to establish himself a kingdom."

Murifri's Apocalyptic view, the idea that the old world was worn out, was a recurring and familiar theme for Dee, a condition personally embodied in two people whose cases had recently been brought to Dee's attention. One was called Isabel Lister. She had tried to mutilate herself with knives, and found herself to be "sore afflicted long with dangerous temptations" to commit suicide. She had come to Dee in the desperate hope that he could help save her from what she thought to be diabolical possession.

The other case concerned an impoverished woman "driven to maintain herself, her husband and three children by her hand labour," presumably because her husband was ill or disabled, and her children too young to earn a living. A "maiden," perhaps a relation of the poor woman, had dreamed of treasure buried in the cellar of the property she was hiring. The lease was about to come to an end, so the maiden and the woman had started digging, but finding certain unspecified "tokens," perhaps human remains, had left off. One of them had then approached Dee to ask if they should continue.

Murifri promised medicine for the first woman, but accused the second of "vanity." "Great hope of this world hath infected the weakling's mind," he said. It was such hope that the miserable Murifri found so absent from the weary world. "The earth laboureth as sick, yea sick unto death. The waters pour forth weepings, and have not moisture sufficient to quench their own sorrows."

However, there was a chance of salvation. Dee, anticipating Laski's imminent royal visit, asked Murifri if the prince should be "confirmed" as a participant of the spiritual actions. "Give him sharp and wholesome counsel. For in him (I say) the state and alteration of the whole world shall begin."

Such an endorsement would have struck Dee as entirely consistent with the context of the divine revelations: the imminent onset of the

"Fiery Trigon." The global "alteration" that this epochal change announced was, according to astrological tradition, to be focused on both Britain and Central Europe. Elizabeth was to lead the Britannic element through the founding of a new British Empire. Laski had evidently been singled out to lead the Continental contingent.

And so it seemed all was ready for a coordinated campaign to take delivery of the divine message, and reveal it to the worldly powers that might implement it.

*　　*　　*

TWO DAYS LATER and just ten days before Laski's princely progress would bring him to Mortlake, Kelley's brother Thomas arrived at Mortlake early in the morning with a message, which threw Edward into "a marvellous great disquietness of mind, fury and rage."[12] A warrant had been issued for Kelley's arrest "as a felon for coining of money." He had also heard that he was under attack from his former friend, John Husey of Blockley, who was now accusing Kelley of being a "cosener, and had used very bitter and grievous reports of him now of late."[13] Joanna, Kelley's unloved wife, had been staying in Blockley at the time, but had been forced to flee to her mother's at Chipping Norton.

Kelley's furious response to these reports, his display of such a "revenging mind and intent," shocked Dee, but also provoked "a great pang of compassion." He knew that it would bring great discredit to himself for "embracing the company of such an one, a disorderly person." However, he was more concerned that it could mean that the "good service of God" that Kelley and he had been commissioned to perform would be taken away from them, which might expose them to "great danger, both in body and soul." He therefore resolved to stand by Kelley.

Later the same day, the two of them engaged in another action, during which a female spirit called Ath appeared. If Kelley stayed at Mortlake and was arrested, it would ruin everything, Dee pointed out. What should he do? "It is written misery shall not enter the doors of him whom the Highest hath magnified," Ath reassured. Dee then asked if it might help if he approached Richard Young.

Young was a relative of Dee's and a rising member of the judiciary.[14] "Trouble yourself when you need," Ath replied.

For the next few days, Mortlake was suspended in a state of nervous anticipation, with the commissioners sent to arrest Kelley expected to bang on the door at any minute. On 9 June, Dee went to his oratory and prayed long and hard for "answer or resolutions of divers doubts." He waited for word from Kelley, who was at his station in the study, gazing into the crystal, but "answer came none." The stone remained empty. "But I held on in pitiful manner," Dee wrote, waiting to see if this meant that the spirits had deserted them.

"At length a voice came from behind E. K. and over his head." "The judgements of our God are most profound," said the voice, "and hard in the understanding of man. There is silence above." Dee "became in a great and sorrowful heaviness." Their actions seemed poised to come to an end, leaving only the silence.[15]

There was nothing further for five days. Then on 14 June, Dee and Kelley suddenly found themselves reprieved. A vision appeared in the stone as soon as Kelley looked at it, revealing an old woman wearing a red petticoat and red silk bodice, her yellow hair "rolled about like a Scottish woman." The woman, who later identified herself as "Galvah," was undertaking a long journey, during which she met a series of people: an old man with a "long grey beard forked"; a young man sitting at the side of a ditch, weeping, whose tears she licked away; a group of children clustered around a table laden with meat, pulling at her clothes in their efforts to reach the food; a thin, feeble man, staggering along, leaning on his staff, who collapses before her; a man climbing a hill, whose clothes have been torn off by brambles and briars, whose hands and feet are sore "with his excessive travail," who falls back down the hill under a hail of stones hurled at him by little ugly "maumets" or dolls. "Unto him that hath no weariness, there belongeth no sorrow," says the man, picking himself up and continuing his climb. The meaning of the vision was more obvious than usual. In the face of all obstacles and impediments, Dee must persist.

The following day, a Saturday, Laski arrived on the queen's barge. He stayed for a few hours, presumably in the company of Sidney and perhaps Bruno. While the august visitors were in attendance, Kelley went missing and did not reappear until 6 P.M., after the visitors had left. When Dee asked him what he had been up to, he replied that he had gone fishing.

❧

K ELLEY was certainly a keen angler,[1] but whether it was fish he had been out to catch that afternoon of Laski's visit is questionable. Over the past few days his fortunes had somehow been transformed. The charges leveled against him ten days before had evaporated. This may have been due to Dee's intervention, a judicious word dropped in the ear of Justice Young causing the commissioners to be called off. But the nature of the charge itself suggests another possible explanation, one that links Kelley's occult subterfuges with Laski's ostentatious progress.

One of the distinctive features of the spy network inherited by Walsingham from William Cecil, and now operating with full, lethal efficiency, was the use of "projectors."[2] In an era that uses the word to refer to machines that show films, its rich resonances have been lost. In the sixteenth and seventeenth centuries, a projector was a financial speculator, the sponsor of one of the infamous bubble companies that promised the wealth of the Americas and the Orient to naive investors. Projection was itself an alchemical word, referring to the projection of the Philosopher's Stone, the powder that Kelley even now imagined he had found, upon base metals to turn them into gold.

In Elizabethan espionage, a projector was an agent provocateur, someone employed to provoke spies into revealing themselves. The playwright Christopher Marlowe is considered by some, notably by Charles Nicholl in *The Reckoning*, his forensic examination of Marlowe's death, to have been such a projector, working on the government's behalf to infiltrate and flush out Catholic insurgents. This role has been linked to his murder in 1593—an event that involved many of the names entangled with Dee's life, including Justice Young himself.

Marlowe was, like Kelley, accused of coining and, like Kelley, escaped punishment. It has been argued that in Marlowe's case, the charges had been trumped up, probably to reinforce his cover as a Catholic activist. Coining was a convenient instrument for such stratagems, as it was just the sort of thing that a Catholic spy might be expected to engage in, as the forging or clipping of coins defaced the image of the queen herself.

If Kelley was employed in a similar role, such charges were probably used not as a cover so much as an incentive, trumped up by Cecil or Walsingham to coerce Kelley into spying on Laski. The timing fits, as the charges arose when Laski, under the observation of the government informer William Herle, made his first surreptitious contacts with Dee.

This might explain why Kelley's reaction when informed of the charges was fury rather than terror; the reaction of a man who had been lured into the labyrinth of Walsingham's spy network, and could not find a way out. It would also explain why, the day before Laski's arrival on the royal barge, Walsingham's agent Charles Sledd, the spy who penetrated the English College in Rome, had come to Mortlake and stayed the night. He was there to give Kelley a final prod. He evidently had some sort of falling out with his hosts, and suffered a serious nosebleed "upon my charitable instructions giving him to virtue and godliness," Dee noted.[3]

Following Kelley's return from his fishing expedition, another action took place in which Laski was the theme. The spirit Galvah, who now seemed to be in charge of proceedings, confirmed the palatine's prospects as a future king of Poland and Moldavia, which was currently under the control of the Ottoman Empire, and therefore seen as lost to Christendom.

Three days later, Dee recorded in red ink in his diary the commencement of a new book of angelic revelations, the *Liber Logaeth*, "which in your language signifieth Speech from GOD," the spirits explained.[4] He had obviously been forewarned that something important was to happen, as he had made elaborate preparations.

He had put on his "holiday clothes," and Galvah, who had appeared out of a "great gladsome shining of the Sun" streaming through the west window of the study, had apparently responded in kind, adorning herself in a "gown furred with foins" or decorative spikes. Dee had also set up a series of hourglasses to measure how long the action would take.

Dee began the proceedings with his usual prayers and devotions, a common feature of all the actions, which he insisted on conducting in the manner of a religious service rather than a mystical rite. "Amongst the angels there may be error, and sin may make them fall from the brightness of their glory," Galvah announced. "But to the soul of man (being once glorified) sin is utterly, yea most largely opposite: Neither shall that dignity ever be lost, stained, or defaced." This was a clear statement of one of the features of the actions that is often misunderstood: the angels were not infallible emissaries. Just like human testimony, the spiritual sort could not be taken at face value. It could be corrupt, incoherent, inconsistent. Some angels were fallen, some really demons in disguise. Furthermore, as Galvah implied, while sinful humans could be redeemed, fallen angels could not.

Galvah gave some of the practical instructions concerning the book of revelations Dee had so desperately sought: "The first leaf . . . is the last of the Book. And as the first leaf is a hotchpotch without order, so it signifieth a disorder of the world. . . . Write the Book (after your order) backward, but alter not the form of letters." Dee was worried by this instruction, but Galvah continued. "Write the 49," she said, referring to the number of pages in the book. "You have 48 already. Write first in a paper apart." The forty-eight pages Dee already had were the ones communicated over the previous months.

Having announced the delivery of the final page, Galvah's head "sparkleth and glistereth as when an hot iron is smitten on an anvil." And as she began to recite the twenty-one words that would make up the final page, "the beasts and all the creatures of the world every one showed themselves in their kind and form: But notably all Serpents, Dragons, Toads and all ugly and hideous shapes of beasts." The sight of this monstrous bestiary was too much for Kelley. Despite Dee's attempts to calm him, he suffered "excessive disquiet and suspecting of the verity or goodness of Galvah." "I do it with all humility and sincerity of mind, and beseech God to help me with his grace," Kelley cried out, "for myself I cannot do so, yet I am Thomas Didymas, I will believe these things, when I see the fruits of them."[5] Thomas Didymas (or Didymus) was the biblical name of Doubting Thomas, the apostle who doubted Jesus.[6]

Kelley's volatility was once again taking its toll on Dee. The following day, Wednesday, 19 June, at the start of another action, Dee beseeched God to make his mind "stable." He was having difficulties controlling his feelings, and begged "to be seasoned with the intellectual leaven, free of all sensible mutability."

There was no time to accommodate Dee's troubles. Today had been chosen as the day when Laski himself would be invited to take part in one of the actions. This was a momentous, and potentially very dangerous, development. What if Laski decided that the actions were demonic? What if he put a traitorous taint on such statements as the warning that "any one that governeth the people upon earth" would have his or her "faults revealed"?[7]

The action began at 2 P.M. without Laski. Kelley proposed that he should make some of the "reprobate" spirits appear before Laski "thereby to shew some experience of his skill in such doings." Dee clearly saw the danger in this, and firmly forbade Kelley from performing such spiritual tricks, which the skryer may have suggested in a desperate attempt to sabotage the entire mission and thereby release himself from any obligations he had made to Walsingham or Cecil.

Dee asked Galvah for advice about Laski's relationship with Cecil, who apparently held a "grudge" against Laski. "What danger may follow?" Dee asked. "The sum of his life is already appointed, one jot cannot be diminished," Galvah replied. "Let him rejoice in poverty," she added, a comment that Dee noted in the margin. Evidently, Laski was not going to help him escape his growing financial problems.

As these preliminaries were taking place, Laski appears to have been waiting elsewhere in Dee's house, perhaps in the reading room of the library. At 5 P.M. he was led into the study and watched as

Kelley summoned up an angel wearing a white robe "holding a bloody cross in his right hand." The angel revealed himself to be Jubanladaech, "the keeper and defender of this man present," in other words Laski's guardian angel. Jubanladaech foretold that "The Jews in his time shall taste of this cross: and with this cross shall he overcome the Saracens . . . For I will establish one faith."

At that point, however, the action was interrupted. Laski had been called out of the study to take a message delivered from the court by William Tanfield, who was acting as one of his servants. As Laski read the message outside, Tanfield suddenly appeared at the doors leading into the study, on the pretext of having some "commendations" for Dee from someone in London. There he discovered Dee and Kelley still sitting next to the crystal.

The intervention briefly threw the proceedings into turmoil. Dee was terrified of the "rash opinion" Tanfield would form of what he saw. As Dee perhaps knew, Tanfield had shady connections. A few weeks later, while Laski was still engaged in his actions with Dee, the Privy Council would give him immunity from arrest on a charge of debt default, a sure sign that he was engaged in secret government business.[8] His appearance that day intensified feelings that the actions were summoning spies as well as spirits, sending whispers back down the Thames to the privy chambers of Cecil and Walsingham. As soon as Tanfield left, Jubanladaech was reinvoked, and predicted that in five months' time the messenger's carcass would be devoured by fish from the sea. Jubanladaech also said that though Elizabeth "loveth [Laski] faithfully," Leicester (Robert Dudley) "flattereth" him, while Cecil hated him "unto the heart, and desireth he go hence." The queen and her first minister had fallen out over the matter, the spirit added. "When this Country shall be invaded, then shall you pass into his Country, and by his means shall his Kingdom be established. . . . The second coming is not long unto, and then shall he be wonderful." With this apocalyptic prophecy, the angel disappeared, sinking into the table "like a spark of fire."

On 2 July, Madimi, the flirtatious sprite who had provided the first spiritual endorsement of Laski, brought more warnings.

"Look unto the kind of people about the Duke [Laski]: and the manner of their diligence," she said.

"What do you mean by that? His own people, mean you?" Dee asked.

"The spies," Madimi replied. Cecil and Walsingham now considered him to be a traitor, she added. And he was not the only one under suspicion. Walsingham was "alienated marvellously" from Dee, she said. "The Lord Treasurer [Cecil] and he are joined together and they hate thee. I heard them when they both said thou wouldst go mad shortly." They were preparing to come and search his house. "Trust them not," she advised, "they shall go about shortly to offer thee friendship." The prospect terrified Dee, and he wondered whether he should take steps to clear the study of any evidence of their spiritual practice.

He also wondered if he and Kelley should follow Laski to Poland, and if so, what should be done about their families. It was the first mention of such an expedition, and the first sign that Dee felt he had no future in his beloved homeland.

*   *   *

AT AROUND THIS time, a book appeared entitled *A Defensative against the Poyson of supposed Prophecies*. It was written by Henry Howard, earl of Northampton, and a member of the leading Catholic family in the country. The book attacked prophecies of all sorts, including astrological, principally because they had been the instrument used to incriminate his two kinsmen, the earl of Surrey and the duke of Norfolk, in Catholic plots that led to both being executed. Howard's book also condemned the practitioners of such arts, naming no names but apparently pointing in the direction of Dee with its references to the "distemper of the brain" suffered by mystics who communed with the angels and cast horoscopes.[9]

During an action on 29 June 1583, Dee received a message from a spirit about Kelley. It was dictated as a series of Greek characters, apparently so Kelley would not understand it. It warned that Kelley had packed his bags and was preparing to leave.

A week later, Dee returned from London, where he had been to court and to see Laski. He found Kelley prepared to "ride forth," intending to go away for five days. When Dee questioned him about his intentions, Kelley took offense. "They have told me that if I tarry here I shall be hanged, and if I go with this Prince he will cut off my head," he said. "I cannot abide my wife," he added for good measure. "I love her not, nay I abhor her." With that he mounted his mare, and set off for "Brainford" (Brentford in Middlesex).

Three hours later, Dee found him back in the house and reassuringly "unbooted." "I have lent my mare out," he said disconsolately, "and so am returned."

"It is well done," said Dee.

Laski came to stay for five days in mid-July, during which a series of further actions were performed.[10]

At the end of the month, the queen took a boat trip from Greenwich toward Syon House, the former home of the dukes of Northumberland, which would soon revert to the family with the granting of the lease to Henry Percy, ninth earl of Northumberland, called the "Wizard Earl" because of his interest in alchemy and astrology. She stopped off at Mortlake en route to talk to Dee. There is no record of what they discussed, but the following day she sent a gift of money via the earl of Leicester's secretary—appropriately, forty angels. Sir Walter Raleigh also sent a letter with reassurances of Elizabeth's "good disposition" toward Dee.

Such comforts failed to allay Dee's feelings of insecurity. His diary entries for August are sparse, among them a report of "a great tempest of wind at midnight" on the same day as Kelley was in a rage with his wife. The following month he spent two weeks going through the endless shelves of his library, the dark corners and hidden nooks of each chamber, drawing up the first comprehensive catalog of his collection. The result was a 170-page document that still stands as one of the greatest works of bibliography to come out of the Renaissance.

The reason he decided to do this at this time becomes clear in a diary entry dated 21 September. Next to the star tables showing Aquarius, the sign of the water carrier, in the ascendant, Dee wrote: "We went from Mortlake, and so the Lord Albert Laski, I, Mr E. Kelly, our wives, my children and family, we went toward our two ships attending for us, seven or eight mile below Gravesend."[11] From there they were to depart on a journey that would lead them all into fantastic, frightening spiritual as well as geographical domains—a journey from which none would return the same, and from which Kelley would not return at all.

XXII

⚜

As Dee and his household made their preparations to depart the country, the royal court was distracted by the wedding of the poet, courtier, and warrior Sir Philip Sidney to Frances Walsingham, the daughter of Sir Francis. Laski may have been in attendance, as would have been many of Dee's closest associates and friends, such as Sir Edward Dyer.

Sidney was now one of the most popular and glamorous figures in Elizabeth's court. He was also a friend and possibly former pupil of Dee's, whom he half-jokingly described as "our unknown God"—by which he apparently meant the inspiring figure of his literary circle, the mysterious "Areopagus."[1]

The Areopagus got its name from the hill near the Acropolis in Athens where the city's rulers would meet. According to a letter from the poet Edmund Spenser to Gabriel Harvey, it was adopted as the name of a literary circle set up by Sidney and Dyer to silence "bald Rymers" and proclaim new "Laws and rules of Quantities of English syllables for English Verse."[2] Whether the Areopagus ever really existed, or was a figment of fizzling literary imaginations, is a matter of debate.[3] But a program of poetical reform certainly did exist, and its manifesto was Sidney's *Defense of Poesie*. Sidney described how the poet,

> lifted up with the vigour of his own invention, doth grow, in effect, into another nature; in making things either better than nature bringeth forth, or quite anew; forms such as never were in nature, as the heroes, demi-gods, Cyclops, chimeras, furies, and such like; so as he goeth hand in hand with Nature, not enclosed within the narrow warrant of her gifts, but freely ranging within the zodiac of his own wit.

Poetry would open up fantastic, artificial universes to rival that of God. "New worlds shall spring from these," as the angels put it in their first revelations to Dee, the meta incognita of the vulgar tongue so spectacularly breached in Sidney's own *Arcadia*, the *Faerie Queene* of Spenser, and the plays of Marlowe and Shakespeare. And it is in Spenser's *Faerie Queene* that an homage to the "unknown God" of the Areopagus can be glimpsed. He sits in a room in the House of Temperance

> . . . *whose walls*
> *Were painted faire with memorable guests,*
> *Of famous Wizards, and with picturals*
> *Of Magistrates, of courts, of tribunals,*
> *Of commonwealths, of states, of policy,*
> *Of laws, of judgements, and of decretals;*
> *All arts, all science, all Philosophy,*
> *And all that in the world was aye thought wittily.*
> *Of those that room was full, and them among*
> *There sat a man of ripe and perfect age,*
> *Who did them meditate all his life long,*
> *That through continual practise and usage,*
> *He now was grown right wise, and wondrous sage.*
> *Great pleasure had those stranger knights, to see*
> *His goodly reason, and grave personage,*
> *That his disciples both desir'd to be.*[4]

Was the man of ripe and perfect age Dee? Were the stranger knights Dyer and Sidney, his disciples Spenser and Harvey? And what would they make of what was happening now, on the day of Sidney's wedding, of this man who had grown so "wondrous sage," together with Kelley and their wives and children, standing on the banks of the Thames on a summer's afternoon, passing from waterside to a waiting barge crates of books, trunks of clothes, and a case containing the newly completed table of practice and the set of magic seals wrapped in red silk? There is a clue in the same poem, following a verse marveling at the discoveries in the New World. These places, Spenser pointed out, had existed

. . . when no man did them know;
Yet have from wisest ages hidden been:
And later times things more unknown shall show.
Why then should witless man so much misween
That nothing is, but that which he hath seen?
What if within the Moon's faire shining sphere?
What if in every other star unseen
Of other worlds he happily should hear?
He wonder would much more: yet such to some appear.[5]

Beyond the New World there may be yet another, whose existence is no more dependent on its discovery by man than were the Amazon, Peru, and "fruitfullest *Virginia.*" Spenser called it the "fairy land."

*   *   *

DEE'S JOURNEY BEGAN on 21 September 1583: St. Matthew's Day, as he noted in his diary. By 3 P.M., their belongings were stowed and they had set off down the Thames toward London. The serpentine curve of the river as it approaches Hammersmith provided Dee with a last chance for a lingering view of his beloved house, the place where the queen had posed before his magical mirror, where members of the court, travelers, and adventurers had stopped for advice, where he had performed his experiments, read his books, where his mother had died and his three children been born (the youngest, Roland, just nine months before), the place where he had built up his reputation and great collection, and which he had now commended to the custody of Jane's brother, Nicholas Fromonds.

Laski met them on the river and they waited for nightfall. Under the cover of dark, "in the dead of the night" as Dee put it, they and Laski loaded their goods onto "wherries" and sailed through London, past the leaded windows of the palaces and castles lining the shore, through the narrow arches of London Bridge, beneath the dangling floors of the houses perched along its sides, past the Tower and Traitor's Gate toward Greenwich, where they stopped to "refresh" themselves at the house of a friend of Dee's, one "Goodman Fern," a local potter.

This clandestine departure then involved a transfer to yet another vessel, a "great tilt-boat" (a large rowing boat with an awning) that Dee had hired with a "Mr Stanley." The presence of the Stanley name adds to the sense of intrigue. The Stanleys, based in Lancashire, were a notoriously factious dynasty linked to a number of Catholic plots and rebellions. Could this be one of their number? Was "Mr Stanley" Sir William Stanley, a mercenary who defected to the Catholic cause in the Low Countries in 1587? Or Ferdinando Stanley, Lord Strange, heir to Henry Stanley, the fourth earl of Derby, the great theatrical patron whose troupe premiered the works of Marlowe and Shakespeare, and who wittingly or unwittingly became embroiled in Catholic plots that would reach as far as Dee's destination, Bohemia? These were the two men who awarded Dee the living at Leadenham, so he evidently knew them, and they evidently thought highly of him. Or was it the son of the late Lord Mounteagle, himself a Stanley, whose mysterious books Kelley had tried to recover? The "Mr" gives little clue; Dee, like many Elizabethans, was lax with his use of titles.

Whoever it was, the motive for slipping away from the country in this covert manner was and remains as opaque as the muddy river waters that slipped along the sides of the great tilt-boat as it carried its cargo out to sea. Some have suggested Dee's reasons for leaving were financial: he and Kelley were basically drawn by the prospect of a good wage and a secure living as part of Laski's household in Poland. But Dee knew some time before he started planning his departure that Laski was insolvent.[6]

On a number of occasions Dee hinted that he was embarking on a private mission on behalf of the queen, suggesting that he may have been, perhaps in combination with Kelley, acting as a spy, or more accurately an "intelligencer," detailed to use his position as part of Laski's entourage to gather sensitive foreign information.[7]

On other occasions he claimed to have been driven out by the hostility of certain "nobles"—perhaps referring to Cecil, or to Henry Howard, earl of Northampton, whose *Defensative against the Poyson of supposed Prophecies* revived suspicions that he was dabbling with demons.[8] As far back as 1577, he had complained that the slanders leveled against him meant he was no longer counted "a good subject, or a commendable (nay scarce a tolerable) Christian" in his own country, which meant that all his achievements, his "acts and travails," had become marginalized.[9]

As the sun rose over the North Sea, the tilt-boat approached two ships moored seven or eight miles beyond Gravesend, at the mouth of the Thames. Dee, Kelley, their families, and Laski boarded the larger, a Danish "double fly-boat," a fast-sailing coastal vessel. Dee's and Laski's servants, two horses, and the luggage were loaded into the smaller, a Flemish "boyer." As soon as the passengers and cargo were aboard, they immediately set sail for the Low Countries, borne by a light wind.

At midnight, a storm blew up, which drove the ships back toward the English shore. Dee's ship dropped anchor in an attempt to keep a safe distance out to sea, but the anchor dragged, forcing the sailors to cut the cable, hoist sail, and attempt to make their way to the nearest harbor at Queenborough, at the mouth of the Thames estuary.

They finally reached the harbor the following morning, and the passengers disembarked on two dinghies that came alongside. The mast of the dinghy carrying Dee and Kelley became entangled with the ship's ropes, and as powerful winds and currents pulled it out to sea, it began to lean over and take on water. Kelley desperately started bailing with a "great gauntlet" while the crew attempted to free the mast. In the midst of the commotion, the boatman lost one of his oars, which quickly floated beyond reach. Eventually the dinghy was freed and floated to a "crooked creek," where they moored. The boatman jumped out, and offered to carry the passengers to the shore, but as he lifted Dee out they both fell, leaving Dee "foul arrayed in the water and ooze."

They spent the rest of the week holed up in lodgings, waiting for the delivery of a new anchor from London, leaving Dee plenty of time to contemplate the implications of such a farcical start to their mission. On Wednesday, 25 September, he consulted the angel Michael. "Let the winds open their mouths, and let the raging waters open their deep and powerful currents into all parts of your vessels," Kelley reported Michael as saying, "yet they shall not prevail, because I shall give you my overwhelming power."

The following day, they returned to their ships. They spent the night at anchor, and sailed the following morning. They had reached the coast of Holland by 28 September, but neither the ship's master nor the pilot could recognize the terrain, so they decided to sail back out to sea "with great fear and danger." They landed at Brielle in Holland the following the day, and, after spending a night in Rotterdam, sailed farther up the coast to Amsterdam, and then through the Zuider Zee to Enkhuizen, where Dee's servant Edmund Hilton was sent ahead to Denmark with some of the luggage, possibly including the huge caskets containing the 800 or so books Dee had packed.[10]

The passengers proceeded by boat to Harlingen, on the opposite side of the Zuider Zee, and by boats up to Dokkum and toward Emden, now in Germany. Emden was a port at the end of the Ems River estuary. It had strong connections with England through the cloth trade, and had been chosen by Dee and his companions as the departure point for their coming inland journey through northern Germany and toward Laski's domains in Poland. They arrived in their boats at 6 P.M. on 17 October, only to find the town's gates locked, forcing them to spend the night back on board, though Laski managed to find lodgings on the opposite side of the estuary. The following day, they entered the town. It was not a particularly prosperous place, with an "old rotten church at the town end."[11] They found lodgings, Laski at the White Swan on the waterside, Dee, Kelley, and their families at the Three Golden Keys, neighboring the "English house," a meeting place for English merchants.

At 8 A.M. on Sunday, 20 October, Dee and his companions set off for Bremen. They left Laski behind with the earl of Emden, apparently trying to extract some money.[12]

Without stopping for rest (perhaps to reduce their traveling costs), they rode through Oldenburg and "a very simple village" called Oppen and arrived in Bremen on Tuesday, 22 October, where they finally allowed themselves some respite from the road, staying at an old widow's house at the sign of the Crown. With Laski now in attendance, they departed on 2 November, riding for Osterholz, where they looked round a "great nunnery," reaching Harburg on the banks of the River Elbe two days later. The following morning they loaded their wagon onto a ferry and crossed the river for Hamburg.

There was time only for a brief stay in the city before they were off again. Dee's family and servants had gone ahead toward Trittau, a village four miles up the road, where they were all to meet up and continue with their journey. Dee arrived to find no sign of them, "to my great grief."[13] Night fell, and an anxious Dee sent out messengers for news. They were all finally reunited at midnight.

And so their slow, perilous progress continued, through Lübeck, Rostock, Stettin (or Szczecin), over the Polish border, where they spent Christmas, southeast to Poznań, where Dee found some time to tour the cathedral and admire the library and the "beautifully carved" monuments to Polish kings in the crypt. At the end of January, freezing weather was hampering their progress. At Konin they had to cross a wooden bridge over the River Warta, which was about to collapse after some of its rickety supports had been swept away by pack ice. They then had to hire twenty-five men to clear a two-mile stretch of road to enable their coaches to pass, before finding themselves marooned outside Vinew, which was surrounded by floods.

On 3 February 1584, after traveling nearly continuously for over four months, by ship, boat, coach, horse, and foot, having endured storms, blizzards, separations, though miraculously no serious injuries or illnesses, they arrived in Łask, Laski's hometown. This, Dee assumed, was to be their destination, at least for the time being, and he summoned the angels to tell him what he should do next.

The actions had, in fact, continued throughout their journey, though in a necessarily punctuated fashion. Many of them were about the land they had left behind, which seemed to become more threatening and hostile as it became more distant. In October 1583, while they were at Dokkum, the angel Gabriel himself had appeared, and warned that "In England they condemn thy doings, and say, Thou art a Renegade. For they say, Thou hast despised thy Prince."[14] On 1 November 1583, while they were in Bremen, Kelley had a vision of Vincent Seve, Laski's brother-in-law, in London walking from Charing Cross down Whitehall toward Westminster Palace, where horses could be seen grazing in the gardens, and crowds of people gathered at the entrance to the abbey. Seve was grandly dressed in a "great ruff," and talking to a group of men on horseback armed with rapiers. No sooner had this "shew" appeared than it was "vanished away," leaving the impression that Seve was up to something.

A few days later, a spirit told Dee that Jane's brother Nicholas Fromonds, who had been left in charge of Dee's house and library, had been imprisoned, and was at that moment under cross-examination. His interrogators were telling him that Dee "hast hid divers secret things" in the house and they demanded that Fromonds reveal their location. There was also a threat that Dee's "house may be burnt for a remembrance of thee [i.e., Dee] too."[15] The truth of these angelic reports is hard to verify, but Fromonds certainly faced threats and incursions while at Mortlake.

After their arrival in Łask, a new spirit called Nalvage appeared, with the face of a child and hair like down. Dee had been suffering from a severe fever for the past few days, and asked Nalvage for medical advice. Nalvage responded with a terrifying vision. Six or seven people wielding torches crouched like apes on the roof of a house—it must have been the cottage at Mortlake. "They are like shadows," Nalvage said. "They start to thrust their torches into the sides of the house, which begins to blaze.

"Now your wife runneth out, and seemeth to leap over the gallery rail, and to lie as dead. And now come you out of the door, and the children stand in the way toward the church. And you come by the . . . door; and kneel, and knock your hand on the earth. They take up your wife; her head waggleth this way and that way. The stone house quivereth and quaketh, and all the roof of the house falleth into the house. Your wife is dead, all her face is battered. The right side of her face, her teeth and all is battered. She is bare-legged, she hath a white petticoat on."

Dee asked what this meant, whereupon a "wench" appeared, dressed in white and sitting on a bench. She was Madimi, the girl who first endorsed Laski's role in Dee's spiritual mission. She now told Dee she had been in England, "at your house where they are all well." "The Queen said she was sorry that she had lost her philosopher," she added. "But the Lord Treasurer answered: He will come home shortly, a-begging to you." His study and its secrets were safe, Madimi reassured. The queen had commanded it to be "sealed up."[16]

Intermingled with these unsettling revelations were the all-important angelic tables, the "Cabala of Nature," as Nalvage called it. They now came faster than ever, Dee's fingers racing across the notebook paper as he struggled to scratch down the spewing stream of divine data. After each session, he would spend further hours on his own, trying to incorporate what he had been told with the information he had already received, drawing together the results in the finished books of revelations that he would later hide away in the secret drawer of his cedar chest. This was the promised language of Adam and of Eden, which would reveal the keys to the cosmic code, delivered in a stammer back in England, but here flowing like vespers from a distant chapel. "It is so terrible, I tremble to gather it," he wrote after one particularly intense session.[17]

* * *

ON 19 MARCH 1584, Dee, recovering from his attack of feverish "ague," set off for Kraków with his family, but without Kelley. The city, 100 miles south of Łask, was, Madimi had declared, a "place sanctified."

In the sixteenth century, Kraków was the capital of Poland, its status proclaimed by the "Wawel," the imposing hilltop fortification that loomed over the surrounding countryside. The Wawel was the kingdom's spiritual as well as temporal nucleus of power, containing within its walls the Renaissance palace that acted as the chief residence of the country's monarchs, and a cathedral, their Romanesque mausoleum.

Beneath the Wawel bustled a thriving city. Years of religious tolerance and civic autonomy had fostered a vibrant mercantile and intellectual climate. The city's university was one of the finest in Europe, a center of natural philosophy, once home to Nicolas Copernicus and now boasting an important collection of scientific instruments.

The travelers arrived on 23 March, and spent the following week at a boardinghouse next to a church in the suburbs, while Dee looked for lodgings in the city. He eventually found a house at an annual rent of 80 guilders in St. Stephen's Street, just a short walk from the spacious market square and the university's Collegium Maius, its main college.

Kelley followed on 6 April—the Friday of Easter Week, as Dee noted, calculated according to the new Gregorian calendar, which the Poles used (in England, Easter was still set to the old Julian date of 19 April). Now reunited, the two immediately resumed their actions in a room set aside in Dee's modest lodgings, the passing traffic of Kraków's busy citizens quite unaware of the strange business being conducted behind closed doors by these foreign visitors—at least for the time being.

The angel Nalvage reappeared; his childlike appearance was now explained by his acquiring the "physiognomy" of the English boy-king Edward VI. He began to deliver further tables, instructing Dee to write down a series of word squares. But as Kelley delivered the angelic formulas, he seemed to be interrupted by another voice, heard not through his external senses, through which he claimed to behold the visions of the angels, but internally, through the "imagination." The experience evidently unsettled him, and later in the same action he confessed to feeling "very angry."[18]

A few days later, his mood worsened. He once more told Dee he doubted the actions. He said he "would no more sit to receive ABC" and left the room. Over the following week Dee continued to work in his "upper study" at transcribing and interpreting the tables. On the morning of Thursday, 19 April, he heard Kelley on the stairs and invited him to come and look at the work he had done. He showed Kelley the books and "how I had some understanding of those holy words their significations." Kelley was not reassured. He told Dee he had confessed his doubts in a letter to Laski, and wanted to return to England.[19]

Laski himself arrived in Kraków the following Wednesday, staying in a "little wooden lodging" in the gardens of St. Stanislaw Church, south of the Wawel. If he had received a letter from Kelley, he clearly had not taken it seriously, and the actions continued. However, so did Kelley's volatile mood. Some days he was happy, telling the spirits he was content with his "friend here, Master Dee" and "very well persuaded of these actions."[20] Other days he would be in a "great storm," or lock himself in his study and refuse to come out. He even produced evidence to show that some of the information imparted by the spirits had been copied from books in Dee's own collection. This was not the first time Kelley had tried to discredit his own visions. However, as before, his admission was not couched as a confession of actual fraud, rather as proof of spiritual mischief, and Dee dismissed it.

During one session, Dee received very clear instructions on the binding of one of the books of tables he had compiled from the actions. It was to contain forty-eight pages, he was told, eight by seven inches in size, and be covered in leather tooled with silver. "What shall I do with the book after I have bound it?" Dee asked the spirit. "I will answer for him," Kelley interjected. "Burn it."[21]

As moods deteriorated inside Dee's study in St. Stephen's Street, so did the political situation outside. On 7 May, Dee watched sixty coaches wind their way around the Wawel and into the city. The enormous train was an escort for a "closed" (windowless) carriage covered with a red cloth carrying the rebel Samuel Zborowski. Zborowski had been arrested by the chancellor Jan Zamoyski on the orders of the Polish king Stephen Báthory on charges of treason. He had led a faction of Polish nobles sympathetic toward Báthory's enemy Rudolf II, the Holy Roman Emperor, whose dominions stretched across Germany and Bohemia, up to the borders of Poland. Zborowski was a popular figure in Poland, and his arrest sent a frisson of rebellion through the city that rattled the doors of Dee's home, startling him from his spiritual actions.

Laski was widely believed to be a supporter of Zborowski, and Dee became worried that this put him and his family in danger.[22] In St. Stephen's Street, he interrupted at least one action because he thought he heard footsteps in the chamber adjoining the study, noting that the door at the bottom of the stairs had been left open.[23] He had every reason to be concerned. The spirits themselves were now openly hostile toward the Polish king, accusing him of being in league with the Ottoman Empire. "Go to the Emperor," Nalvage told Dee, meaning Rudolf, who had set up his court at Prague, which was 300 miles to the west.[24]

But Dee could not afford to go to Prague. Laski's fortunes, which had always been precarious, now deteriorated further. He was in a "low estate from high," in other words, out of favor with the king. He had run out of money, and taken refuge in the Franciscan monastery, where he was frequently visited by Kelley. "Go to the Emperor," the spirits were insistent, but Dee could not see how.

On 13 July 1584, Dee's fifty-seventh birthday, Gabriel announced that Dee now had the keys of God's "storehouses . . . wherein you shall find (if you enter wisely, humbly and patiently) Treasures more worth than the frames of the heavens. . . . Now examine your Books, confer one place with another, and learn to be perfect for the practice and entrance." In other words, the raw material for the "Book of Enoch," as the holy writ was now called, had finally been delivered, and it was up to Dee to generate the sacred text.

The following day, Dee's son Roland fell gravely ill, and by 1 P.M. that afternoon seemed "ready to give up the ghost . . . his eyes set and sunk into his head." Roland recovered, but to Dee it could only be interpreted as a warning, one that was reinforced the following evening. While he was sitting in his chamber, he saw flashes of fire dancing around his chamber that cast no light. "Who commanded thee to be gone?" a spirit angrily asked Dee through Kelley on 23 July, finding them both still in Kraków. "I take the commandment to have been from God," Dee replied. "Thou hast broken the Commandment of God," the spirit replied.

On 31 July, the angelic fury erupted once more. "Were you not commanded to go after ten days?" the spirit said, fire spewing from its mouth. "I have brought madness into the house of the unjust," it added. Dee noted that Kelley had been stricken by this madness, but was now recovered. He had managed to scrape together the money to get himself and Kelley to Prague, if not his family. The problem was Laski, who was supposed to finance the whole trip.

He had apparently not even managed to make provision for himself. Should they go without him?

"Thus sayeth the Lord, if you tarry, it is because I am, which am strength and triumph against mine enemies, and so against the enemies of those that put their trust in me," replied the spirit, unhelpfully.

"Lord, show us the light of thy countenance, and be not wrathful," Dee beseeched.

"Move me not, for I am gone," the spirit replied.

And so, in a day's time, was Dee.

PART EIGHT
CAESAR'S COURT

✤

At the far end of the earth is Bohemia
A fair and exotic dominion
Full of deep and mysterious rivers.

KONSTANTIN BIEBL,
Protinožci

XXIII

✦

RAGUE gave the world Kafka and the robot.[1] Both are icons
of mechanized modernity, but both had their origins in the
city that Dee and Kelley now journeyed toward. The capital
of the Kingdom of Bohemia pulsated with mad machines, capri-
cious powers, and hidden influences, where a skeleton standing
nonchalantly next to the town hall's astrological clock marked time
with the yank of a rope and the turn of an hourglass, where Rabbi
Loew was said to be at work in the Jewish Ghetto building the
Golem, a figure of clay that he would bring to life by placing a
tablet inscribed with the name of God in its mouth, where Rudolf
II, the great-grandson by two lines of descent of the Spanish queen
Joan the Mad, sat in demented isolation in his castle on the hill, the
haughty and impenetrable Hrad, while around him visitors and
ambassadors circulated in maddening labyrinths of courtly ritual.

Prague had become a focus of power since Rudolf moved his
court there from Vienna in 1583, the year before Dee was commanded to gain an audience with this remote, melancholy emperor
or "Caesar," as the spirits dubbed him, harking back to the pagan
Roman emperors whose authority he was supposed to have inherited. He was the joint leader of the now all-powerful Hapsburg
dynasty, which divided most of Continental Europe between its
two branches: in the west Philip, king of Spain, champion of
Catholicism, and onetime husband of Queen Mary of England,
with dominions that now stretched across the Atlantic to the New
World, and in the east Rudolf, Holy Roman Emperor and ruler of
Austria, Germany, Hungary, and Bohemia.

Rudolf was the product of the loveless marriage between
Emperor Maximilian and Maximilian's cousin Maria of Spain. He

had spent his teenage years in the Spanish royal household, and was cultivated by his stern uncle Philip II in Catholic discipline and Castilian manners. He grew up into a thoughtful, somber, cautious prince, with an unusually good command of the languages, if not the peoples, of his dominions, including Czech.

When his father died in 1576, he inherited a realm made up of a patchwork of principalities and palatines so loosely knit as to threaten continual disintegration.[2] It was also riddled with religious dissent, thanks to the policy of theological lenience fostered by his father, the ecumenical emperor Maximilian II, whose free-thinking attitude Dee celebrated by dedicating to him the *Monas Hieroglyphica*.

Rudolf had climbed the steep hill leading up to Prague's castle or Hrad to remain aloof from the chaotic dominion he had inherited. Through the lofty windows of his recently modernized palace, all the chaos and confusion was reduced to a distant uniformity. Yet it was through these very same windows in 1618 that the rebellious spirits now stirring below would throw out—literally—the Catholic governors appointed over them by Rudolf's successor, this famous "defenestration" initiating the holocaust of the Thirty Years' War, the "first total European war."[3]

Perched on the edge of this precipice, Rudolf became increasingly enclosed and inscrutable, a man of few words, in Philip Sidney's estimation, "sullen of disposition, very secret and resolute, nothing the manner his father had in winning men in his behaviour."[4] He retreated from practical matters, and instead started to dabble in more cerebral ones—science, art, collecting, spiritualism, Hermeticism, and alchemy.

*   *   *

ON 1 AUGUST 1584 Dee left Kraków with his servant Edmund Hilton, Kelley, and Kelley's brother Thomas. Joanna Kelley, Jane Dee, and the children had been left behind in the house on St. Stephen's Street. The date of departure was significant for Dee. This, the spirits had promised, was when the first book of revelations would be delivered to Dee—assuming they were using the new calendar, 1 August falling in another ten days by the old reckoning. Either way, Dee's arrival in Prague coincided with a momentous point in his spiritual mission.

It took eight days by coach to complete the 300-mile journey, following the course of the Vistula River, skirting the foothills of the Carpathian Mountains, through the rolling landscape of Moravia, from Kraków to Prague. They entered a city that was in some respects similar to Kraków, its streets falling under the shadow of a hill topped by a castle and cathedral, the indomitable Hrad. The heart of the city lay not on the hill, but on the other side of the sluggish Vltava River. There, in the medieval streets of the Old Town, Prague's maverick, mysterious character could be seen seeping out through architectural details—petrified bells, rams, skeletons and stars, odd dioramas, and mysterious allegories in stone or *sgraffito*, a form of wall painting peculiar to Bohemia. Celetná Street, the main thoroughfare to the Old Town Square, and the serpentine alleys and dark passages that disappear into the city's interior, were once lined with taverns named after mysterious creatures and strange objects—the Unicorn, the Stone Table, the Blue Star, the Vulture, the Spider, suggesting that visitors were entering not just a foreign city, but a fabulous other world.

During Rudolf's reign, this sense of unreality intensified, as a host of "charlatans, knaves and blowhards," as one bewitched visitor put it, were drawn to the city's gates by the promise of rich pickings and lax regulation. In came people like the Greek Mamugna of Famagosta, who passed himself off as the son of an Italian martyr and paraded the city streets pulled by a pair of black mastiffs, and Geronimo Scotta, "especially known for his diabolical legerdemain," who arrived in a train of three red carriages drawn by forty horses and ended up in the town square "selling salves, stag-horn jelly, vitriol of Mars and cassia pulp" from a wooden stall. Such characters seemed to stand on each street corner and wander every sentence of the city's literature, becoming more fantastic with each reappearance.[5] It was in this Bohemian brew that Dee and Kelley now immersed themselves.

Dee found lodgings in the home of Thaddeus Hajek, Emperor Rudolf II's physician. Hajek's house stood on a corner of Bethlehem Square in the Old Town, near the Bethlehem Chapel, where the fifteenth-century Czech martyr Jan Hus, inflamed by the teachings of John Wycliffe, preached against the corruption of the Catholic Church.[6]

Hajek had inherited the property, called the "House at the Green Mound," from his father, the alchemist Simon Bakalar.[7] Bakalar had decorated the walls with strange inscriptions and motifs, including his own name majestically rendered in Latin, *Simon Baccalaureus Pragensis*, imprinted in letters of silver and gold, surrounded by hieroglyphs, pictures of birds, fishes, flowers, fruits, leaves. Over the door was written the verse:

> *Immortal honour and equal glory are due to him*
> *By whose wit this wall is adorned with colour.*

And on the south side of the room, high up, was written:

> This art is precious, transient, delicate and rare. Our learning is a boy's game, and the toil of women. All you sons of this art, understand that none may reap the fruits of our elixir except by the introduction of the elemental stone, and if he seeks another path he will never enter nor embrace it.[8]

Dee was in his element. He was also once more in the Continental intellectual environment he had found so convivial in his younger years. His host was the foremost astronomer of Central Europe, and shared very similar interests.[9] Hajek's observations of the Nova of 1552 were among the most accurate made, and he kept detailed records on the passage of the comet of 1577. He investigated the use of clocks to measure celestial positions, published a series of astrological ephemerides, drew up a report on alternative calendars following the introduction of the Gregorian system, and wrote on metoposcopy, the study of assessing a person's character and fortune from their face. He was also a Protestant, a follower of Jan Hus, belonging to the moderate "Utraquist" faction.

Dee could not have hoped for a warmer welcome. He and Hajek had probably corresponded since the discovery of the nova, and Hajek gave his guest generous access to both his home and his network of imperial contacts. It is unclear what Hajek knew of Dee's mission, but he evidently allowed Dee and Kelley the privacy they needed to continue their work in his father's old study.

Their first Prague action took place on 15 August, and began with an extraordinary series of alchemical visions: a furnace with an opening the size of four or five city gates belching a "marvellous smoke," a seething lake of black pitch, from which emerged a creature with seven heads and the body of a lion, a great hammer with a seal embedded in its striking surface. Madimi appeared, "bigger than she was." No longer was she the skittish girl or humble "wench" Kelley had described before. She was in apocalyptic mood: "Woe be to women great with child, for they shall bring forth monsters. Woe be unto the Kings of the Earth, for they shall be beaten into Mortar. Woe be to such as paint themselves." The list went on and on. "Woe be unto false preachers, yea seven woes be unto them, for they are the teeth of the Beast. . . . Woe unto the Virgins of the Earth, for they shall disdain their virginity, and become concubines for Satan. Woe to the merchants of the earth . . . they are become the spies of the earth, and the dainty meat of Kings. . . . Woe to the books of the earth, for they are corrupted."

Worse woe was to come. Satan was in a great rage, and set upon overthrowing Dee. "He seeketh the destruction of thy household, the life of thy children," Madimi warned. "Yea, he tempteth thy wife with despair, and to be violent unto herself." To prevent such terrible happenings, Dee was instructed to bring his family to Prague, and write immediately to Rudolf, "saying that the Angel of the Lord hath appeared unto thee and rebuketh him for his sins."[10]

Dee was left in a state of turmoil by these terrifying revelations. Over the coming days, he asked the spirits repeatedly about the welfare of his family, and agonized over how he could deliver to

Rudolf, the all-powerful emperor in whose domain he was now so vulnerably placed, the angelic revelation and reprimand required.

On 20 August, following another plea for help with drafting the letter to Rudolf, Uriel appeared. The angel was in as doleful a mood as Madimi had been, and chastised the failures of those who considered themselves wise, those who "dig into Nature with dull mattocks" in a vain attempt to understand it. "You have received this Doctrine in chambers and in secret places. But it shall stand in the great City, and upon 7 hills and shall establish herself as truth." In other words the doctrine delivered to Dee shall one day be accepted even in Rome, the home of the Catholic Church.

The words echoed scriptures that Dee had been pondering, which he had copied into the opening pages of the notebook recording the Prague actions. In his first letter to the Corinthians, St. Paul had appealed to fractious followers to unite. "Is Christ divided?" Paul had demanded to know. "Where is the wise man? Where is the scribe? Where is the debater of his age? Has not God made foolish the wisdom of the world?"[11]

After much agonizing, Dee finally completed a letter for Rudolf, and was apparently rewarded on 21 August with news from Krakow that his wife and children were well. His letter to the emperor was couched using the conventional obsequies: "To the serene and potent Prince and Lord, Rudolf by the grace of God, Emperor of the Romans ever august, and of Germany, Hungary, Bohemia, &c." Dee offered to present himself "at the feet of your Caesarean Majesty abjectly to kiss them, extremely happy if in anything I shall be able to be pleasing and useful to so great an Emperor of a Christian republic."

He made no mention of the angels, nor of Rudolf's need for reformation. Instead, he pointed out that he had known Rudolf's predecessors: his grandfathers Charles V and Ferdinand I, meeting the first "when I was young" at the court in Brussels, and the second in Pressburg, Hungary. "And I began to take a particular delight in the most clement Emperor Maximilian, the father of your Caesarean Majesty," Dee noted, a man "worthy of immortal glory"—perhaps, Dee implied, for his religious tolerance.

Dee also mentioned the *Monas Hieroglyphica*, which was dedicated to Maximilian, pointing out that "in the protracted performance of this work, my mind had a presentiment of the House of Austria," that is, that the Hapsburgs would produce one "in whom, for the benefit of the Christian polity, the best and greatest thing would, or might, become actual"—a veiled suggestion of expectations that Rudolf would preside over the reunification of the church. "Therefore," Dee concluded, "to your Caesarean Majesty, the fourth of the Roman emperors from the noble family of Austrian princes who were flourishing in my lifetime, here am I, also the fourth letter of each of the three alphabets"—Greek, Roman, and Hebrew.

Dee chose an unlikely, indeed potentially dangerous intermediary to deliver this fateful epistle: Don Guillén de San Clemente, the Spanish ambassador. San Clemente was a powerful figure in Rudolf's court, representing the emperor's uncle, King Philip II of Spain, the custodian of Catholicism and scourge of Elizabethan England. San Clemente had every reason to distrust Dee. A Dutchman dining at his table had leaned over to whisper a word or two into the ambassador's ear about Dee's reputation as a conjurer and a "bankrupt alchemist." Dee might also have been a spy, sent by Walsingham to foment trouble in the Hapsburg heartland.

Despite this, San Clemente developed a real and abiding fondness for Dee. He invited the philosopher to his residence on several occasions, and became godfather to Dee's child Michael, born in Prague the following year. Dee even showed San Clemente the crystal used to summon the angels, and two of his notebooks recording the actions, which San Clemente approvingly perused, commenting that he was descended from one who would appreciate the true meaning of this strange Cabala, the great Spanish mystic and poet Ramon Lull.

On 24 August, St. Bartholemew's Day, Dee sent Emericus Sontag, a secretary of Laski's assigned to work for Dee, to the ambassador with the precious missive. Three days later, several letters arrived: one from the elusive Laski, another from Dee's wife, Jane, and another from her brother Nicholas Fromonds, bringing news from England of how Adrian Gilbert, Charles Sledd, and the book-seller Andreas Fremonsheim had "used me very ill in divers sorts"—Dee's first direct indication of the damage being done to his home and library in his absence. After sunset, another letter arrived. It was from San Clemente: he had delivered the letter to Rudolf, and was promised a response in three or four days.

Ten days later, the response came, written by one of Rudolf's secretaries:

> To the noble and most excellent master—master most deserving of respect: The Emperor has just signified to the Spanish Ambassador that he will summon your Lordship to him at 2 of the clock, when he desires to hear you. If your Lordship is able to come at the aforesaid hour, you will be admitted at once to the Noble Octavius Spinola, who is his Imperial Majesty's Stall-Master and Chamberlain. He will introduce your Lordship to his Majesty. For the rest, I commend myself to your Lordship with the utmost possible devotion.

The timing was terrible. The previous evening, Kelley had got drunk and threatened to cut off the head of Alexander, one of Laski's guards. Alexander had responded by drawing his sword and threatening to slice Kelley into pieces. By the following morning the two had sobered up, and Dee tried to stage a reconciliation. But Kelley blew into a rage and "in his doublet and hose, without a cap or hat on his head," chased Alexander into the street, where he hurled stones at the soldier and challenged him to a fight. "Nolo, Domine Kelleie. Nolo!" the retreating Alexander had cried. The scene had not gone unnoticed by the city watchmen, who warned Dee "to have a care of the peace keeping"—all this within a few hours of Dee's appointment with the emperor.

Dee, with his secretary Emericus, rushed across the Charles Bridge and up the steep, winding road leading to the gate of the castle. He was ushered into the "Ritter Stove" or guardroom at the gate. There was evidently some confusion as to who he was, and Dee and Emericus were told to wait. After a while Dee asked Emericus to go and find out the time. As Emericus wandered around the courtyard outside the palace, looking for a clock, he was spotted through a window by the emperor's chamberlain Octavius Spinola.

Spinola came down to ask Emericus his business, and was told that Dee was waiting in the guardroom, whereupon Spinola came to offer his greetings. By now it was 3 P.M., as Dee noted, an hour after the time appointed for his audience, an hour to think about the coming ordeal. Spinola returned to the emperor's chamber to announce the philosopher's arrival, and came back to fetch Dee.

Gently taking a fold of Dee's gown, Spinola led the way through the labyrinthine courts and passages of the palace toward the inner sanctum where its solitary sovereign lurked, as Dee summoned all his courage to deliver to Caesar himself a message he knew his host would not want to hear.[12]

* * *

NEXT TO THE moat surrounding the palace, an African lion was imprisoned in a den, its impotent roars echoing across the city.[13] It belonged to an assortment of exotic creatures, fantastic art, and strange objects that Rudolf had accumulated since his arrival in Prague. The collection was spread throughout the palace, and comprised endless cabinets of curiosities. There was a six-foot narwhal bone, the dried remains of a dragon, samples of "bezoar," the strangely formed gastric calculuses of antelopes, the toxic roots of the mandrake plant that had miraculously grown into homunculus shapes, an agate basin in which the veins of the stone formed the word "Christ," dissected frogs, hippopotamus's teeth, samples of *terrae sigillate* or medicinal earth, an amulet filled with a plague remedy made of toads, virginal menstrual blood, white arsenic, orpiment, dittany, roots, pearls, coral, and Eastern emeralds.[14]

As well as these works of nature and science, there were equally wonderful works of art. Rudolf was a generous patron of painters and craftsmen. This was where Arcimboldo, the Leonardo of the Rudolfine court,[15] designed miraculous hydraulic machines and musical instruments, dabbled with codes, and painted the emperor's face as a collection of fruit, where Bartholomew Spranger, Rudolf's court painter, worked on his erotic couplings of bearded old men and voluptuous maidens, where Dürer's meticulous studies of dead birds hung alongside Brueghel's exquisite rural vistas, where nests of delicately engraved "glyptics" or gemstones glittered alongside collections of rare coins.[16]

There was also an extensive library, rivaling even Dee's, with such precious volumes as a copy of Trithemius's *Steganographia*, Hoefnagel's *Four Elements*, with its opening image showing the grotesque hairiness of Petrus Gonzales, a man afflicted with hirsutism, and a copy of the mysterious Voynich manuscript, possibly acquired from Dee. This, rather than the lands stretching away beneath the palace's ramparts, was Rudolf's world, and Dee now found himself passing through it, as he approached the imperial quarters.

The chamberlain finally led him through a dining hall and into Rudolf's privy chamber. The emperor sat behind a table, upon which lay a wooden chest, a silver inkstand, some letters, and a copy of Dee's *Monas*. Dee craved his majesty's pardon for presuming to write to the emperor, and Rudolf replied that he was sure of Dee's affection for him. He "commended the book *Monas*" but had found it too hard for his "capacity"; and added that the Spanish ambassador had told him that Dee had something to say that he would find useful.

"So I have," said Dee, and looked around the chamber to check they were now alone, which they were.

He began by filling in the background to the declaration that was to follow, the story of his forty years spent "in sundry manners, and in divers countries, with great pain, care and cost" trying to gain "the best knowledge that man might attain unto in the world," his realization "that neither any man living, nor any book I could yet meet withal, was able to teach me those truths I desired and longed for," his decision to look elsewhere for enlightenment, to the angels, to God "by whose commandment I am now before your Majesty and have a message from him to say unto you: and that is this:"

The Angel of the Lord hath appeared to me, and rebuketh you for your sins. If you will hear me, and believe me, you shall triumph. If you will not hear me, the Lord, the God that made heaven and earth (under whom you breathe and have your spirit) putteth his foot against your breast, and will throw you headlong down from your seat.

Moreover, the Lord hath made this covenant with me (by oath) that he will do and perform. If you will forsake your wickedness, and turn unto him, your Seat shall be the greatest that ever was, and the Devil shall become your prisoner: which Devil I did conjecture to be the Great Turk.

This my commission is from God. I feign nothing, neither am I an hypocrite, or ambitious man, or doting or dreaming in this cause. If I speak otherwise than I have just cause, I forsake my salvation.[17]

XXIV

※

TWO days after the audience with Rudolf, Dee announced to the spirits that he had fulfilled his mission. The angel Uriel appeared in the stone, his face covered with a black blindfold, to cover his face from those "as defile the seat of the soul, and are suffocated with drunkenness"—Kelley, in other words. "In the year 88 shall you see the sun move contrary to his course, the stars increase their light and some fall from heaven," Uriel announced, leaving Dee wondering if he meant 1588. "In the mean season will I be merciful unto Rudolf and will bring into his house such as shall be skilful unto whom I will give my spirit to work God, Silver and the Ornaments of his house. And he shall perceive that I bless him."[1]

Rudolf's response to Dee's impertinent revelation had been surprisingly humble. According to Dee, the emperor had "said he did believe me, and said that he thought I loved him unfeignedly, and said that I should not need so earnest protestations: and would not willingly have had me to kneel so often as I did." A week later, he received a letter from Spinola, the emperor's chamberlain. Dee was told that the "business" was to be entrusted to "the magnificent Master Dr Curtz."[2]

The "magnificent" Jakob Kurz von Senftenau was one of Rudolf's most trusted courtiers, soon to become imperial vice-chancellor. He was a keen botanist, the garden surrounding his house being stocked with exotic fruits and flowers, including a magnificent pear tree.[3] He was also interested in astronomy. In the coming years, Kurz would deal with Tycho Brahe just as he was now being asked to deal with John Dee.

On 15 September, Dee arranged to go to Kurz's house in the Malé náměstí, a small square in the Old Town, a short walk from

Hajek's house in Bethlehem Square. He arrived at 1 P.M., and was shown into the reception room where there was a table with two chairs. Dee was acutely sensitive to the balance of power that would prevail in the coming interview, and minutely inspected his host's actions for signs of disrespect. But Kurz was friendly, and deliberately offered Dee the position of "pre-eminence" at the head of the table.

Kurz said that he had heard of Dee's "fame" and seen his writings, and was "very glad of the opportunity now of my coming to this city," and not just for the emperor's sake. For the next six hours Dee explained to Kurz his mission, showing him excerpts from his books of actions and the crystal stone. These books now numbered eighteen (only a few of which have survived), and contained a complex description of a completely unknown language, with its own alphabet, words, rules of pronunciation, grammar, method of writing, and system of use. It was by any standards an impressive production—not, as later critics would characterize it, a "rhapsody of . . . Whimsies," but, at the very least, a magnificent folly, a labyrinthine structure spread across the landscape of Renaissance thought.

But what did Kurz make of it? In the coming days, Dee began to fear that he did not regard it as seriously as he should. Again and again, Emericus was despatched to the palace for word of Kurz having made his report to the emperor, and each time he returned breathlessly with none.

At 7 A.M. on 27 September, a servant appeared at Dr. Hajek's house and told Dee that Kurz was on his way. Kurz came on horseback at 9 A.M., and was shown into the study where Dee and Kelley performed their actions. He was invited to sit in Kelley's chair, Kelley himself having for some reason hidden in his bedroom. Dee was by now in a frenzy of anxiety and suspicion, and complained to Kurz of "envious malicious backbiters" rubbishing his name. Kurz claimed to have heard nothing of this. He had heard from the emperor, however, who wanted to see the books of actions. Presumably because of his distrust of Kurz, Dee refused, saying he could only deliver copies, which he would produce "at leisure."

Despite these sharp exchanges, the meeting ended amicably. Dee showed Kurz his *Propaedeumata Aphoristica*, and offered to lend him a copy of a work cowritten with Federico Commandino, the mathematician and translator of Archimedes. However, Kurz's visit marked a decisive turning point in Dee's relations with Rudolf's court.

In a subsequent meeting with Kurz, Dee was more or less dismissed, being told that Rudolf considered his sins to be a matter for himself and his confessor.[4] Rudolf did say he would act as Dee's benefactor, but nothing came of the offer.

The mood in Prague became increasingly hostile. Rumors were spreading about the nature of Dee's mission, that he prophesied, as one Bohemian noble noted, "a miraculous reformation" across the Christian world that would "prove the ruin not only of the city of Constantinople but of Rome also."[5]

Early in 1585, Dee somehow intercepted a private report written by one of Rudolf's secretaries that confirmed his worst suspicions. It was a digest of a letter from Johannes Franciscus Bonomo, bishop of Vercelli. Bonomo was the first papal "nuncio" or ambassador in Bohemia for over a century, appointed by Pope Gregory XIII to reestablish the Catholic Church's influence over a region of Europe that had managed to remain stubbornly beyond its reach since the time of Jan Hus. The instrument for this project was Rudolf himself, whose personal commitment to Catholicism it was Bonomo's job to translate into political action.

Bonomo's letter had been sent to the emperor in late 1584—around the same time as Dee's interview with Kurz. Bonomo had heard the rumors concerning Dee, in particular that he had summoned spirits "with the aid of certain magical characters." According to Catholic orthodoxy, "good spirits are not enchanted and moved to appear" by such means, Bonomo pointed out. Therefore Dee must be acting on behalf of evil ones. Furthermore, Dee was married "and was thus given to the cares of this life and to worldly matters"—in other words, lacking the essential purity that enabled the celibate Catholic priesthood to mediate between God and His flock.[6]

As the letter clearly demonstrates, Dee's problem was not that he was considered mad or deluded. In fact, Bonomo noted that Dee's intellectual abilities and accomplishments carried the endorsement of none other than Jakob Kurz, who described the philosopher as "extremely learned in a great number of subjects." Indeed, at around this time, Kurz was said to have personally arranged for Dee to receive a doctorate from the University of Prague and a monthly stipend of 40 florins.[7]

Dee's problem was that the nuncio had identified him as a threat to the ongoing mission to bring Prague back into the Catholic fold. He might muddle the emperor's mind, interpose his spirits between Rudolf's personal preoccupations and his imperial duties.

In 1585, Bonomo was replaced as nuncio by Germanico Malaspina, Bishop of San Severo, who was equally concerned about Dee's influence. Within weeks of his appointment, Malaspina decided he must deal with this inconvenient foreigner, and set a trap to dispose of Dee and his unruly gang of spirits once and for all.

XXV

‰

ONE writer described Francesco Pucci as an "anglicised Italian pervert."[1] He was certainly unorthodox. He was born in 1543 to one of Florence's most powerful Catholic dynasties, but turned his back on a career in the church in favor of the itinerant life of a merchant and intellectual. He moved to Paris in 1571 to study theology, and there beheld one of the formative events of his life and of the Reformation: the St. Bartholomew's Day massacre, which saw the slaughter of thousands of French Protestants during one night of frenzied violence in August 1572. Pucci abandoned Catholicism and began to cultivate his own religious doctrines. He wrote a treatise entitled *Forma d'una republica catholica* calling for a universal Christian republic ruled by an enlightened, divinely inspired council.[2]

In the early 1570s, Pucci went to study at Oxford. However, he was suspected of Catholic sympathies, and was expelled after taking his M.A. He continued on his restless travels, which took him to Antwerp, Basel, a London prison, and finally to Kraków, where he embarked on a series of disputes with the Jesuits. In the summer of 1585, his eccentric orbit became entangled with that of Dee and Kelley, which, unbeknownst to his new companions, set all three on a collision course with the papal nuncio Malaspina.

Dee had by now managed to bring his entire family from Kraków to Prague, and had settled them in lodgings near the river in Salt Street, close to Hajek's house in Bethlehem Square.[3] However, soon after Jane and the children had arrived, Madimi announced that Dee and Kelley must immediately return to Kraków. This hiatus was upsetting. Jane had just given birth to another child, Michael, after a difficult pregnancy, and Dee was desperately short of money. He presented to the spirits a plea written by Jane, in which she described how the family had been forced "to lay such things as are the ornaments of our house, and the coverings of our bodies, in pawn."[4] Despite these entreaties, the trip back to Kraków went ahead.

Dee and Kelley arrived amidst a series of whirlwinds "writhing up the dust with great vehemency on high and shooting forward still, and then mounting into the air," which Dee considered portentous.[5] The atmosphere in Kraków was also disturbed. Following the arrest and execution of Samuel Zborowski, King Stephen Báthory's relations with the Polish nobility had crumbled. His ambitious plans to merge Poland with Moscow and Transylvania to create an Eastern empire to rival Rudolf's had come to nothing, and in the following weeks he would withdraw from Kraków altogether, brooding on the ingratitude and intractability of his subjects at his country palace in Niepołomice. It was while he was there that he invited Dee and Kelley to come and perform an action in his presence, which they did, summoning spirits that condemned him as roundly as they had Rudolf.

In Kraków, Dee and Kelley began to develop connections with the Catholic Church. Kelley had shown an unexpected interest in Catholicism while they were still in Prague. On 27 March, he had asked Dee for a copy of an action delivered in England, because he wanted to show it to the Jesuits. The Society of Jesus was a leading force in the Catholic Counter-Reformation, and Dee was astonished Kelley wanted to reveal such a sensitive document. He insisted that he must ask permission of the spirits before showing "anything of theirs" to "their enemy." Kelley was furious, and tried to lock Dee in his study. Dee grabbed Kelley by the shoulders to prevent him, and called out to the rest of the household to witness the "violence offered unto me."

Passions were eventually calmed and divisions repaired. Kelley never got the document he so desperately wanted. Even the spirits he summoned denied his requests. However, in Kraków he and Dee started to attend the local Catholic church of St. Stephen's, where on 22 April Kelley "received the Communion" to Dee's "unspeakable gladness and content," and sought confession from a Jesuit priest for "the crimes and grave errors of his entire antecedent life."⁶ Dee was constantly concerned about the state of Kelley's soul, and was obviously happy to overcome misgivings he had about the Jesuits' political role if exposure to their religious devotions helped improve his skryer's spiritual health. It is an indicator of his devoutness and religious tolerance that he considered any form of holy communion to be better than no holy communion at all.

During this sparsely documented and confusing period the first sighting of Francesco Pucci flits into view, in connection with some astrological work Dee was apparently commissioned to perform on behalf of a Florentine client.⁷ Within a month, Pucci had somehow managed to gain Dee's trust, and had followed the philosopher back to Prague. There, on 6 August, he was allowed to witness a spiritual conference, a privilege granted to very few. It proved to be an important action, as Uriel used it to give his angelic assessment of the Reformation.

Dee did not regard the angels as infallible. The only protection he had from being deceived was that the messages they delivered came to him through a stone that he believed to have been blessed by God, and contained important insights to the way the world worked that had eluded him through conventional study. Thus, he must have taken Uriel's assessment of the role of the church very seriously.

Uriel's pronouncements at first had a distinctly Catholic tinge. The scriptures, the angel said, must be understood "by Ordinance and spiritual tradition." This clearly meant that the church was an important intermediary between God and humanity. The will of God was communicated "unto his Church taught by his apostles nourished by his Holy Ghost, delivered unto the World and by Peter brought to Rome by him, there taught by his successors." But the church did not have a monopoly on divine truth. "Partakers of the heavenly visions and celestial comforts"—people like Dee—had a role too.

Furthermore, Uriel agreed that the Pope may be capable of evil, but argued that those who claimed him to be an Antichrist "rise up amongst yourselves." This, of course, was a reference to Protestants, and Uriel's attitude toward them was less clear. "Luther hath his reward. Calvin his reward. The rest, all that have erred, and wilfully run astray," he said. This would suggest that Luther and Calvin, the founders of the Reformation, did not fall into the same category as other nonconformist theologians. However, it is unclear what "reward" Luther and Calvin had received.

Whatever was to be made of Uriel's statement, it was certainly heretical. Thus Dee had every reason to keep out of the way of the Catholic authorities, which with each day were increasing their influence over Rudolf's court. The nuncio Malaspina had made it clear for some time that he was interested in Dee's activities. As soon as Dee and Kelley returned from Kraków, he had bombarded them with flattering invitations. He "desired passionately to enjoy some friendly conversations," Dee's "fame" having "so much and for such a long time been resounding round his ears."[8] Dee procrastinated. He did not dare refuse, but he had heard "bad reports" that the nuncio "was preparing violence and laying an ambush for me." He was also "aware of the very great controversies obtaining between our Princes." In late 1585, Robert Dudley, the earl of Leicester, had left England with an expeditionary force bound for the Netherlands, where he was to help the Dutch fight forces sent by Rudolf's uncle, Philip II of Spain. England had formally allied herself to a Protestant coalition against Catholic Spain.

By the spring of 1586, Dee was back in Prague, where the pressure on him to meet the Catholic authorities intensified sharply. On 20 March, the "Most Reverend Lord Germanicus Malaspina became very severe," sending a "great nobleman" to summon Dee. The reason for the change of mood was that Malaspina had been recalled to Rome, and no doubt wanted to have something to report to the Pope. But still Dee did not respond. Then, two days later, another intermediary appeared on Malaspina's behalf: Francesco Pucci.

Pucci had apparently met Malaspina only a few days before. But his decision to act as the nuncio's emissary, even if apparently in the interest of his friends, must have come as a shock to Dee. In the face of such pressure, he relented. At 6 A.M. on 27 March, Dee sent Pucci to the nuncio's residence to say he would come that morning. The nuncio immediately sent a carriage to pick him up, but Dee would not take it, presumably fearing a kidnap plot. He arrived with Kelley at Malaspina's residence at 7 A.M. The greetings were cordial, and they were shown into a room where four chairs awaited them, one each for Dee and Kelley, one for Malaspina. The fourth, it soon emerged, was for Pucci.

The nuncio began with an eloquent address clearly aimed at luring Dee into an indiscreet admission. "Who does not see how much the condition of the Christian religion is in distress and danger?" he asked, half-rhetorically. If the king of Spain were to die, he doubted that "Rome and the Apostolic See" would even survive—a sentiment that clearly, and perhaps to Dee alarmingly, echoed the opinion of some of the spiritual messengers. This much was obvious, but, despite "diligent enquiry," despite the efforts of the Pope and the emperor, the authorities had failed to find a way of bringing "succour to the Christian religion in its so mournful condition." So, what to do? The nuncio professed he had not a clue. "Therefore, if you, gentlemen, with whom (by a singular favour of God) blessed angels often are present, and to whom God himself reveals His mysteries, if you have received any counsel, or if you can think of any help to be employed against those evils affecting us all, I beg you to disclose them to me; I shall indeed gladly and with the greatest attention listen to you."

Dee would not be drawn by such silky words. He may have been happy to berate an emperor, but he knew better than to challenge the Catholic Church. "It is indeed true that iniquity still prevails, and that that chaste Bride of God, who has suffered great violence, is compelled to withdraw almost into solitude," he said. "Yet it is not in our hands to give counsel or to suggest remedies against such great evils and so prodigious a calamity." He admitted that "very great and very many mysteries and counsels of God are known to us of which all human talents conjoined could not invent or expect," but was pledged to keep them to himself. "We lead a monastic life, and it is with the greatest reluctance that we let such manifest evidence of our inward joy be known."

Dee ended with "a few more civilities" and a patriotic statement of loyalty to his queen. The nuncio seemed satisfied with the reply, and expressed his gladness that they had at last had an opportunity to meet. Dee had apparently escaped the trap.

Then Kelley intervened.

It seems to me [Kelley said] that, if one looks for a counsel or remedy that might bring about a reformation in the whole Church, the following will be good and obvious. While there are some shepherds and ministers of the Christian flock who, in their faith and in their works, excel all others, there are also those who seem devoid of the true faith and idle in their good works. Their life is so odious to the people and sets so pernicious an example that by their own bad life they cause and promote more destruction in the Church of God than they could ever repair by their most elaborate, most long, and most frequent discourses. And for that reason their words do not carry the necessary conviction and are wanting in profitable authority.

May, therefore, the doctors, shepherds, and prelates mend their ways; may they teach and live Christ by their word as well as by their conduct. For thus (in my opinion) a great and conspicuous reformation of the Christian religion would be brought about most speedily.

The words were worthy of Luther himself. However, the nuncio remained calm, quietly accepting them as "concordant with the Christian and Apostolic doctrine." Malaspina then signaled that the meeting was at an end, and thanked Dee and Kelley for coming. "I shall call on you at your house where (I hope) we may then have a longer conversation on such matters," he added, as they rose to leave.

Dee, who had an effective network of informants, later discovered that the nuncio's true feelings were very different from the "honey-sweet and humble words" he had uttered at the meeting. Kelley's speech had "so filled that Most Reverend Lord with inward fury" that, "if it had not been for certain respects," he would have resorted to the popular Prague tactic of having Kelley "thrown out of the window" then and there. However, Dee's own diplomacy had evidently left the nuncio unable to take immediate action, which would have required the endorsement of the emperor.

Nevertheless, they were still vulnerable. A month later, during Lent, Kelley went on a strict fast. He was preparing to visit a Jesuit priest, to whom he wanted to make confession. This was yet another swerve in Kelley's twisting spiritual journey, and when he announced his intentions, it must have left Dee completely perplexed.

However, at this stage, the relationship between the philosopher and skryer was at its closest and most affectionate. For the first time, Dee referred to Kelley in his records as "Edward." Where before he had seen Kelley as the mere instrument of spiritual communication, he now embraced him as an equal partner in their enterprise. He therefore accepted Kelley's sudden conversion to Catholicism at face value, as "a humble act of contrition."

The confessor took a different view, at least according to Kelley's account of the encounter to Dee. The priest demanded that Kelley admit "of a certain very great crime which he had not yet confessed." Despite Kelley's protests that he had confessed to everything in Kraków, and there received absolution, the priest persisted: Kelley had communicated with spirits, which must be wicked, as "it was not probable or credible that we should have any intercourse with good angels."

Kelley objected, pointing out that the Scriptures themselves provided the test of whether or not the spirits were sent by God. "By this you know the Spirit of God," says John in his first letter, "every spirit which confesses that Jesus Christ has come in the flesh is of God, and every spirit which does not confess Jesus is not of God. This is the spirit of the antichrist."[9]

The impetuous Kelley then mentioned that there were "copious volumes" recording the angelic revelations. The priest immediately demanded that they be handed over for inspection by himself, the nuncio, and the rector of the Jesuits. Kelley refused, saying they were private, "kept in the custody of my friend, the Doctor." The priest then suggested a "fraud and stratagem" to get them, which Kelley rejected. The priest also wanted to know where Dee and

Kelley were getting their money from. The question was a revealing and pertinent one. Dee and Kelley had recently enjoyed a dramatic improvement in their material circumstances. They had moved into a new and much grander residence, the old fortified medieval palace overlooking the Cattle Market in Prague New Town owned by the imperial physician and pharmacist Johann Kopp van Raumenthal. It is now called the "Faust House" in recognition of its historic links with alchemists and mystics.[10] How had they come by such wealth? "Divine favour," was Kelley's answer, which apparently did not convince the priest.

Eventually, Kelley became "so heated in his zeal" that he challenged the priest to a sort of spiritual duel: they would both go to some "convenient and secret place" and "each after his own manner, invoke Almighty God, the Creator of heaven and earth." Whoever was guilty would be struck down by heavenly fire. The father refused the offer. Dee was furious with the priest, shocked to find "so poisonous an egg" ready to hatch at the center of the Christian world. His fury increased when he heard that, on returning to the Jesuit's College to see his confessor once more, Kelley was blocked by Francesco Pucci. Pucci soon after apologized for intervening, and Kelley forgave him, but Dee was by now convinced that the Italian was traitorous.

The spirits apparently agreed, because following Easter they staged, apparently for Pucci's benefit, a theatrical effect every bit as compelling as the mechanical dung beetle engineered to ascend into the heavens in Dee's production of Aristophanes's "Peace."

*   *   *

DEE RELATES THE story without comment, apparently accepting what in hindsight appears to be an elaborate and ingenious charade mounted by Kelley to persuade Pucci that the incriminating books of mysteries demanded by the Catholic authorities had been destroyed.

It began at 8 A.M. on 10 April, when Dee was in his study, a "small heated room, truly elegant and commodious," at the top of a tower, preparing for an action. He was joined by Kelley, who settled himself before a "new and very fine" table, and Pucci, who sat on a bench that ran along a wall.

A spirit appeared that launched a scathing attack on human hubris. "You are ignorant. You cannot read," it said, referring to the Book of Nature that it had been the mission of the angels to restore through Dee. "You all have become gods and mighty giants, and you are full of the spirit of your father, the devil." "Arise then," the spirit instructed Dee. "Place before me the books and all that which you have received from me, and then you will learn what else I shall tell you and how, by one look. I shall destroy the eyes of your adversaries at the very time when they think they see most sharply."

Dee went downstairs and fetched a large, white box filled with the volumes that he had so meticulously written over the past four years. The spirit then commanded him to destroy them, having first removed the record of that day's action. Dee did as he was told, ripping apart one by one each of the twenty-eight volumes, destroying "all the things which, from the first hour of our conjunction until the present hour, had been revealed and shown to us by God's faithful." By his own hand, he destroyed the book of the forty-eight angelic keys, written entirely in the angelic language, a "most clear interpretation" on the use of the language written in English, one containing the "wisdom and science" first revealed to Enoch, and a very short book, but the most precious of all, containing "the Mystery of Mysteries and the Holy of Holies," which alone "contained the profoundest mysteries of God Himself and of the Almighty Divine Trinity that any creature will ever live to know." The spirit next instructed Dee to fetch the powder and book that Kelley had discovered at Northwick Hill, and that were now reverently contained in a bag made of "black fustian" cloth and secured like a purse by metal clasps. This command was so unexpected that Kelley was "overcome with helpless amazement." "Oh Lord," Kelley protested, "I did not receive these from Thee."

After much persuasion by Dee and Pucci, Kelley reluctantly surrendered the bag, which was placed on the table next to the twenty-eight volumes. The spirit then commanded Kelley to place the volumes in the bag.

"Now you, Kelly, will rise and you will remove the stones from the mouth of that furnace, and where those stones now are you will place this," said the spirit. There were four or five fire-bricks placed in the opening of the fire used to heat the room. Kelley removed them, and placed the bag in the furnace.

"Rise, Pucci, join him, and see to it that he puts them into the very fire," said the spirit. "You will not withdraw until the fire entirely penetrates them." Dee fell to his knees and prayed as he watched the "holocaust" of his precious papers. As they were consumed, Kelley stared into the fiery furnace and saw the shape of a man walking among the flames. He seemed to be plucking the pages out of the fire.

The spirit now commanded Dee to throw in any remaining unbound papers, which he gathered together and handed to Kelley and Pucci. The spirit's final instruction was to remove the crystal stone from the table of practice, and suspend the table on the wall "where there is a chapel of the enemies," in other words, on the wall adjoining the chapel of the Jesuit college.[11] There it would hang as a "token and memorial" to the spiritual mission that now had apparently been brought to a peremptory end.

Nearly three weeks later, at 1:30 P.M. on 29 April, Kelley was looking out of a window in the gallery next to his chamber, and saw a man pruning trees in the vineyard, whom Kelley assumed to be the gardener. The man walked over to the house and, without revealing his face, called up to Kelley, telling him to tell his "learned master" Dee to come into the garden. The man then walked over to a rock next to some cherry trees, and there "seemed to mount up in a great pillar of fire."[12]

Kelley told his wife to go down to the garden and see if there was anyone there, but she returned saying she could find no one. Kelley reported what he had seen to Dee, fearing that he was being disturbed by a wicked spirit. They both went into the garden, walking to the banqueting hall in the grounds, and along a cliff-side to a bank next to a pile of vine stakes and an almond tree. Dee and Kelley sat there together for a quarter of an hour, looking for a further sign of the spirit's presence. Then Dee noticed something white, like a sheet of paper, tossing to and fro in the wind. He went over to find out what it was and found beneath the tree three books. They were three of his books of mysteries, the Book of Enoch, the forty-eight Angelic Keys, and the "Liber Scientiæ Terrestris Auxilii et Victoriæ."[13]

The gardener whom Kelley had seen earlier now reappeared, and led Kelley off into the vines. Dee stayed under the almond tree, and awaited Kelley's return. Kelley eventually reappeared carrying the material that had apparently been destroyed in the furnace. It had been found, he told Dee, in the mouth of the furnace.

The following day, Dee and Kelley resumed their actions. A spirit confirmed that these were to continue, but not with Pucci, who was "defiled." "For behold, you are yet in the wilderness," the spirit warned. "Therefore be silent."

*   *   *

THE SPIRITUAL WARNING came too late. On the very day that Dee had recovered his books, Filippo Sega, successor to Malaspina as papal nuncio in Prague, wrote to the Pope warning that Dee had managed to infiltrate the imperial court, where he was spreading a "new superstition."

There may also have been growing suspicions in court that Dee was acting as a spy. On 6 May, Dee had departed on a trip to Leipzig, where he expected to meet up with his servant Edmund Hilton, who was evidently acting as a courier, carrying letters between Dee and the English court. Dee arrived on 11 May, and made contact with an English merchant, Laurence Overton, who had the previous year sought refuge in Dee's house in Prague while suffering from an illness, and been nursed back to health by Jane. Overton said that Hilton had not yet arrived, and was not expected for another sixteen days. Dee decided he could not wait, and left a letter to be given to Hilton when he turned up. It was addressed to Sir Francis Walsingham, the queen's secretary of state and chief spymaster. "I am forced to be brief," he wrote. "That which England suspected was also here." He does not specify what was suspected, but it was connected with Dee having been for the past two years "pried and peered into" by imperial spies. Dee also asked Walsingham to send Thomas Digges, Dee's former pupil and close friend, "in her Majesty's behalf," to perform "some piece of good service." Again, Dee offered no specifics.

The following month, Walsingham received another report from Germany, this time written by the financier and traveler Sir Horatio Palavicino, which said: "The bearer will tell you verbally about Doctor Dee and 'Kele' [Kelley]."[14]

By 24 May, Dee was back in Prague, where he received a warning that the nuncio had submitted to the emperor a portfolio of evidence charging Dee with necromancy and "other prohibited arts."[15] The accusations that had dogged him since his days at Cambridge had now reached across Europe to Prague. On 28 May, Dee wrote to Rudolf, pleading his innocence. His pleas had no effect. The following day, a clerk arrived from the court with a decree signed by Rudolf himself banishing Dee, his family, and Kelley from the empire. They had just six days to get out.

PART NINE
RAVISH'D BY MAGIC

✢

In flesh at first the guilt committed was;
Therefore in flesh it must be satisfied:
Nor spirit nor angel, though they man surpass,
Could make amends to God for man's misguide,
But only man himself, who self did slide.

EDMUND SPENSER,
Hymn of Heavenly Love

XXVI

✣

TRAILS of unusually thick smoke were often to be seen rising from the chimneys of Třeboň Castle. Lying amid the tranquil fishponds and lush meadowlands of southern Bohemia, almost equidistant between the imperial power centers of Prague and Vienna, the quiet town of Třeboň was an ideal location for the undisturbed practice of alchemy. And on 14 September 1586, it became a new home for Dee.

The previous four months had been tough for Dee and his family. He, Kelley, Kelley's wife, Joanna, Jane, and Dee's four children, including the infant Michael, had been packed together with all their possessions into two coaches and forced to leave Bohemia without anywhere to go. They had endured accommodation that was "sordid and cramped," as well as dangerous.[1] They had to cover hundreds of miles in search of a new home. And they had been pestered by Pucci, who had followed them as far as Erfurt in Germany, where he had tried to persuade them to return to Prague. He claimed that it was the emperor, rather than the nuncio, who was responsible for their banishment—an assertion Dee knew to be contradicted by other sources. Pucci even suggested that they should all go to Rome to present their case there, claiming that they were sure of a sympathetic hearing.

Dee was having none of it. He had developed an uncharacteristically intense personal dislike for Pucci, not just for "his blabbing of our secrets," but because of "household behaviour, not acceptable to our wives and family."[2] He did not specify exactly what this behavior was, but it was the reason the Italian would be later branded a "pervert." Dee refused to have anything to do with Pucci's pleas, and sent him back to Prague empty-handed.

The exiles finally found a convivial temporary home in Hesse-Kassel, a German principality run by the eccentric Calvinist Count Moritz, the province's "Landgrave" or ruler. Moritz had a passionate interest in astrology and alchemy.[3] Kassel, the capital of the province, had become an intellectual center to rival Rudolf's Prague, and Dee was welcomed there almost as a trophy to add to Moritz's impressive collection of philosophical friends.

However, Dee was determined to go back to Bohemia, and in August received news that the emperor had given permission for their return. It had been secured by the fabulously wealthy Vilem Rozmberk, the ruler of the lands surrounding Třeboň. Vilem was Bohemia's most powerful noble.[4] He had held the crown at Rudolf's coronation in 1575, and received the Order of the Golden Fleece, the Hapsburgs' highest honor for chivalry. He was a Catholic, but like so many in Bohemia, was relaxed in his views. "Festina Lente" was his motto, make haste slowly.[5]

Dee's first recorded meeting with Rozmberk had taken place in Prague just days after the nuncio petitioned the emperor for the philosopher's banishment. It was May Day, and a carriage had been sent to deliver Dee to the beautiful terraced gardens Vilem had recently completed along the slopes beneath the imperial palace.

Among the spring blooms and budding saplings, they sowed "good seeds for the service of God," discussing Vilem's past and future, his "loose life" and his marriage prospects. The Rozmberk line was faced with extinction. Vilem had married three times, and failed to produce an heir. He now had an eye on Polyxena, the daughter of the Bohemian chancellor, Vratislav von Pernstein, and was wondering whether he would have any more success with her. The failure of Europe's princes to produce heirs was a continuing source of anxiety, and also taken as a further sign of the great cosmic disturbance signaled by the nova of 1572. Elizabeth remained unmarried, as did Rudolf, though the latter had fathered several illegitimate children. Even Philip II, who had passed through four marriages, producing two heirs, had been found wanting: his first son, Don Carlos of Austria, had turned mad and against his father; the second, Philip, had rejected his royal obligations. It was as if the divine right was being withdrawn, and Rozmberk was clearly interested in seeing if Dee could somehow summon spiritual intervention to halt this relentless process of dynastic entropy.

It was Rozmberk's yearning to reproduce, as much as the promise of unlimited wealth, that drew him to becoming one of Bohemia's most generous patrons of alchemical research, rivaling even the emperor Rudolf. Murals on the walls of his sumptuous castle at Český Krumlov, his principal town, explored the theme of fertility using alchemical as well as astrological and biblical symbolism. Indeed, the entire city became a virtual shrine to the art of transmutation. Its houses were covered with occult symbols, and the magnificent round tower overlooking the city was painted in vivid colors thought to have alchemical significance.[6]

To pursue his interest, Vilem financed no fewer than six laboratories scattered around his domains. The one at Třeboň, about twenty-five miles northeast of Český Krumlov, was now to be made available to Dee and Kelley.

*   *   *

ACCORDING TO LEGEND, the German philosopher Cornelius Agrippa, the author of *De occulta philosophia*, would pay merchants with gold coins that shone remarkably bright, but which invariably turned into slate or stone within twenty-four hours. Stories like these are linked with many Renaissance philosophers: Ramon Lull, Trithemius, Paracelsus, and Dee himself.[7] Alchemy was a peculiar preoccupation of sixteenth-century Europe. Most monarchs and many nobles financed alchemical experiments. The puzzling feature of this trend was that it continued even though such experiments invariably failed or were revealed to be fraudulent. Renaissance metallurgists had reliable methods for testing or "assaying" for gold by the process of "cupellation," which involved melting the sample in a "cupel" or dish, and then blasting it with hot air, which would oxidize impurities, including other metals such as lead, copper, or tin.[8]

One possible reason for the popularity of alchemy was that it tapped into a "silver rush" that had been released by the discovery of a number of mines in Bohemia and Poland, many of which were to be found on the extensive Rozmberk estates. Metallurgy, which had proved very effective at extracting precious metals from the dark ores being lifted from the earth, was regarded as a form of alchemy, and the yields of the one seemed to confirm the fundamental soundness of the other.

Another reason for irrepressible alchemical optimism was that success depended on the right spiritual as well as chemical conditions. Laboratories were often positioned next to chapels or "oratories," one to prepare the chemicals to be experimented upon, the other to prepare the experimenter himself. If the experiment failed, then it was easy to claim that it was the alchemist, rather than alchemical principles, that was at fault. Hope sprang eternal that just as soon as practitioners became pure, then lead would be transformed into gold, the dead into the living, and—this being the focus of Rozmberk's interest—the sterile into the fertile.

Kelley's interest in alchemy was probably more pecuniary than procreative. Nevertheless, he may have been drawn by the art's "vitalistic," often sexual imagery, the depiction of alchemical processes as a union of feminine and masculine principles for the production of a "child." Dee himself uses the symbolism of the fertilized egg in his alchemical allusions in the *Monas*.[9] Kelley believed Joanna, the wife he had so reluctantly taken, to be barren, and this became a growing preoccupation during his time at Třeboň. Perhaps as well as the prospect of riches, it was the prospect of children that encouraged him to join Dee in the pursuit of the Philosopher's Stone.

They began experimenting soon after their arrival at Rozmberk's castle, using the mysterious red "powder" Kelley had found buried at Northwick Hill, which he had committed to the furnace and miraculously recovered in Prague. These were not the first experiments of this sort that Dee had undertaken. There are several earlier references to alchemical secrets and activities in his diaries and other writings, and the *Monas* suggests that his interest in the subject was more than merely academic as far back as the early 1570s. However, the work he undertook at Třeboň marks the beginning of a systematic attempt to explore the field under spiritual guidance.

The actions had for some time touched on alchemical themes, particularly in Prague, where Kelley beheld furnaces with doors made of crystal, rivers of quicksilver, streams of colored water, giants with legs made of gold and lead, miners digging up lodestones and alabaster.[10] The spirits had also commanded Dee to tell both Rudolf and Stephen Báthory that he had discovered the Philosopher's Stone, promising him that he would soon do so.

In Třeboň, they now had the time and resources to start work on fulfilling the spirits' promise. Over the coming two years, Dee would fill his diaries with innumerable coded jottings about his experiments using combinations of salts and rare earths suspended in water, horse manure, and menstrual blood.[11] Rozmberk ordered his engineers to construct a laboratory in one of the gate houses of Třeboň castle specifically for Dee and Kelley. Dee also toured other Rozmberk alchemical facilities, such as the laboratory in Reichenstein, Silesia.[12]

On 19 December 1587, three months after their arrival at Třeboň, Kelley revealed how advanced their alchemical work had already become. Two brothers unknown to Dee, called Edward and Francis Garland, had just arrived from England. They had come to tell Dee that Fyodor Ivanovich, Ivan the Terrible's successor, was offering him the post of philosopher to the Muscovy court at a magnificent annual salary of £2,000 supplemented with a further 1,000 roubles from the imperial Lord Protector. As before, Dee was not drawn by the offer.[13]

In any case, if it was riches he wanted, Kelley himself suddenly seemed to have even greater wealth at his disposal. For the benefit of the Garland brothers, Kelley, drawing on the same skills that made him such an effective skryer, put on the first of many demonstrations of his newly acquired alchemical powers. He produced a speck no larger than a grain of sand of the "Philosopher's Stone." Presumably it was a sample of the red powder.[14] He placed the sample into one and a quarter ounces of the mercury held in a crucible. Thereupon almost one ounce of the "best gold" was produced. This was divided up between the Garlands, Dee, and Kelley, with the crucible given to Edward as a souvenir.

Such impressive demonstrations inevitably set tongues wagging. Rumors spread through Třeboň that Kelley and Dee were dealing with devils, some of them evidently spread by jealous members of Rozmberk's household. Jakub Krčín was Rozmberk's powerful estates manager, responsible for building farms, breweries, and laboratories. During Dee and Kelley's time in Třeboň he had also built a dam one and a half miles long and over 150 yards thick, which had created an enormous artificial lake around the south side of the town. Dee and Kelley were taken on a tour around the lake in July 1588, and when the drunken driver tried to turn their coach around on the dam's narrow causeway, the coach toppled and the entire party fell into the water.[15] Krčín took a strong dislike to the "privileged scoundrels" Dee and Kelley, and refused to attend a marriage supper at Třeboň's town hall because they would be there.[16]

News of Kelley's powers also spread farther afield, soon reaching the English court, which buzzed with reports of the miraculous transmutation of coins, pewter dishes, flagons, even bedpans, of games of quoits played with silver ingots, of his possession of a magic powder so powerful one ounce could yield 272,330 ounces of gold.[17] Such rumors produced an unexpected frisson in the Lord Treasurer William Cecil, who in coming years would do everything in his power to lure Kelley back to England.

Dee featured in none of these stories—indeed, he claimed no more ability to transmute base metal than to summon spirits. He was now cast in the role of helper rather than adept, the sorcerer's apprentice rather than the sorcerer. At 9 P.M. one February evening in 1588, Dee records in his diary receiving a summons from Kelley to "his laboratory over the gate: to see how he distilled sericon," an order that clearly showed that by this stage the philosopher had become little more than a spectator.[18]

While alchemical tales worked their magic abroad, in Třeboň Kelley underwent an appropriately miraculous transformation of his finances. Within a month of Dee and Kelley's appearance in Třeboň, Francesco Pucci had turned up. Dee and Kelley, who were now convinced he was acting as a spy, decided to try and buy him off. Pucci refused their offers, so Dee called upon him to come to the court house in Třeboň and publicly proclaim before witnesses, including Lord Rozmberk himself, that he had no claim over them. There two large bags of money were placed before him, out of which 800 florins were counted. Pucci found the sight of such glittering bounty irresistible, although, as he heaved the heavy bags off the counting table, he stipulated that it was "received in the name of God and from us as servants of God." It was not, however, the last they were to see of Pucci.

* * *

DURING THE OPENING months of 1587, Kelley made regular visits to Prague on his own. On 18 January, he returned from a trip with more evidence of his newfound wealth: a fabulous gold necklace of Rozmberk's, sparkling with jewels valued at 300 ducats, which he presented to Dee's wife, Jane. The gallant gesture was a significant one, as it anticipated a new theme that began to insinuate itself into the continuing but now sporadic spiritual actions.

On 21 January, Kelley left Třeboň once again for Prague, and then for Poland. While away, he wrote to Dee, ending the letter, "I commend me unto Mrs Dee a thousand times, and unto your little babes: wishing myself rather amongst you than elsewhere." Dee happened to be riding to the nearby town of Newhouse[19] when the letter arrived, and Jane sent a messenger to take it to him, together with a covering note:

> Sweetheart, I commend me unto you, hoping in God that you are in good health, as I and my children with all my household am here, I praise God for it. I have none other matter to write unto you, at this time.

This short, affectionate note is one of Jane's very rare appearances in the pages of his spiritual actions, and the only one that hints at the affection she felt for her husband. She surfaces elsewhere usually in connection with illness or arguments. Dee variously describes her as impatient, testy, fretting, and angry. She was also a stern mother, on one occasion boxing her daughter Katherine's ears so violently the girl suffered a profuse nose bleed lasting more than an hour.[20]

However, Dee was obviously devoted to and dependent upon Jane. His reports of her outbursts are those of an anxious or bewildered partner rather than a carping or critical husband. He "sank into low spirits" when she was angry with him.[21] He fretfully noted any sickness or worry that afflicted her.[22]

But the challenges of living with a spirited wife were as nothing compared with the difficulties of living with an obsessive philosopher. Through the unflattering prism of Dee's diaries and notebooks, a domestic life is portrayed that is totally determined by the demands of her husband's work. His entire spiritual enterprise, as well as his intellectual and consulting work, was conducted at whichever location Dee currently called home. It was her onerous task to create a hospitable setting for the reception of Dee's angelic as well as noble visitors, a place where spirits could be received in an atmosphere of sanctified peace and privacy while guests were entertained in lavish style. But the demands upon her went further still.

Paracelsus, the alchemist and pioneering physician who strongly influenced Dee's work, wrote: "In the heavens you can see man, each part for itself; for man is made of heaven. And the matter out of which man was created also shows the pattern after which he was formed."[23] And the same applied to woman, even more so. Menstruation in particular seemed to mark a close link between the female and lunar cycles. It was in this spirit that Dee kept a detailed, coded record of Jane's periods, carefully logging in the margins of his astrological tables when they occurred. He would even observe how heavy they were, whether or not the "show" was "small" or "abundant." He also noted when they had sex, using a symbol combining the astrological signs for Venus and Mercury, giving not only a date, but a time.[24]

One of the earliest references to a spiritual visitation in Dee's diaries was a dream of Jane's, which she told to Dee. An angel had come to her, touched her, and said, "Mistress Dee, you are conceived of child: whose name must be Zacharias: be of good cheer, he shall do well as this doth."[25] According to the Bible, Zacharias (or Zecharia) was the husband of Elizabeth, who was barren but became pregnant with John the Baptist following a visit by the angel Gabriel.[26] Dee clearly considered the dream significant, and also sensitive, as he recorded it in his diary in coded form.

In the coming years, Jane would make a number of appearances in the actions. On one occasion, Gabriel apparently re-created a version of her dream about Zacharias. He appeared and announced that Jane was pregnant, which indeed she was. He also explained the reasons why she was having difficulties with the pregnancy. When she had been "a milky substance" in the womb, he said, her mother had contracted a disease, which meant she had developed a "second vessel" or vagina "so thin, and tied short, that it is not able to keep in or retain the simile and quiddity of her own substantial being and seed."[27]

It was the angel Madimi who, within six months of Dee's arrival in Třeboň, would draw Jane into the angelic conferences in a way that even Dee had never anticipated, and in the process help bring the entire spiritual mission to a ruinous end.

XXVII

⁂

J ESUS said, "if any man come to me, and hate not his father, and mother, and wife, and children, and brethren, and sisters, yea, and his own life also, he cannot be my disciple."[1] Jesus' disdain for domestic life is the reason why Catholic priests are celibate, and presumably why on 4 April 1587 at Třeboň an angel that appeared before Dee and Kelley felt obliged to curse those who love their families above God. "Woe be unto you that so do: and woe be unto the generations that shall follow you." Dee would have been familiar with this doctrine, but the reason why it emerged so forcefully now would only gradually become apparent.

"Be obedient," the spirit commanded. "Be full of humility, and abandon pride. Bow thine ears unto the poor. Be often sorry for thy days misspent. Be strong in me." There was a pause. Then the spirits said to Dee: "Thy wife is even at the door of sickness: But behold, I am even he, that is the Lord of Health." Then the spirit turned its attention to Kelley. "As unto thee, barrenness dwelleth with thee, because thou didst neglect me." This is the first reference in Dee's records to Kelley's failure to have children.

Since the beginning of Lent, which that year had begun on 11 February, Kelley had prayed each day "to be made free," to be released of his skrying duties. "O foolish man," said the spirit, recognizing the reason to be Kelley's newfound wealth and status. "By how much the heavens excel the earth, by so much doth the gift that is given thee from above excel all earthly treasure.

"Thou art made free," the spirit continues, "and the power which is given thee of seeing shall be diminished in thee, and shall dwell upon the first-begotten son of him that sitteth by thee." In other words, Dee's seven-year-old son Arthur was to take over from Kelley as Dee's skryer, to complete the spiritual mission of receiving the holy books. In fourteen days, they were all to return, when Kelley was to hand over the magic powder and cease practicing. "Behold, thou art a stumbling-block unto many," the spirit added.

Over the coming days, Dee did his best to prepare his son. He asked Kelley for help, but it was refused. So Dee tried to train the child himself, making him recite prayers and stare into the stone set upon the table of practice. The idea of using a child as a skryer was not particularly unusual. It was a task best performed by a receptive sensibility, by a malleable mind unburdened by the limitations of rationality. That is why Kelley, with his juvenile tantrums and uncontrollable passions, seemed such a convincing candidate.

Arthur, however, proved less capable. Over the coming weeks, Dee subjected the poor boy to a punishing schedule of three sessions a day. Arthur tried valiantly to do his father's bidding, but saw very little, and for hours on end nothing at all. To Dee's immense relief, on 17 April, the day before the two-week deadline appointed by the spirit, Kelley turned up "by extraordinary good fortune—or perhaps by divine will," and resumed his position before the stone.

With Arthur still present, Kelley beheld a message written as if on the side of a distant globe that "turneth so swiftly that I cannot well read it." The message read: *All sins committed in me are forgiven. He who goes mad on my account, let him be wise. He who commits adultery because of me, let him be blessed for eternity and receive the heavenly prize.* The following day, the meaning of this disturbing phrase became clearer. Once again, Arthur was in attendance. Madimi appeared, at first with the other angels, then on her own. She parted her cloak, to reveal that she was naked beneath, "and showeth her shame." Dee told her to go.

"In the name of God, why find you fault with me?" Madimi asked.

"Because your yesterday's doings and words are provocations to sin, and unmeet for any godly creature to use," Dee replied.

At some point during these erotically charged proceedings, poor

Arthur fainted, perhaps because he had been fasting in preparation for the action, perhaps because, as Madimi suggested, he had been "touched" by her.

There followed a vision of four heads upon a pillar: the heads of Dee and Kelley and their wives, Jane and Joanna. Madimi produced a half moon brought from the heavens, bearing an inscription: *Nothing is unlawful which is lawful unto God.* She went into an orchard, where she cut off the branches of one tree, and grafted them together.

Dee interpreted this performance to mean that the four of them were to be united "after the Christian and godly sense." But Kelley offered a different interpretation, one he claimed so utterly to abhor he could have nothing more to do with the spirits. They were, he told Dee, to share their wives. Dee did not understand. Share in what sense? In the sense of "carnal use (contrary to the law of the commandment) or of spiritual love and charitable care and unity of minds, for the service of God advancing"?

A vision that Kelley then beheld in the stone settled the matter: "Upon a scroll, like the edge of a carpet, is written: 'I speak of both.'"

"The one is expressly against the commandment of God: neither can I by any means consent to like of that doctrine," Dee cried. "Assist me, O Christ. Assist me, O Jesu. Assist me, O Holy Spirit."

Another inscription appeared, another holy writ:

> If I told a man to go and strangle his brother, and he did not do it, he would be the son of sin and death. For all things are possible and permitted to the godly. Nor are sexual organs more hateful to them than the faces of every mortal. Thus it will be: the illegitimate will be joined with the true son. And the east will be united with the west, and the south with the north.

The action was over, leaving Dee in a state of "great amazement and grief." He could not believe that angels he had always assumed to be good could propound "so unpure a doctrine."

*   *   *

KELLEY NEVER SO much as hinted that his visions were fabricated. But he repeatedly cast doubt on their veracity. He often told Dee that they were produced by devils rather than angels, and even suggested that they might be evidence of Satanic possession.

During the first months of their actions together, there are clear signs that Dee, too, entertained suspicions, not as to whether or not the spirits were from God, but whether or not Kelley saw spirits at all. However, such suspicions were somehow dispelled. Dee became and remained utterly convinced that Kelley was really seeing something. This was partly because Kelley's performance was so convincing. His very body seemed to be a medium for spiritual communication. Before and during his visions, he often reported physical sensations— of pangs, heart palpitations, "a great stirring and moving" of the brains, things running in his head, his belly being "full of fire." Some encounters even left marks, such as the occasion when Dee discovered "two circles as broad as groats very red" imprinted on Kelley's arms where a demon had "nipped" him.[2]

To modern eyes, these symptoms would be quickly recognized as having psychotic or neurological causes, but such conditions were unknown in Dee's time. There was no concept of an internal subconscious agency or even of a nervous system that could spontaneously misbehave in this fashion. Such symptoms were the product of celestial as well as physical forces at play in a sensitive instrument.

Ultimately, however, Dee's faith in the actions rested not on the quality of Kelley's performance, but on the visions themselves. The material he had received may have sometimes been incomprehensible, but it was, for him, too compelling, too philosophically sophisticated, too intricate and elaborate to be invented. It fitted perfectly the patterns he witnessed through his work and his life: the novas and comets, the ecclesiastical schisms and bloody wars, the acclamations and denunciations, the ancient texts and new worlds, the arrests, the burnings, the loss of friends and the making of enemies, the spying, the ciphers, the secrets. The world was on the brink. Such an outpouring of spiritual activity was inevitable.

But not this. This idea of sharing wives did not fit at all.

"Your own reason riseth up against my wisdom," Madimi had told Dee. "Behold, you are become free. Do that which most pleaseth you." He had become free. Throughout his career, Dee had struggled to reconcile reason with wisdom, understanding with faith. The angels had apparently provided him with the means of reconciling the two. His faith had delivered the message, his understanding would enable him to make sense of it.

Many years later the kind old crone of Mortlake, Goodwife Faldo, would hail Dee a great peacemaker. But he could make no peace here. He must choose. "Your own reason riseth up against my wisdom. Do that which most pleaseth you." It was a test of his faith. Dee had to decide whether it was a divine instruction, which his faith must lead him to believe, or an elaborate deception, as his reason might otherwise conclude.

In undertaking the actions, Dee had "offered my soul as a pawn," as he put it—sold it, in other words, for the gift of divine knowledge. But who was the pawnbroker? God, or Kelley? Angels or demons? Was he a prophet being primed to deliver a divine message, or a philosopher whose selfish yearning for knowledge was driving him to pawn not just himself but his own wife to the devil? Was he Enoch, the patriarch? Or was he Faust—whose story was this very year popularized by the publication of Johann Spies's book *The History of Dr Faustus, the Notorious Magician and Master of the Black Art*?

Dee knew of the strong feelings his wife aroused in Kelley. Was the entire episode an invention of Kelley's, a means of escaping the actions and his skrying duties—or, worse, of fulfilling his wanton lust for Jane? "Assist me, O Christ! Assist me!" But no such assistance was or could be given. Dee was alone, and must decide for himself. "Behold you are free." A lifetime was focused on this decision, like a beam of light projected into a darkened room.

At dinner that evening with Jane and Joanna, Dee mentioned as casually as he could the "great grief" of that day's actions, "the common and indifferent using of matrimonial acts amongst any couple of us four." The women thought it strange, and hoped it would prove to have an innocent explanation.

After dinner, Kelley retired to the laboratory, and spent four hours alone there. A glass retort bubbled away, distilling wine. The purified alcohol was needed to fuel lamps, experiments, and, no doubt, Kelley. The distillation of one spirit seemed to produce another. A creature called Ben a cubit high emerged from the alcoholic fumes and hovered above the still. Ben claimed to be the angel who had led Kelley to the powder. He prophesied the destruction of Elizabeth and England, and an invasion by "one of the house of Austria made mighty by the King of Spain his death"—Rudolf. Furthermore, Francis Garland, who had been sent with his brother Edward to inform Dee of the Russian tsar's invitation, was a spy acting for William Cecil. Ben also accused Dee of doing "evil" in requiring "proof or testimony now that this last Action was from God Almighty." Dee should be "led prisoner to Rome" for his lack of faith.

At two in the morning, Kelley emerged from the laboratory and told Dee what he had seen. Dee was skeptical, finding "much halting and untruth" in the report. Dee then went to bed. He found Jane awake, wanting to know what had happened.

"Jane," said Dee, "I see that there is no other remedy, but as hath been said of our cross-matching, so it must needs be done."

Jane trembled and wept for quarter of an hour. Dee tried to pacify her, "and so, in the fear of God, and in believing of his admonishment, did persuade her." She resolved "to be content for God's sake and his secret purposes." Later that night, presumably after many hours spent staring at the ceiling, pondering on what her husband had said, she told him she would do as commanded, but only "in one chamber," so that she could be close to Dee. "I trust," she added, "though I give myself thus to be used, that God will turn me into a stone before he would suffer me, in my obedience, to receive any shame, or inconvenience."

Later that night they made love.

Two days later, Dee produced a covenant, solemnizing the pact, which he wrote out in his book containing the notes of the actions.

We four ... do most humbly and heartily thank thee, O Almighty God (our Creator, Redeemer and Sanctifier) for all thy mercies and benefits hitherto received, in our persons, and in them that appertain unto us: And at this present, do faithfully and sincerely confess, and acknowledge, that thy profound wisdom in this most new and strange doctrine (among Christians) propounded, commended, and enjoined unto us four only, is above human reason.

Kelley added a disclaimer, saying that he had "often and sundry times" warned Dee to beware of the spirits, and declaring that he would "from this day forward meddle no more" with spirits.[3]

Two days later, Kelley did meddle. A creature appeared in the stone, surrounded by fire, a man "with flaxen hair hanging down upon him," "naked unto his paps" and splattered with blood. "Your unity and knitting together is the end and consummation of the beginning of my harvest," he said. "For I will not dally with you, but I will be mighty in deed amongst you. And lo, I will shortly open your eyes, and you shall see; and I will say, ARISE, and you shall go out. What I am, I am."

After the creature had gone, Kelley reported feeling "that his body had in it like a fiery heat, even from his breast down unto all his parts, his privities and thighs."

On 3 May, Dee drew up a new covenant, which he, Kelley, Jane, and Joanna all signed. Three days later, as an insurance against demonic contamination, he went with Kelley before the table of practice, which was set up in the castle chapel, and "read over the covenant (verbatim) before the Divine Majesty and his holy angels."

Madimi appeared. "Are you ready?" she asked.

"We are ready," Dee replied.

"It is decided. Make haste. Let everything be in common among you."

On 20 May, there were still difficulties with the covenant.

"Behold, I have prepared a banquet for you," said a spirit, "and have brought you even unto the doors; but because you smell not the feast you disdain to enter." The spirit then addressed Dee. "He that pawneth his soul for me loseth it not, and he that dieth for me, dieth to eternal life. For I will lead you into the way of knowledge and understanding: and judgement and wisdom shall be upon you, and shall be restored unto you: and you shall grow every day wise and mighty in me."

The following day, Dee wrote two words in his diary: "Pactum factum," pact fulfilled.

XXVIII

✤

TWO days after the "cross-matching" was consummated, Kelley once more knelt before the table of practice and summoned the spirits. A horseman appeared, and there followed an exchange, recorded by Dee in his notebook, but scored out:

"Kelly, was thy brother's wife obedient and humble to thee?" the horseman asked.

"She was," Kelley replied.

"Dee, was thy brother's wife obedient unto thee?"

"She was obedient," Dee replied.

The horseman rode off into a "great field," and Madimi appeared. She was suspicious of Dee's answer.

"Dee, dost thou lie or say truth, in saying she was obedient?" she demanded to know.

"I counted her obedient for that she did whereof she thought her obedience to consist; for that she did not come after as I thought she would, she might seem in some part disobedient; but if it offended not God, it offended not me, and I beseech God it did not offend him," Dee replied.

This admission released the most explicit vision Kelley had yet delivered, a fantasy frothing with lust. It featured a Golden Woman, the "daughter of Fortitude" who had been "ravished every hour from my youth."

Few or none that are earthly have embraced me, for I am shadowed with the circle of the sun, and covered with the morning clouds. My feet are swifter than the winds, and my hands are sweeter than the morning dew. I am deflowered, and yet a virgin. Happy is he that embraceth me: for in the night season I am sweet, and in the day full of pleasure. My company is a harmony of many cymbals. I am a harlot for such as ravish me, and a virgin with such as know me not. . . . I will open my garments and stand naked before you, that your love may be more inflamed toward me.

The Golden Woman departed through the same endless green field as the horseman and Madimi.[1] This was the last recorded spiritual action Dee was to conduct with Kelley.[2] However, a moment that should in every sense have been climactic failed to produce a culminating confrontation or moment of truth. It just slowly dribbled away, leaving nothing but a stain.

Over the coming months, a rift formed between the Kelleys and the Dees. The peacemaker Dee wrote "charitable letters" to both Kelley and Joanna in an effort to normalize relations, but apparently to no avail. The situation could not have improved when Jane gave birth to a boy on 28 February 1588, forty weeks almost to the day after the pact had been consummated. He was christened Theodorus Trebonianus Dee, "gift of God at Třeboň." At no point does Dee allude to the paternity of the child.

There was a form of reconciliation with Joanna on the anniversary of the pact, but the following day Dee makes a mysterious entry in his diary referring to "threats" involving Joanna, and a dagger symbol next to the diary entry.[3]

On 20 July, Edward Dyer, Dee's friend and the godfather of his oldest child, Arthur, arrived at Třeboň. Dyer approached offering the warm embraces of Elizabeth's court, but walked straight past Dee into the arms of Kelley. England was agog with reports of the skryer's alchemical skills, and William Cecil, Lord Burghley himself wanted Kelley to come back home and work his magic there. Dee had apparently been forgotten.

By now, Třeboň was crowded with English visitors: Joanna Kelley's brother, Edmund Cooper; the mysterious Francis Garland, identified by the spirits as Cecil's spy; one Thomas Southwell, who claimed to have been given a lump of the Philosopher's Stone; John Basset, hired as Arthur's grammar teacher, who turned out to be working under an assumed name. They buzzed around Kelley like bees around a bloom, probing for a taste of the tinctures and elixirs promised by his colorful demonstrations.

Dee was offered glimpses of Kelley's skills, and apparently believed in them. "I saw the divine water, by the demonstration of the magnificent master and my incomparable friend Mr Ed. Kelly," he proudly wrote one day. "Hope confirmed. Donum Dei, et Domini E.K.," he wrote on another.[4]

One moment Dee and his "incomparable friend" were thus in conjunction, but the next in opposition. "Great friendship offered for money, and two ounces of the thing [the Philosopher's Stone]," Dee noted in his diary in December of 1588, casting a different interpretation of their amity. This was written in Greek characters, so Kelley could not read it.[5]

The following month, Kelley showed Dee a letter from Lord Rozmberk. It showed that Dee was now estranged from his noble patron. "Mr Kelly did before my wife confess, that my Lord's desire was that I should not have come hither, from the very beginning of our coming."[6] Dee was now expected to leave Třeboň as soon as he could.

In mid-February, Dee wrote a terse entry recording that Kelley had gone to Prague. Dee would never see him again.

*   *   *

KELLEY RODE OUT of Třeboň and into Bohemian history.

Within the year, he had been made a baron of Bohemia, and was claiming ancestry with the "knightly kin and house called Imaymi in the county of Conaghaku in the kingdom of Ireland." He also acquired extensive estates, including a castle, nine villages, and two houses in Prague.[7] Unaware or unconcerned that Kelley was the conduit for the angelic remonstrations delivered by Dee, Rudolf himself now sought Kelley's services. He wrote personally to Rozmberk to ask if Kelley could supervise some alchemical experiments the emperor was undertaking at his own laboratories.[8]

Meanwhile, reports continued to filter back to England of Kelley's prodigious progress. Lord Willoughby, ambassador to Prague and himself a patron of alchemy, reputedly brought back a bedpan to present to Elizabeth, with a section that Kelley had transmuted into gold. He also claimed to have seen Kelley make gold rings out of pieces of wire, one of which was valued at £4,000, which he gave to one of his servants.

Cecil redoubled his efforts to lure Kelley back. Spies were instructed to report on him, letters were despatched commanding, then imploring that he return.[9] "Sir" Edward's responses were candid. On 24 July 1590, he observed to Cecil that "being in security, and that in a country full of peace and liberty, seized in lands of inheritance yielding £1,500 yearly, incorporated to the kingdom in the second order, of some expectation and use more than vulgar of his Majesty's privy council . . . , Chief Regent in and over all the Lands and Affairs of the Prince Rosenberg: I can not see how I might easily and honestly depart, much less to steal away." Quite so. The following month, he wrote again, spelling out the message in case Cecil had failed to comprehend it: "I am not so mad to run away from my present honour and lands. . . . To deal plainly, I find myself well at ease. And can well content myself with my present state and will not remove but upon greater reasons than I yet find."[10]

Cecil was not put off by such impertinent rebuffs. He repeatedly ordered Edward Dyer back to Prague to retrieve the unruly adept. At first, Dyer found the atmosphere in Rudolf's court too hostile to stay. "I used all my best means, to have gotten some medicine to have satisfied her Majesty by her own blissful sight: but Sir Edward feared to consent thereto," he reported. Kelley was apparently frightened of kindling jealousy in the court "whereof he being now of the Emperor's privy council he hath more regard than in time passed."[11] However, during a second attempt he managed to secure a foothold in Kelley's laboratory, where he saw for himself some of the work under way.

The experience left Dyer utterly convinced of Kelley's abilities. Back in England, he tried to persuade the Archbishop of Canterbury himself of Kelley's powers. "I do assure your grace, that . . . I am an eye-witness thereof; and if I had not seen it, I should not have believed it. I saw Master Kelley put of the base metal in a crucible; and after it was set a little upon the fire, and a very small quantity of medicine put in, and stirred with a stick of wood, it came forth in great projection, perfect gold; to the touch, to the hammer, to the test."[12]

Cecil was by now beginning to get impatient. "I have cause to thank you, and so I do very heartily for your good, kind letters sent to me by our countryman, Mr Roydon, who makes such good report of you (as does every other man that has had a conversation with you)," he wrote in May 1591. Matthew Roydon was a poet and a friend of Christopher Marlowe whose name was linked with Lord Strange and the so-called "School of Night," a circle of free-thinking writers and philosophers named after a reference in Shake-speare's *Love's Labour's Lost*.[13] "Yet I have the same mingled with some grief," Cecil continued, "that none of them can give me any good assurance of your return hither; the thing most earnestly desired of all well disposed to the Queen's Majesty." There followed a detailed report on Cecil's gout, which some have interpreted as a coded reference to Kelley's alchemical "medicine," since Cecil studiously avoided any direct references to transmutation for fear of his letters being intercepted.[14]

Cecil also wrote to Dyer. Rumors had apparently reached Prague that Sir Christopher Hatton, the Lord Chancellor, had "uttered divers reproachful speeches even before her Majesty" regarding Kelley. Cecil was at pains to point out that Hatton had been "notably wronged." But doubts were beginning to surface about Kelley's powers, and Cecil started to put pressure on Dyer to deliver. If Dyer could not get Kelley to return, Cecil warned, "I must certainly think that he cannot perform that which you conceive of him, but that by some cunning or, as they say, legerdemain, both you and all others have been deceived."[15] In fact, Kelley was unable to return, not because he could not "perform," but because he had been arrested.

On the morning of 30 April, a unit of guards gathered at the gates of Prague castle, ordered by the emperor himself to go to Kelley's house "with commandment to bring him up bound, the cause concealed." Because of Kelley's status, the captain and lieutenant of the castle, Prague's provost and the Bohemian secretary of state were called upon to supervise the arrest, and at noon the entire detachment marched down the steep cobbled streets leading from the castle to Kelley's house.

When they arrived, they found he was not there. He had apparently been tipped off and made his escape. "The officers finding not the principal, seized on the accessories; bound his servants, and led them up to prison in sight of the whole town: sealed up the doors of every chamber," as an account filed by an English traveler put it.[16] Among those "accessories" was Dyer himself.

Rudolf was furious at the news of Kelley's escape, and, cursing "in the Dutch manner," ordered a search. Kelley was finally tracked down to an inn at Sobeslav, en route to Rozmberk's estates in southern Bohemia. According to another English report, the guards found him asleep in his bedchamber, and cut his doublet open with a knife. They told him that "they were by the Emperor's commandment to carry him back again, dead or alive, which they cared not." He was taken to the imposing hilltop castle at Krivoklát, where he was imprisoned in a cell with "no air, but that which comes through a hole, through which he was fed food bit by bit."[17]

The reason for Kelley's arrest was the cause of endless speculation. Sir Horatio Palavicino, one of Cecil's most reliable "intelligencers," put it down to Kelley's transmutations being revealed as fraudulent. Other theories were more colorful: that he had fallen out with a rival alchemist, who accused him of trying to poison the emperor; that he owed 32,000 dollars (thalers) to two merchants from Cologne for jewels; that a bogus alchemist executed by the duke of Bavaria had confessed to being in league with Kelley.[18]

Queen Elizabeth asked for Dyer to be released, but made no application on Kelley's behalf. Nevertheless, interest in his fate remained intense and reports continued to flow in from passing travelers, spies, and diplomats. Some of the most detailed appear in letters written by Christopher Parkins, another English expatriate in Prague who Kelley had once falsely accused of conspiring to kill Elizabeth. The forgiving Parkins, "setting aside all passion," wrote a sober analysis of Kelley's state, noting that there were already signs of his rehabilitation.[19]

In the autumn of 1593, the irrepressible Kelley was released, apparently none the worse for wear, being "fat and merry," as another correspondent noted.[20] Cecil once again despatched couriers to make contact, sending William Hall, a mysterious figure whose name some have speculated was an alias for William Shakespeare.[21] Two years later, English merchants and intelligencers were still filing reports, one from Seth Cocks to Cecil's son, Sir Robert Cecil, Walsingham's successor: "I am now within these two days to depart hence and mean to pass by Prague, because I will see Sir Edward Kelley, who they say enjoys his former favour with the Emperor."[22]

He was now reported to be back with the Rozmberks, fighting in an army raised by Vilem's brother Petr Vok against the Turks. However, Kelley's wandering star fell again. On 1 November 1596 he had a fight with the assistant of another alchemist, Kryštof Želinsky ze Sebuzína, who held an influential position at court, and once more "suffered chains and imprisonment," as he put it.[23] This time he was confined to the castle at Most, an imposing fortress that lies near the modern Czech border with Germany.

At this point Kelley melted back into the realm of myth from whence he came. According to one legend, he drugged his guards using opium smuggled to him by his wife, Joanna, or his brother, Thomas, tried to make his escape by climbing from his cell window using knotted sheets, but fell and broke his legs; according to another he faked his own suicide. In coming years, his very existence was in question: on 25 November 1595, Dee heard that he had been "slain," but there were reports that he was still active in 1597. Some said that he had resumed practicing as an alchemist in Russia; others claimed to see his ghost wandering southern Germany.[24]

The last reported sighting of Edward Kelley was in 1598 by the Czech physician and alchemist Matthias Borbonius, but, like the spirits he so successfully conjured up, he would continue to haunt the occult world for centuries to come.[25]

PART TEN
THE LONG
JOURNEY

✦

Stand still you ever-moving spheres of heaven,
That time may cease, and midnight ever come.

CHRISTOPHER MARLOWE,
The Tragicall History of Dr. Faustus

XXIX

On 15 December 1589, after six years, thousands of miles, some triumphs, several disasters, a few accolades, and numerous humiliations, Dee walked back into his cottage at Mortlake to find it in ruins.[1]

The journey home had been an eventful one. The decision to leave Třeboň was made on 3 February 1589, and the following day he handed over "the powder, the books, the glass and the bone" to Rozmberk, who in return gave Dee "discharge in writing of his own hand: subscribed and sealed." The glass was the magic mirror Dee had been given by his old friend William Pickering, and before which the queen herself had once posed. Rozmberk presented it to Rudolf to add to his collection.

On 11 March, Dee and his family finally set off. They departed Třeboň in style, their train comprising three purpose-built coaches drawn by twelve young Hungarian horses, three outriders, and three "wains" or wagons. During the journey across Germany, they also acquired an escort of twenty-four soldiers and six "harquebusiers and musquettiers" (soldiers bearing guns and muskets) from the earl of Oldenburg's garrison to provide protection from marauding gangs.[2]

They passed through Nuremberg and Frankfurt, arriving at the north German port of Bremen on 9 April, where Dee put the saddle horses out to pasture, and sent the twelve coach horses to the landgrave of Hesse-Kassel, who had provided him with a home during his months of exile from Bohemia.[3] He and his family spent the next seven months in hired lodgings in Bremen, meeting a procession of travelers, hearing snippets of news, and writing letters both to England and Bohemia.

Some old troubles returned to haunt Dee. Money, briefly in such lavish supply, began to run short. He had arguments with Jane and his landlord, and was repeatedly warned to leave. He also had nightmares, the most vivid on 12 August, when in the early morning he had a "terrible dream that Mr Kelly would by force bereave me of my books."

On 26 November, he left Bremen for Stade, on the estuary of the Elbe. There he briefly met Edward Dyer, who was on one of his many missions to persuade Kelley to return to England. Dee sailed for England on the *Vineyard* on 29 November. The crossing now involved a date shift of ten days, as England was still using the old Julian calendar. His ship reached the Thames estuary on 22 November, "old style."

He disembarked near Stratford, then a small village to the east of London, where his "brother," Justice Richard Young, lived. He needed help with regaining possession of his house at Mortlake. He evidently had difficulties, as he spent over two weeks in negotiations. He could only peer through the windows of his old home as he passed by it on 9 December, on his way to Richmond Palace for an audience with the queen. He came to a settlement the following day, when it was agreed he could go back as a tenant of Jane's brother, Nicholas Fromonds. Five days later, he finally walked in through his front door.

The house had been ransacked. The reading room, once the humming center of his intellectual empire, was stripped of all its furniture and reading equipment. Most of his scientific instruments had been taken, such as the ten-foot-long "radius astronomicus" used in his astronomical observations, a sea compass, his "excellent watch-clock made by one Dibbley," a "great bladder" containing a "brownish gum" that had been prepared in Dee's own laboratory using multiple distillations, and, perhaps most devastating of all, the celestial and terrestrial globes given to him by his friend Gerard Mercator, upon which Dee had so carefully marked his own discoveries.[4]

In the "appendix," all that remained of his irreplaceable collection of title deeds and official papers were the storage boxes, pulled from the case or "great frame" that had once held them, still bearing the chalk labels describing the papers they no longer contained. In the laboratories, the ingredients and glassware he had collected from across Europe, the "purposely made vessels" of clay, metal, glass, and "mixed stuff" he had brought back in "one great cart laden" from the Duchy of Lorraine, all gone. Only a few, worthless, "spoiled and broken" jars remained.

As for the library, Dee estimated that 500 volumes had been taken, including four books that alone he estimated to be worth £533.[5]

Several theories have been advanced for the ransacking of Dee's library. For years, the accepted story was that a "London mob" had gathered in Mortlake and stormed the property following his departure for the Continent with Laski. This explained the mud found on the pages of several surviving manuscripts, which must have been stained when they were trodden beneath stampeding feet.[6]

In fact, at least some of the culprits of the "spoilation" of the library were known to Dee, and one in particular was identified by Dee himself in a series of annotations he added in 1589 to the library catalog he had drawn up just before his departure in 1583: John Davies, the privateer who had visited Mortlake with Adrian Gilbert. In a copy of Sebastian Muenster's *Cosmographia*, Dee wrote, "Jo. Davis took [this book] by violence out of my house after my going." It was not the only work he had taken. He had helped himself to manuscripts on perspective, commentaries on the Psalms, anything he could lay his hands on—around seventy volumes in all, according to Dee's own estimate.

Davies was the only thief to be positively identified by Dee, but he was not alone. Hundreds of other books and articles went missing. Some of the scientific equipment was later found by a local man called Thomas Jack, such as a fragment of Dee's "magnes stone" (a sample of magnetized iron ore or lodestone).

Perhaps it was Jack who recovered the missing "great sea cumpas" that turned up three years after Dee's return, delivered to Mortlake in the middle of the night with its needle missing.[7] It had come from the home of one Nicholas Saunder, who it turns out had many more of Dee's possessions. In their survey of Dee's library catalog published in 1990, the bibliographers Julian Roberts and Andrew G. Watson showed that many of the works taken from Dee's library subsequently resurfaced with Dee's signature incriminatingly bleached out and replaced or written over by Saunder's. "The presumption must be, therefore, that if Saunder was not a thief he was at least a receiver on a massive scale," Roberts and Watson concluded.[8]

In short, Dee's house had been ransacked not by an ignorant peasant mob, but by pupils and associates. Their motives remain unclear. They may have seized the books to settle outstanding debts, or to discover the secrets they contained, or to hide them from others. However, they did not simply remove valuables; some they vandalized, such as the quadrant Dee had used to compile a book of star positions in 1554, which he found scattered across the floor, "with hammers smit to pieces."[9]

* * *

DEE WAS NOW sixty-two years old. The England to which he had returned was very different than the one he had left. The court was unrecognizable. Many of Dee's old friends were gone. Robert Dudley, the earl of Leicester and Elizabeth's onetime favorite, was dead. Soon to follow were Sir Christopher Hatton and Francis Walsingham. "Good Sir Francis," as Dee dubbed him, passed away at 11 P.M. on 6 April 1590, his agonizing death throes luridly reported by the Catholics his regime had so effectively repressed, one noting that urine erupted from his mouth and nose as his body suffered its final spasms.[10]

There was also a distinct change of mood toward astrologers. The conjunction of Saturn and Jupiter in 1583, inaugurating the era of the Fiery Trigon, was supposed to mark the onset of a period of cataclysmic disaster, culminating in the *annus horribilis* of 1588. The year turned out to be one of the most successful in English history. Catholic plots against the queen had been quelled, Sir Walter Raleigh had founded the first English colony in the New World, at Roanoke Island, and, of course, the great Spanish Armada had been defeated.

A flurry of pamphlets, plays, and books began to appear ridiculing astrological prophecies. "An astronomer," thunders the character Raffe in John Lyly's play *Gallathea*, "of all occupations that's the worst. . . . He told me a long tale of Octogessimus octavus [i.e., 1588], and the meeting of the Conjunctions & Planets, and in the mean-time he fell backward himself into a pond."[11]

Dee soon found that he, too, was toppling in the mire. When rumors of strange, demonic happenings spread across London during an outbreak of plague in the early 1590s, he was identified as the cause.[12] He was also said to have foreseen an assassination attempt against Elizabeth by the queen's Portuguese doctor, Roderigo Lopez, in 1593.[13]

In 1592, a pamphlet published in Antwerp by Catholic exiles started to circulate London's streets, which appeared to make a direct attack on Dee. It was called *An Advertisement written to a Secretary of My L. Treasurer*, and was aimed at discrediting Sir Walter Raleigh. Raleigh was at this time in the midst of a vicious power struggle with the ambitious and ruthless Robert Devereux, earl of Essex, and it was no doubt Essex's partisans who were spreading the rumors the pamphlet promulgated.

It accused Raleigh of setting up a "school of atheism" at Durham House, his sumptuous riverside residence—the school later dubbed the "School of Night." The pamphlet went on to complain "of the conjuror that is master . . . and of the diligence used to get the young gentlemen to this school, wherein both Moses and our Saviour, the Old and the New Testament, are jested at, and scholars are taught among other things to spell God backward."[14] The pamphlet does not identify the "conjuror" by name, and it is usually assumed to be Thomas Hariot, a philosopher and alchemist who worked for Henry Percy, the "Wizard Earl" of Northumberland, whose name was also associated with the "school." However, Dee is a contender too. One of the unidentified authors of the tract was the exiled Sir Francis Englefeld, the man who arrested Dee for "lewd and vain practises of calculing and conjuring" during Queen Mary's reign.[15] Dee certainly seemed to consider himself to be the pamphlet's target, as he indicated in a petition he presented to King James I in 1604.[16]

Dee had a number of links with Raleigh's infamous "school."[17]

Many of its members, such as Christopher Marlowe, would have been known to him. He was closely associated with Raleigh, who took Dee's place in the "Fellowship of New Navigations Atlanticall and Septentionall" that set off to colonize America in the mid-1580s. Dee dined at Raleigh's London home, Durham House, which was the supposed venue of his ungodly academy.[18] He knew Hariot as well, describing him as his "friend," and the two were in contact during this period, exchanging books.[19]

In the spring of 1590, Jane gave birth to a daughter, their fifth child. She was christened Madimia at Mortlake Church on 5 March. Dee managed to persuade an impressive selection of nobles to become her godparents, including Sir Francis Walsingham's widow. However, none of them would have appreciated the significance of their infant goddaughter's name, with the possible exception of one: Sir George Carey. Carey was the son of Henry, Lord Hunsdon, the Lord Chamberlain and the patron of Hunsdon's Men, a theatrical troupe that performed at Newington Butts and later the Cross Keys Inn in the City. Following his father's death in 1596, Sir George took over the troupe, when it became known as the Lord Chamberlain's men, set up shop in the Globe, and began to perform the plays of its chief dramatist, William Shakespeare.

Carey was also a prominent member of Raleigh's irreligious "school." In 1594, George Chapman published *The Shadow of Night*, in which he reminisced about the times his friend "my good Mat . . . reported unto me that most ingenious Derby, deep-searching Northumberland and skill-embracing heir of Hunsdon had most profitably entertained learning in themselves, to the vital warmth of freezing science, & to the admirable lustre of their true nobility."[20]

Ingenious Derby was Lord Strange, deep-searching Northumberland Henry Percy, and the skill-embracing heir of Hunsdon Sir George Carey. And "my good Mat" was Matthew Roydon, a poet, friend of Christopher Marlowe, and author of a moving elegy to Sir Philip Sidney, "A Friend's Passion of his Astrophel." He was also the courier who brought Kelley's letters from Prague to William Cecil in 1591.[21]

Dee had connections with this magic circle, though whether from inside or without remains unclear. But he was certainly interested in stoking the "vital warmth of freezing science," despite the damage it might do to his reputation. With his livelihood at Mortlake destroyed, he came up with an audacious plan to start anew by setting up a sort of secret academy of his own, a real "School of Night."

*　　*　　*

ON 19 JUNE 1591, Dee went to Greenwich to lobby for the job of mastership of St. John's Cross, an almshouse near the famous school in Winchester. The position was already occupied by "the worshipfull Mr. Doctor Bennet," but there were some vacant bishoprics, and Dee felt sure Bennet would eagerly accept any that were offered to him. This idea revived an aspiration that had been thwarted for twenty years, since the queen first promised him the position.

Dee had ambitious plans for St. John's Cross. He wanted to set up a kind of research institute, complete with laboratories and printing presses, overseen by "mechanical servants" (technicians), that would offer a secure place "for our learned men to be entertained and lodged." It would be a place where thinkers who elsewhere might be accused of atheism and necromancy would find themselves "in such a solitary and commodious place, they may dwell in freedom, security, and quietness, under her Majesty's unviolable protection."[22] He also noted that, being in Winchester, it was good for schools, and also the glass factories of Sussex, where he could better "oversee the workmen and workmanship, for better matter and shape of glass works and instruments-making."

Dee was desperate for his plan to be accepted. It represented his only hope of rehabilitation. His finances were now critical. As well as the damage done to Mortlake, he had returned to discover that the living of Long Leadenham had been seized during his absence by John Robinson, Archdeacon of Bedford, depriving him of his only regular source of income.[23] He had issued petitions in an attempt to recover it along with the rectorship of Upton, taken from him during Queen Mary's reign, but his attempts had come to nothing. "Utterly put out of hope for recovering the two parsonages by the L. Archb. and the L. Treasurer," he despondently noted in his diary on 21 January 1591.

The issue of the mastership of St. John's Cross was handed over to Cecil and, while he issued ever more urgent pleas to Kelley to return to England, the Lord Treasurer ruminated at his leisure on Dee's application. He finally produced a vague response in December, a "gentle answer" that the queen was mindful to give him one of the posts that would be freed up by an imminent round of new bishoprics.[24]

As Dee was left to dangle on this thread of reassurance, beneath him the chasm of debt continued to deepen. He had to pawn his plate to pay his bills, raising £20, £14 of which went straight to Thomas Hudson for wood and corn, £4 to Goodman Bedell for "billet, bales and loose faggot," 8 shillings to Goodwife Welder for one month's nursing. He was also propped up by donations from friends and patrons: £20 and a hogshead of claret from the adventurers Richard and Thomas Cavendish; £10 from the alchemist Thomas Smith; £5 in "rials and angels," gold coins, from the Archbishop of Canterbury. The queen herself called by to promise him a princely 100 angels, half of which he received within two days, the other half apparently not at all. He also appears to have resumed his career as a freelance astrologer and adviser. On 1 February 1594, for example, he received "two little double gilt bowls" from a John Ask, whose horoscope he had cast.[25] He carefully weighed them, presumably to calculate their value. On 5 April 1592 he was consulted by Lady Russell, who had been "robbed a little after midnight of pearls, diamonds." "One John Smyth is suspected," Dee wrote, "a young man of 30 years old, very ingenious in many handiworks, melancholic, auburn-haired."

Dee's financial problems were accompanied by a string of domestic disasters. His son Roland fell into the Thames, his infant daughter Madimia dropped out of bed and hurt her forehead, and Arthur, while playing at the home of Dee's neighbor Sir William Herbert, knocked himself out by the "wanton" throwing of a brickbat straight up in the air "and not well avoiding the fall of it again."[26] When they were not having accidents, the children were suffering illnesses: Theodore with "tertian ague" and a bloodshot eye, Arthur with "quotidian gentle ague," which was treated with a bloodletting, Madimia with some unspecified sickliness.[27] Jane, too, suffered, having a miscarriage after being ill for three days, aborting a fetus "nearly as big as an egg," Dee noted.[28]

Dee was strong and healthy for a man in his sixties. He continued to make frequent trips to London and the royal palaces, and welcomed guests to his house on an almost daily basis. His diary also shows that he and Jane regularly had sex. However, he was not immune from occasional aches and pains, suffering from cramps in his calves, "veins or arteries" and rectum, and from kidney stones. A Dr. Giffard treated the stones with enemas, leaving Dee "eased of my grief." He got further relief from the news, received two days after his sixty-fifth birthday, that a certain Mr. Carter of Yorkshire had managed to reach the ripe old age of eighty.

But mingled with such reassurances were insistent reminders of mortality. One of the saddest concerned Dee's melancholic nurse, Anne Frank. She had, he noted in his diary in the summer of 1590, "long been tempted by a wicked spirit: but this day it was evident, how she was possessed of him." Dee attempted to rid her of her demons by performing some sort of exorcising ritual. There was a respite lasting two days before she once more suffered a "great affliction of mind." The following day she had recovered a little, being "well comforted," and the day after that Dee "anointed (in the name of Jesus) Ann Frank her breast, with the holy oil."

Any relief she enjoyed was short-lived. The following week, she asked to be anointed again. Dee "very devoutly" prepared himself with prayers, and tried another application of the holy ointment. "The wicked one did resist a while," he noted. A month later, Anne tried to drown herself in the well, "but by divine providence I came to take her up before she was utterly overcome of the water, shortly after sunset." Dee set one of his maids to watch over her, but three days later, Anne slipped away from her bedchamber and downstairs to the hall in the adjoining "hovel" that Dee had rented. There, behind a door, she slit her own throat. "Lord have pity on us," Dee wrote.[29]

By 1592, Dee began to receive indications that the Lord might indeed have pity on him and his family. On 6 August, he rode to Nonsuch, Elizabeth's dreamy Surrey palace built as a hunting lodge and guest house by her father. The mastership of St. John's Cross was now a good prospect. He might even get compensation for the damage done to his house while he was away, which he estimated to be well over £1,000.

The cause of this newfound hope was Anne, countess of Warwick. She was one of Elizabeth's closest ladies-in-waiting, and had been using her influence to lobby hard on Dee's behalf. The countess was married to Ambrose Dudley, one of the sons of the duke of Northumberland, whom Dee had served in his youth, and it was perhaps this connection that made her such an eager champion of Dee's cause. She may also have known Jane when she served at court.

Dee arrived at Nonsuch to find promising news. The countess had sent word through a Mr. Ferdinando that the queen was favorably disposed toward his application for the mastership of St. John's Cross. Dee also saw the Archbishop of Canterbury there, who confirmed the queen's enthusiasm.

Over the following days, these promising augurs were reinforced by a sudden and apparently spontaneous display of ingratiation by William Cecil. The veteran Lord Treasurer, who had on so many occasions rebuffed Dee, now overburdened the philosopher with hospitality, inviting him to dinner on two nights in succession and sending him a haunch of venison as a gift. There are a number of possible reasons for Cecil's attentiveness, none of them designed to further Dee's interests. Cecil was by now in frequent correspondence with Edward Kelley in Bohemia, and perhaps wanted Dee to use his influence to persuade the alchemist to return home. Another possible reason is suggested by the presence at the dinner table of Cecil's son, Sir Robert Cecil. Sir Robert had replaced Sir Francis Walsingham as Elizabeth's chief spymaster, and would later use his intelligence network to unravel the Gunpowder Plot. There was one particular scheme that Sir Robert was working on that may well have arisen as a topic of dinner conversation, a plot to test the loyalty of Lord Strange.

Strange, whose father had put forward Dee for the rectorship of Long Leadenham in 1558, was from that clutch of nobles celebrated by George Chapman for adding "vital warmth to freezing science." He was part of the Stanley dynasty, long suspected of harboring Catholic sympathies. Strange was also believed to have connections with a number of English papists exiled in Prague, among whose number was one Richard Hesketh, an amateur alchemist and merchant who had moved there in 1590. Sir Robert Cecil had devised a plan to plant a letter calling for Catholic insurrection on one of these exiles for delivery to Strange at his stronghold in Lancashire. If Strange failed to report the letter to the authorities, it would prove that he was a traitor. The unfortunate Hesketh was chosen to be the courier.

The plot was hatched when Hesketh returned to England in 1593. En route to Lancashire, he stopped at the White Lion Inn at Islington, north of London. There he was given a letter addressed to Strange, which he was led to believe contained news concerning his English confederates. Hesketh duly delivered the incriminating missive. Strange handed the letter over to the queen, saving his own skin but condemning that of the unfortunate messenger. On 29 November 1593, Hesketh was hanged, drawn, and quartered at St. Albans.

There is no evidence that Dee was involved in this subterfuge, but it is possible that while he dined with Sir Robert, he was being pumped for information about Prague. He knew of Hesketh, having noted his nativity.[30] Dee had left Bohemia by the time Hesketh arrived there, but there is plenty of evidence to link Kelley with the Catholic cell to which Hesketh belonged. For example, a Jesuit priest in Prague, Thomas Stephenson, wrote a letter to Hesketh that, in the space of a few sentences, mentioned not only the overthrow of Elizabeth, but the current well-being and whereabouts of a "Sir Edward," "Mr Thomas," "Mr Hammon," and "Mr Leigh." It seems certain that "Sir Edward" was Kelley, and possible that the others were Kelley's brother Thomas, John Hammond, a "gentleman" hired by Dee while in Třeboň, and Henry Leigh, who had carried letters between Kelley and Burghley, and who may have been the "Sir Harry Lee" whose brother Dee reported meeting, and who once offered Kelley an annuity of £40 a year to skry.

One further piece of suggestive evidence links Dee with the conspiracy. The agent lurking in the shadows at Islington, who slipped the fateful note into Hesketh's hand via one of the inn's boys, was a "Mr Hickman." One of Dee's first skryers was Bartholomew Hickman. Hickman had government connections, he and his uncle Richard having originally come to Mortlake on the recommendation of Sir Christopher Hatton, the late Lord Chancellor.[31] In fact, Dee had dealings with the whole Hickman clan, not just Bart and uncle Richard, but Bart's brothers William and Ambrose, his daughter Joan, and an unnamed nephew. Bartholomew Hickman reentered Dee's life at precisely this time.[32]

Dee was also a friend of Thomas Webb, one of the agents used by Cecil to report on Kelley's activities in Prague. At the end of 1593, soon after Hesketh's execution, Webb was arrested and sent to the Marshalsea Prison in Southwark for "coining," the same charge brought against Kelley and used by the government as a handy judicial instrument for controlling unruly or unreliable agents. Dee went to visit Webb at Marshalsea, and would go back again when Webb thought he was about to be condemned.[33]

Whatever Dee's role in these machinations, it did not win him any permanent support either from Cecil or his son Sir Robert. The Lord Treasurer continued to fret about the absence of Kelley, and dreamed of being enriched by his alchemical art. He soon lost interest in Dee.

On 9 November 1592, Dee heard that the countess of Warwick had managed to persuade the queen to appoint commissioners to investigate his case for reparations and the mastership of St. John's Cross. She chose Sir Thomas Gorge and Sir John Wolley, her Latin secretary and an old acquaintance of Dee's. They came to Mortlake on 28 November, and Dee laid before them a detailed survey of his writings, his services to the queen and to the nation, and the losses he had suffered, which he calculated to amount to £1,510. A week later, he heard that Sir Thomas Gorge had succeeded in securing for him "speedily" a royal grant of 100 marks. This was welcome, but only temporary relief.

Dee lobbied for St. John's Cross with growing desperation. He went with his wife and all seven of his children to Isleworth to petition the queen. He asked old family friends, such as Lady Scudamore, to apply pressure. Jane even intercepted the queen as she was walking from her private garden at Somerset House up the Strand, and passed her a petition, which Elizabeth apparently accepted "and kept upon her cushion."[34]

In May 1594, Dee finally heard that Sir John Wolley had "moved my suit to her majesty." She had apparently "granted [it] after a sort, but referred all to the [Archbishop] of Canterbury"—an unpromising development, as exactly the same had happened to his ill-fated proposals for calendar reform.[35] A month later, he went to see the archbishop, John Whitgift, at Croydon. Elizabeth had total faith in Whitgift, and Dee had no hope of securing the job without the archbishop's support.

Whitgift said that the previous Sunday he had been with the queen and Lord Treasurer at Theobalds, Cecil's lavish country seat in Hertfordshire, and they had discussed Dee's case. It seems Cecil had decided to continue with the policy of prevarication. No action was to be taken. The indecision was final.

Dee could take no more. "I take myself confounded for all suing or hoping for anything that was," he wrote after returning home from Croydon. "And so, adieu to the Court and courting, till God direct me otherwise."

XXX

✦

ON 17 July 1607, Dee walked over to the cedar-wood chest where he kept his books of mysteries and magical paraphernalia. He unlocked it, and took out the stone he had used with Edward Kelley, his "jewel," newly set in gold. He set it before the man who thirty years before had acted as one of his first skryers and had since returned to become his last, Bartholomew Hickman.

Dee was now seventy-nine years old. He had spent the last decade in Manchester, where Archbishop Whitgift had finally determined he should go, as warden of the fractious fellows of the Collegiate Chapter there. It was virtual exile, placing him far outside the orbit of the queen and her court.

Of the eight children Jane had borne, only three now survived. Michael, born on 22 February 1585 in Prague, had died on 13 July 1594 aged nine years. Dee recorded the boy's last words as "O Lord, have mercy upon me." Theodore, the gift from God born in Třeboň, had given up the ghost in the spring of 1601. Margaret, his youngest, born 14 August 1595, and Madimia seem to have been victims of a plague that passed through Manchester in March 1605. The same disease had also taken his wife, Jane. After twenty-seven years of marriage, she had gone and he was now alone.

It is hard to know what feelings Dee and Jane had for each other in their final years together. The nature of their relationship is so rarely glimpsed, and then very unromantically through Dee's private diary. In a note he made in January 1601, he wrote next to the usual symbol for sex the word "voluntaria" appended to the astrological sign for Venus. The Venus symbol clearly refers to Jane. The meaning of "voluntaria" is less obvious. It could mean that Jane had been "willing." But in what sense? That she had been unwilling before? Or that on this occasion she was more willing than usual? The use of Latin indicates the reference may relate to some spiritual instruction. Following the cross-matching episode, Dee recorded, again in Latin, sexual encounters with Jane as being conducted with "necessary conditions" or "circumstances."[1] Perhaps this meant that such conditions and circumstances no longer applied, that an act in some manner controlled by the angels could once more be undertaken free of restraint.

Two weeks after their voluntary congress, Dee refers to a "reconciliation" between all the members of his family, "and I did declare to my wife, Kath. my daughter, Arthur and Roland, how things were mistaken."[2] Perhaps in these weeks, the bitter aftermath of the cross-matching episode had finally been resolved, and the man Jane had once so touchingly addressed as her sweetheart had been readmitted to her affections.

Now Jane had gone, and so had most of his children, many of his friends, and Queen Elizabeth, who died in 1603, to be replaced by the more austere Scottish King James. Dee decided to leave Manchester, and return to London, to seek out once again the consoling company of the angels.

On his return, he had conducted several actions with Hickman, one at Mortlake, another at the sign of the Three Kings in Covent Garden, another at the home of a mistress Goodman. The apparitions were pallid shadows compared with the blazing visions conjured up by Kelley. Only one angel appeared to Hickman, Raphael, with advice on the treatment of Dee's kidney stones and piles.

Perhaps it was in a desperate attempt to recapture some of the old magic that Dee now produced the stone he had used with Kelley. But as the crystal sparkled before them, it was Raphael again. "I have now, here, in this pearl entered possession," the angel announced, "to serve thee at all times." Raphael also promised Dee that the "key" to the divine revelations left in his keeping and taken from him in the furnace in Prague would once more be restored, so that he would finally achieve "the perfect understanding of the hid knowledge and secrecy of God." "And that dust which thou hast in keeping shall be turned to the right use, from whence it was," Raphael added, referring to a sample of Kelley's magic powder that Dee had kept (apparently without Kelley's permission, as he had been required to hand over the powder in his possession before leaving Třeboň).

"Thou shalt take a long journey in hand," promised Raphael. "And when thou art at thy journey's end amongst such friends beyond the seas as thou knowest, God shall and will raise thee as faithful friends."

Dee prepared for the journey by secreting his books of mysteries away in his locked chest, and burying them in the fields surrounding Mortlake. One day, they would be discovered. One day, they would be understood.

His last days were possibly spent at the home of John Pontois, a new friend who he had appointed his executor. Pontois lived in Bishopsgate Street in London, just a few steps from the bustling lanes of Tower Ward where Dee had been born.[3] According to one report, in the final two weeks of his life, as he lay dying in his bed, his daughter Katherine "conveyed away his books unknown to him . . . which when he came to understanding, it broke his heart."[4] In his final years, he had been dreaming of those books, of being surrounded by them, many newly printed and filled with "strange arguments."[5]

It is not known exactly when he died. The date usually given is December 1608. However, in his diary, a picture of a skull is scribbled in the margin next to 26 March 1609, and the note "Jno Δ." Dee used the triangle, the Greek letter delta, as his personal insignia. Perhaps this is the day he departed on his long and last journey, dutifully noted in Dee's customary manner by John Pontois.

He was buried at Mortlake Church, "middest of the chancel, a little towards the south side," recalled Goodwife Faldo, the woman who would warmly remember the "welbeloved & respected" Dee so many decades later.[6] There was a gravestone, but it is long gone, as is his "cottage." Part of the site is now covered with a small plot of grass and a bench overlooking the River Thames.

Thus Dr. John Dee passed through the curtain of existence and into the company of angels. "Now is there a veil drawn before all," as Kelley once put it at the close of an action, "and all things appear far beautifuller than ever they did."

EPILOGUE

⚜

O NE day in 1642, Robert Jones, a confectioner living at the sign of the Plough in London's Lombard Street, decided to go with his wife, Susannah, to Addle Street, a lane running up from Castle Baynard, the great Norman fort on the banks of the Thames.[1] The street was lined with joiners' shops, and Mr. and Mrs. Jones were out to buy some "household stuff." Their eyes alighted on an item that particularly took their fancy: a "Chest of Cedar wood, about a yard & a half long." The lock and hinges were of such "extraordinary neat work," the chest "invited them to buy it."

They discovered from the shopkeeper that the chest had come from the household of Thomas Woodall, a royal surgeon.[2] Woodall had apparently inherited it from his father, also a surgeon. No doubt impressed by the provenance, Mr. and Mrs. Jones bought the chest and took it back to their home on Lombard Street, where it was to remain, undisturbed, for twenty years.

In 1662, Mr. and Mrs. Jones decided to move the chest to a different position in the room. When they lifted it, they heard a rattle "toward the right hand end, under the Box or Till thereof, & by shaking it, were fully satisfied it was so." Mr. Jones decided to investigate further. In the base of the box, he discovered a "small crevice" or slit. He stuck a knife into it, and a hidden drawer popped out. Inside he found a collection of books, papers, and a small casket containing a necklace of beads made of olive stones, from which dangled a wooden cross.

The Joneses leafed through the books and papers so secretively and devoutly stored for all those years, but could make no sense of them. They had Latin titles such as *48 Claves Angelicae* (The 48 angelic keys), and contained prose written in gibberish, word squares, hieroglyphs, and tables. Mr. and Mrs. Jones put the pile to one side.

Their maid came upon the papers, and thought them particularly suitable for the lining of pie tins and "other like uses." She had worked her way through about half the pile before her employers noticed what she was doing. They put the surviving documents back in the chest, and then forgot about them once more.

Mr. Jones died in 1664. Two years later, the Great Fire of London broke out. As panic spread through the surrounding streets, Widow Jones gathered together as many possessions as she could carry and took them to safe lodgings at Moorfields, to the north of the City wall. The chest was too heavy to move, and was left to be consumed along with her home. However, as the flames started to lick Lombard Street, Mrs. Jones decided to remove the mysterious papers from the chest and take them with her.

Soon after, Mrs. Jones remarried. Her new husband was Thomas Wale, a warder at the Tower of London. She showed him the papers, and, though he could make no more sense of them than she, he recognized their potential value. He knew of a man with an interest in such works, a lawyer and collector called Elias Ashmole.

Ashmole was an expert in astrology, alchemy, and other occult matters. He was also one of the most important antiquarians of the seventeenth century, his collection forming the basis of the magnificent Ashmolean Museum in Oxford. On 20 August 1672, while he was with his friend the astrologer William Lilly at Lilly's country house in Hersham, Surrey, his servant Samuel Story turned up with a parcel containing the papers preserved by Wale's new wife. Wale wondered if Ashmole would be prepared to swap them for a volume on the Order of the Garter.

When Ashmole unwrapped the parcel, he immediately knew his answer. He rushed up to London to meet Mr. Wale, where he heard the story of the papers' discovery. It confirmed his hopes. John Woodall, father of the surgeon Thomas and former owner of the chest, had been the last known custodian of the collection of Dr. John Dee.[3] The books hidden in the chest were Dee's books of mysteries.

Ashmole was fascinated by Dee, intending at one point to write a life of the philosopher. It was he who had visited Goodwife Faldo, and extracted her fond reminiscences of Mortlake's "welbeloved & respected" magus.

Over the coming months, he poured over Dee's strange manuscripts, in the hope of revealing their secrets.

> This night I began to consider of the 12 Names of God, being the first in the Book[4] & found them in the middle lines of each of the 4 great Squares in the first Table on either side about the black Cross. When I was in bed I conceived the Characters of divine Imposition in the Liber Scientiae Auxilij & Victoriae Terrestris, (which formerly I had found extracted from out ye second Table placed at the beginning of the Book) by taking the Letters in the Squares about the black Cross of the first Table, (which the several Characters traced out) might be a word, which next morning I found to be so.[5]

Despite the occasional nocturnal glimmer of understanding, he made little headway.

*   *   *

ASHMOLE'S WERE NOT the only manuscripts of Dee's to surface. Some time in the 1610s or 1620s, another antiquarian and collector, Sir Robert Cotton, decided to excavate the fields around Dee's house, where he found a stash of documents. They were badly damaged by damp, but still legible.

They moldered away for years before Sir Robert's son, Sir Thomas Cotton, gave them to the scholar Meric Casaubon, urging him to copy them before they disintegrated.[6] Meric did as he was asked, and discovered that they contained detailed transcripts of Dee's spiritual conversations, including every sensational detail concerning Dee's audience with Rudolf, and the "cross-matching" agreement with Kelley. After consulting the bishop of Armagh on the theological implications of releasing such apparently diabolical dialogues, Casaubon decided to publish the papers. They appeared in 1659 under the title *A True and Faithful Relation of What Passed for Many Years Between Dr John Dee and Some Spirits*.

The *True and Faithful Relation* brought Dee's spiritual activities to public notice for the first time, and set the seal on his reputation.

"What is here presented unto thee (Christian Reader)," Casaubon's preface began, was a book "that might be deemed and termed *A Work of Darkness.*"[7]

Casaubon believed that Dee had been deluded rather than evil, and justified the publication of these mystical actions on the grounds that they would act as a warning against "presumptuous unlawfull wishes and desires" being entertained by other philosophers. Dee's delusion did not lie in his belief in the spirits' existence. No learned man, in Casaubon's opinion, "can entertain such an opinion (simply and seriously) that there be no Divels or Spirits." Dee's "only (but great and dreadful) error" was that he "mistook false lying spirits for Angels of Light, the Divel of Hell (as we commonly term him) for the God of Heaven."

Subsequent opinion was less sympathetic. In his burlesque poem *Hudibras*, the poet and satirist Samuel Butler wrote:

> *Kelly did all his feats upon*
> *The Devil's looking-glass, a stone,*
> *Where playing with him at bo-peep*
> *He solved all problems ne'er so deep.*[8]

Thomas Smith, author of the first biography of Dee, published in 1707, considered his subject insane, while the historian Anthony á Wood found himself "overwhelm'd with melancholy" when contemplating Dee's spiritual adventures.

From there, it was further downhill. In the eighteenth century Dee was dismissed as "extremely credulous, extravagantly vain," in the nineteenth as "weak and wrongheaded . . . all but an idiot withal," in France he was accused of *fourberie*, trickery, in Germany of being a "Dummkopf."[9]

Such a Dummkopf deserved no place in history, and Dee would subsequently be erased from the annals of Elizabethan policy, geography, mathematics, astronomy, just about every one of the innumerable fields that he influenced. The message contained in the surviving books of mysteries given to Ashmole, if they contained one, remained undisclosed.

The one place where Dee's reputation thrived was in the world of modern mysticism. He has been credited with being a founder of the Rosicrucian movement, a secret brotherhood claiming to possess esoteric wisdom handed down from ancient time. In the nineteenth century he was declared to be an English Nostradamus, the prophet of an earthquake that would destroy London in 1842, and a devastating plague expected in 1899.[10] He was adopted by the Victorian "Hermetic Order of the Golden Dawn," hailed as the originator of "Enochian magic," brought back to life by Gustav Meyrink in his novel *The Angel from the West Window* and commemorated by Aleister Crowley, who considered himself to be, among many strange things, the reincarnation of Kelley.

"'Tis magic, magic that hath ravish'd me," cried Marlowe's Faust at the moment he submits to the forces of the occult. And so it had Dr. Dee's reputation.

In more recent years, various researchers have attempted to rescue Dee from the hands of the hard-headed rationalists and muddle-headed mystics. The most influential has been eminent historian Dame Frances Yates, who argued that Dee was the true Renaissance man. Yates showed that Renaissance thinking, far from being overcome with rationalism, was suffused with magic, and Dee embodied this better than any other English thinker. "John Dee has to the full the dignity, the sense of operational power, of the Renaissance magus," she proclaimed. "And he is a very clear example of how the will to operate, stimulated by Renaissance magic, could pass into, and stimulate, the will to operate in genuine applied science."[11] In other words, natural magic as practiced by Dee did not forestall the coming scientific revolution, but enabled it. It is certainly true that most of the figures now associated with the foundation of modern science had interests similar to Dee. Copernicus cited the mystic prophet Hermes Trismegistus to justify his heliocentric universe, Tycho Brahe wrote treatises on the astrological significance of his astronomical discoveries, Johann Kepler devised his theory of elliptical orbits in an effort to confirm Pythagorean notions of cosmic harmony, and Isaac Newton tried to discover the secret of the Philosopher's Stone.

Others have emphasized Dee's more practical, political side. William Sherman criticized the portrayal of Dee as a "Merlin at the Tudor court" and offered instead a less picturesque but perhaps more realistic image of him as "the first English think-tank . . . a retailer of special (often secret) knowledge, an 'intelligencer' in the broadest sense."[12]

But even the most matter-of-fact assessment of Dee cannot completely dispel the aura of mystery. An understanding of Tudor political discourse, even of Renaissance magic, may shed light on Dee's work, his intellectual legacy, his philosophical milieu, but it makes no sense of his eager embrace of Kelley's astonishing phantasmagoria. Many Renaissance thinkers dabbled in magic, some even conjured up spirits, but none other than Dee claimed to summon the divine secrets of the universe from angels and archangels.

Was, then, Dee a dupe? On 8 May 1583, Kelley had a vision of a beautiful palace out of which came a "tall well favoured man, very richly apparelled with a brave hat and a feather on his head," followed by "a great number, all like courtiers." The man said: "How pitiful a thing is it, when the wise are deluded." Was that a teasing reference to Dee?

There is plenty of evidence that Dee had to some extent fallen under Kelley's spell. His unruly, retrograde skryer obviously had a way of captivating his clients, particularly men like Dyer, Cecil, Rozmberk, and Rudolf, and Dee was by no means immune. However, Dee's faith in Kelley cannot be solely ascribed to the skryer's charms. The sophistication of the Enochian language, the huge cast of spiritual characters, the flamboyant personalities, the sheer quantity of material, all conjured up from a stone, apparently without recourse to prompts or prewritten scripts, were compelling.

It was not just the intensity of Kelley's visions that made them so bewitching. It was the way they fitted into the context in which they were delivered. There was the local setting: the room, the ritual, the light, the magical apparatus, the intense aura of piety produced by Dee's rituals, prayers, and supplications. And there was a global context, to which Dee could rightly claim to be, at least in England, uniquely sensitive. His collection of books and scientific instruments, his contacts with Europe's most powerful monarchs and courts, his philosophical, geographical, political and mystical works, his imprisonment, his religious struggles, his involvement with ciphers and spies, all of these meant that he could see as well as anyone, perhaps better, that the world was in a state of transformation, and the angels captured this perfectly.

"Behold, these things shall God bring to pass by his hands whose mind he hath now newly set on fire," the spirit Medicina Dei had said. "The corners and straights of the earth shall be measured to the depth: and strange shall be the wonders that are creeping in to new worlds. Time shall be altered, with the difference of day and night. All things have grown almost to their fullness."[13] Dee had seen with his own eyes the world spill off the edge of the map, and the universe burst out of its shell. And as the cosmos had spread into infinity, so he had seen his, everyone's position in it correspondingly reduced. For the first time in more than a thousand years, anyone with the learning to see (and there were still very few) beheld a universe that no longer revolved around the world, and a world that no longer revolved around humans.

Dee's magical journey with Kelley can be seen as a response to this traumatic demotion. Magic was the way that people could be reconnected with an alienated cosmos. It was the hidden mechanism by which God operated in the world, the invisible force that joined the spiritual realm to the material one. It was the continuum between life and death, the penumbra of human existence, the "strange participation," to use Dee's phrase, in which the body and spirit, the natural and the artificial, the real and the imagined were engaged.[14]

Dee had hoped that science, and in particular mathematics, would reveal the mechanism of this strange participation. Math would, he thought, correct the cosmic misalignment, restore the divine order. His proposals for calendar reform, synchronizing human time with divine "radix" of time, the birth of Christ, were a practical example of this.

"O comfortable allurement, O ravishing persuasion," he wrote in his preface to Euclid, "to deal with a Science, whose Subject is so

Ancient, so pure, so excellent, so surmounting all creatures, so used of the Almighty and incomprehensible wisdom of the Creator, in the distinct creation of all creatures: in all their distinct parts, properties, natures, and virtues, by order, and most absolute number, brought, from Nothing to the Formality of their being and state."[15]

But, as Dee himself came to realize, not even the "ravishing persuasion" of mathematics was equal to the task. As he told Emperor Rudolf, he had spent forty years "with great pain, care and cost" trying to discover the secrets of the universe, and mankind's position within it. "And I found (at length) that neither any man living, nor any book I could yet meet withal, was able to teach me those truths I desired and longed for."

There was only one other way to turn, to God himself. Through his angels, he would guide us back to the universe we were leaving behind. This was Dee's hope, and Kelley's promise. Together, they would navigate a northwest passage to universal truth before, with the onset of the modern, mechanistic age his own work helped to inaugurate, unity would become irrecoverable, and the magic would go out of the world forever.

"If mankind had to choose between a universe that ignored him and one that noticed him to do him harm," warned the great scholar of Elizabethan literature, E. M. W. Tillyard, "it might well choose the second. Our own age need not begin congratulating itself on its freedom from superstition till it defeats a more dangerous temptation to despair."[16]

NOTES

✤

1. There are two copies, one in the BL MS Sloane 1782, f31, another in the Bod MS Ashmole 1788, f137; what follows is based on the latter, which was probably copied by Elias Ashmole.
2. Bod MS Laud Misc. 674, f74ʳ; see "Horoscopes and History," North.
3. *The History of London in Maps*, Barker and Jackson, p. 12.
4. Bod MS Ashmole 174 ff439–45.
5. John Dee did not acknowledge any brothers or sisters, though it is possible that he had a brother. Francis Dee, Bishop of Peterborough, was the son of either a brother or a cousin of John's. See *John Dee*, Calder, chapter 3, note 5.
6. According to John Aubrey, Dee's grandson described Roland as being a "vintner," see *Brief Lives*, Aubrey, p. 210 and note, but this was probably a reference to Dee's son, also called Roland. According to Aubrey, Ashmole recorded under which "sign," i.e., trading name, Roland traded, but the information is sadly illegible. A census document or "Book of Assessment" drawn up by the civic authorities identifies Roland Dee was a resident of the Tower Ward in 1548. See *CSP, Domestic, 1547–1580*, p. 621. Roland served an apprenticeship under William Strathorne and gained admittance to the Company of Mercers in 1536. See *Register: List of Mercers 1347 to 1914*, Mercers' Company, Mercers Hall, London; *Survey of London*, Stow, p. 152.
7. *Survey of London*, Stow, p. 157.
8. St. Dunstan's was destroyed in the Second World War. There is a view of it in the Agas map, showing the spire and churchyard. See *The A to Z of Elizabethan London*, Prockter and Taylor, p. 25.
9. All the mercers' buildings were destroyed in the Great Fire, rebuilt, and destroyed again in the Second World War.
10. A century and a half later, the first Astronomer Royal, John Flamsteed, would establish the Royal Observatory at the top of Greenwich

Hill and overlooking the palace, casting a horoscope to mark the moment that one of the world's most prestigious scientific institutions was founded.

11. See pedigree drawn up by Dee, BL MS Harleian 5835 f4–6. Sewer has sometimes been mistaken for "server."

12. Catherine had been previously married to Henry's brother, Prince Arthur, and according to Lev. 20:21, it was "unclean" for a man to "take his brother's wife . . . they shall be childless." When Henry had married Catherine, she had claimed that her union with Arthur had been unconsummated, so the biblical injunction did not apply. Henry now believed that the injunction must apply, as this would explain the failure of his marriage to Catherine to produce a male heir.

13. For an account of the Felipez episode, see *Catherine of Aragon*, Mattingly, p. 185f.

14. *Encyclopaedia*, William Caxton, quoted in *The Elizabethan World Picture*, Tillyard, p. 47. Caxton's calculations were probably based on Ptolemy's *Almagest*, or Campanus of Novara's thirteenth-century edition. Ptolemy put the distance of Saturn as 19,865 times the earth's radius. The stars lay "at a distance of five myriad myriad [i.e., 10,000 myriad] and 6,946 myriad stades and a third of a myriad stades" beyond that— around 50 million miles. See *Measuring the Universe*, Ferguson, p. 41.

15. See *Diaries*, entry for 1 February 1594, in Fenton, ed., p. 264 and note.

16. Bod MS Ashmole 356, Item 5. The tract is unsigned but attributed to Dee because the style of the handwriting matches his own. It carries later annotations, possibly added by Frances Sidney, Sir Philip's widow, who acquired it after her husband's death.

17. See *John Dee*, Calder, chapter 10, section 4.

18. *Ptolemy's Tetrabiblios*, Ashmand, pp. 59 and 18. For a more contemporary account of astrological practice, which largely conforms to Ptolemy, I have also referred to *Christian Astrology*, Lilly, in particular book 1, pp. 25–93.

CHAPTER II

1. See "Erasmians and Mathematicians at Cambridge in the Early Sixteenth Century," Rose, pp. 47–55, and *A History of the University of Cambridge*, Leader, pp. 294–336.

2. *CR*, chapter 1.

3. *Brief Lives*, Aubrey, p. xxix. Quoted in "The Mistaking of 'the Mathematicks' for Magic in Tudor and Stuart England," Zetterberg, p. 85.

4. *Stars, Minds and Fate*, North, pp. 187–192; "The Harmonic Roots of Newtonian Science," Penelope Gouk, and "Newton, Matter, and Magic," John Henry, *Let Newton Be!*, Fauvel, pp. 100–125 and 126–145.

5. *Praeface*, Aii^v.

6. "Peace," Aristophanes, pp. 160–175.

7. Dee mentions a work entitled *Trochilica inventa mea*, written in 1558; it has not survived. *CR*, chapter 6, item 27.

8. See "The Academic Drama at Cambridge: Extracts from College Records," Moore Smith.

9. *CR*, chapter 1.

10. *Winter's Tale*, V, iii, 85–91.

CHAPTER III

1. See *Diaries*, Fenton, p. 305 and note. The folio by Ashmole entitled "A transcript of some notes Dr Dee had entered in Stoffler's Ephemerides beginning 1543 and ending 1556" is at MS Ashmole 423, f294.

2. *CR*, chapter 1.

3. Quoted in *The Civilization of Europe*, Hale, p. 282.

4. Ascham used Louvain as the benchmark to assess Cheke's achievements at Cambridge. See *The Cambridge Connection*, Hudson, p. 54.

5. Like many Flemish scholars, Frisius had adopted a Latin name. He was born in Frieseland as Reiner Gemma.

6. *History of Mathematical Sciences*, Ivor Grattan-Guinness, p. 194.

7. Museum of the History of Science at Oxford, accession no. 33–73.

8. Mercator was born Gerard de Cremer or Kremer.

9. This projection did not mean that medieval cartographers believed the world to be flat, as has sometimes been assumed.

10. For example, the Beatus and Henry of Mainz world maps. See *Medieval Maps*, Harvey, pls. 17 and 18.

11. Quoted in *John Dee*, Sherman, p. 6. See "Propaedeumata aphoristica," Dee.

12. *John Dee's Library Catalogue*, Roberts and Watson, #768.

13. Dee outlines the principles of the device in *CR*, chapter 7.

14. *John Dee*, Sherman, p. 5 and fig. 3. An annotated facsimile of the album is held at Pembroke College, Cambridge, MS 2.113.

15. *CR*, chapter 2.

16. See *Annals*, Strype, volume 2, pt. 1, p. 529.

17. For example, a copy of Petrus Ramus's *Prooemium mathematicam* contains inscription indicating that Sir William Pickering sent Dee the book from France; see *John Dee's Library Catalogue*, Roberts and Watson, p. 93.

18. *CR*, chapter 2.

19. *CR*, chapter 2.Though no independent account of Dee's lecture has survived, he seems to have had various testimonies on the event, as he mentions presenting them to the commissioners sent by the queen in 1592.

20. *John Dee's Library Catalogue*, Roberts and Watson, pp. 93 and 3.

21. *Diaries*, October 1547, Fenton, p. 305.

22. *CSP*, Spanish, volume 9, pp. 146 and 222. Quoted in *The Later Tudors*, Penry Williams, p. 42.

23. *De Caelestis Globi amplissimis commoditatibus* (1550) and *De Planetarum, Inerrantium stellarum, Nubiumque a centro terrae distantiis: & stellarum omnium veris inveniendis magnitudinibus* (1551).

24. Dee notes this in his copy of Cardano's *De supplemento almanach* (*John Dee's Library Catalogue*, Roberts and Watson, #440). A transcription of the notes appears in "Books from John Dee's Library," Prideaux, pp. 137–138.

25. Quoted in *Dictionary of National Biography*.

26. Calder, chapter 4, note 34.

27. The information about Dee's connection with Pembroke comes from his copy of Girolamo Cardano's *Libelli quinque*. See "Books from John Dee's Library," Prideaux, pp. 137–138.

28. He was the first man of nonroyal blood to bear the title of duke. See *Children of England*, Weir, p. 131.

29. In the tribute in his "Praeface" to Dudley's eldest son, also called John, Dee was clearly writing as a teacher fondly remembering a student. Discussing the use of mathematics in the military sciences, he lauded "the Noble, the Courageous, the loyal, the Courteous John, Earl of Warwick." He went on to write about how hard young John had worked to understand "feats and Arts" that would be of service to his country, an achievement that no one, other than Dee himself, "can so perfectly and truly report."

30. *Index Britanniae scriptorum*, Poole.

CHAPTER IV

1. Dee noted this in the margin of a volume, now in the Folger Shakespeare Library in Washington, which contains a number of mystical texts by authors such as Ficino. See *John Dee's Library Catalogue*, Roberts and Watson, pp. 9 and 85.
2. The wedding was on Whit Sunday, which fell on 21 May by the Julian calendar.
3. Quoted in *Children of England*, Weir, p. 153.
4. *Acts of the Privy Council*, volume 4, 1552–1554, entry for 21 August 1553. The entry reads: "A lettre to the Lieutenant of the Tower willing hym to . . . send hither Thomas Thirlande, John Tomson and Rolan Dye [Dee], to be ordered by the Lords of the Counsaill." Thirlande may have been Thomas Thurland, a canon, and John Tomson an auditor of the Royal Exchequer. Dye was the spelling of Dee used for both John and Roland in the council's records.
5. Population statistics are unreliable for this period, as there was no official census. The estimates are taken from *Population and Metropolis: The Demography of London 1580–1650*, R. Finlay, Cambridge, 1981, and "The Population of London, 1550–1700: A Review of Published Evidence," *The London Journal* 15 (1990): 111–128.
6. *Letters and Papers*, ed. Gairdner, 1903, volume 19, pt. 1, p. 371.
7. *Original Letters*, Ellis, p. 34.
8. See *Children of England*, Weir, p. 262.
9. The *Catholic Encyclopedia*, Herbermann, entry on Bonner.
10. The *Catholic Encyclopedia*, Herbermann, quotes these lines in its entry on Bonner, which tries to rehabilitate him by pointing out he was in fact reprimanded by the council for being too slow to prosecute those sent to him for examination.
11. *Acts and Monuments*, Foxe, volume 7, p. 80.
12. *Acts and Monuments*, Foxe, volume 7, p. 82.

CHAPTER V

1. For Englefeld, *CSP*, Domestic, volume 6, Addenda 1547–1565, p. 342, and his exile from England, *Annals*, Strype, volume 1, pt. 2, p. 50.
2. *Acts of the Privy Council*, volume 4, 1552–1554.
3. Dee described Christopher Cary as "my scholer" in a marginal note in his copy of *Ars demonstrativa* by the Spanish philosopher and mystic Raymond Lully.
4. *CR*, chapter 5.

5. *Brief Lives*, Aubrey, p. 167.
6. In 1574, Elizabeth's chief secretary of state William Cecil intercepted a letter that listed the names of English exiles in Spain who had been given pensions by the king of Spain. Among the names listed are Dee's old enemy Frances Englefeld and "M. Pridieux." See *Annals*, Strype, volume 1, pt. 2, pp. 53–54.
7. See *The Diary of Henry Machyn*, Machyn, entry for 4 January 1553 and notes.
8. There were several reports circulating at this time about wax effigies of the queen; another was apparently unearthed at the house of a priest in Islington, who was reputed to be a conjuror, see *Annals*, Strype, volume 2, pt. 2, p. 206.
9. Under the treaty solemnizing Mary's marriage to Philip, she remained sovereign of England.
10. *Acts and Monuments*, Foxe, volume 7, p. 126.
11. See "Necessary Advertisement," Dee.
12. *Acts of the Privy Council*, volume 4, 1552–1554.
13. *Upton*, Hurle, p. 31.

CHAPTER VI

1. *Survey of London*, Stow, p. 312. The mound, called Mount Calvery, is just south of Islington and shown on the Agas map of London.
2. *London Encyclopaedia*, p. 757.
3. *Acts and Monuments*, Foxe, volume 7, p. 605ff.
4. *Acts and Monuments*, Foxe, volume 7, p. 612.
5. *Acts and Monuments*, Foxe, volume 7, p. 613.
6. *CR*, chapter 5.
7. *Acts and Monuments*, Foxe, volume 7, p. 736.
8. Dee noted the date of Bonner's death at Marshalsea on 5 September 1569, ironically in the margin of his copy of *De Scriptoribus Anglicae*, written by the radical Protestant antiquarian and dramatist John Bale. The book survives in the library of Christ Church, Oxford (ref W.b.4.8); *John Dee's Catalogue*, Roberts and Watson, #274.
9. The book was a mathematical treatise by Andreas Alexander, which Dee had bought in 1551. *John Dee's Library Catalogue*, Roberts and Watson, p. 4.
10. On Henry's theological conservatism, see, for example, *Henry VIII*, Scarisbrick, pp. 408–409.
11. Quoted in *Elizabeth the Queen*, Weir, p. 54.
12. *Catholic Record Society*, Miscellanea, volume 7, 1911, pp. 52–53.

13. Sir Stephen Powle to Francis Walsingham, 8 April 1587, Bodleian MS Tanner 309, ff67b–68.

CHAPTER VII

1. *Cambridge Antiquarian Communications*, volume III, p. 157. Quoted in *John Dee*, Calder, chapter 5, §1.
2. BL MS Cotton Vitell. C.VII., f 310 et seq; printed in *Chetham Miscellany I*, p. 46ff. It is possible that the work appeared a year later, as New Year's Day in England was still officially 25 March. However, Dee often adopted the Continental practice of observing New Year's Day on 1 January.
3. *John Dee's Library Catalogue*, Roberts and Watson, pp. 19–20.
4. *John Dee's Library Catalogue*, Roberts and Watson, p. 6.
5. Wayne Shumaker published a translation of *Propaedeumata Aphoristica* in his *John Dee on Astronomy*, Berkeley, 1978. This volume has a useful introductory essay on Dee's mathematics and physics and his place in the scientific revolution by J. L. Heilbron. Much of what follows comes from Nicholas Clulee's discussion of Dee's natural philosophy in *John Dee's Natural Philosophy: Between Science and Religion*, p. 40ff.
6. *Religion*, Thomas, p. 341.
7. *MP*, ci^r. Dee observed that this phenomenon "is not by me first noted, but by one *John Baptist de Benedictis*."

CHAPTER VIII

1. *Chronicles*, Holinshed, volume 6, p. 492.
2. Arguably Henry I's daughter Matilda was the first queen regnant, but she was never crowned.
3. Quoted in *The Later Tudors*, Williams, p. 427.
4. Quoted in *Religion*, Thomas, p. 405.
5. *Troilus and Cressida*, Shakespeare, I, 3, 101–103, 109–110.
6. See *Acts and Monuments*, Foxe, volume 7, p. 642.
7. This information is contained in a private letter to Robin Cousins by the Rev. B. J. Bennett of Leadenham.
8. Quoted in *Elizabeth the Queen*, Weir, p. 31.
9. Elizabeth fashioned herself as a "prince" rather than a princess, the term then applied to the abstract idea of a monarch's role as much as a king or queen's male offspring.
10. There is no record relating to Roland Dee's death. John was admitted to the company of mercers by patrimony in 1555, which may indicate

that Roland died then or soon after. John's eldest son, Arthur, was also admitted by patrimony in 1605, when he was twenty-six, just three years before John died.

11. *Annals*, Strype, volume 1, pt. 2, p. 44.

CHAPTER IX

1. He did publish a new edition of his *Propaedeumata*, dedicated to Elizabeth.
2. See *Giordano Bruno*, Yates, p. 93. A full discussion of the Cabala is found in *Major Trends in Jewish Mysticism*, Scholem.
3. *T&FR*, Preface, p. 23.
4. The paper was entitled *Cabbalae Hebraicae compendiosa tabella*. See Dee's list of unpublished works in *CR*, #29.
5. In *Religion*, p. 69, Thomas points out that the distinction between a prayer and a spell was still unclear in Dee's time, being the subject of intense debate among sixteenth-century Protestant theologians, who argued that words had no power in themselves, but only if heard by God.
6. When Dee was in Antwerp on another occasion he asked his friend Abraham Ortelius to direct correspondence via the Birkmanns' servants in Antwerp. See "John Dee and the Secret Societies," Heisler; *Ecclesiae Londino-Batavae Archivum*, volume 1, pp. 157–160 and 787–791.
7. *Evangelium regni*, Niclaes, pp. 3–4.
8. See, for example, *John Dee's Library Catalogue*, Roberts and Watson, p. 13; "John Dee and the Secret Societies," Heisler. Hamilton wrote that Dee was "the one English scholar who may well have sympathised with Continental Familism," *The Family of Love*, Hamilton, p. 154.
9. See *Renaissance Curiosa*, Shumaker, p. 92ff. Shumaker's account of Trithemius's life is based on Klaus Arnold's biography, published in 1971.
10. *Renaissance Curiosa*, Shumaker, p. 97, Shumaker's translation.
11. One suggestion is that the Hungarian was Johannes Sambucus (János Zsámboky in Hungarian), who had connections with the publishing trade in Antwerp, but he was not a nobleman. Another possibility is Count Balthasar Batthyany, a generous patron with an interest in alchemy. I am grateful to the Hungarian Dee scholar György Endre Szônyi for his advice on this subject.
12. PRO, State Papers Domestic 12/27, no. 63. It is printed in *Notes and Queries*, ed. J. E. Bailey, series 5, volume 11, 1879, pp. 401–402 and 422–423.

13. *Europe and England in the Sixteenth Century*, Morris, p. 17.
14. *Steganographia*, Trithemius, p. 27. This example comes from "Solved," Reeds, p. 2.
15. *Renaissance Curiosa*, Shumaker, p. 95, Shumaker's translation.
16. *Steganographia*, Trithemius, p. 95.
17. For example, D. P. Walker, one of the most influential scholars on Renaissance magic, wrote, "The Third Book, which is unfinished, does not, like the other two, contain any examples of enciphered messages; one is told to say the message over the picture of a planetary angel at the moment determined by complicated astronomical calculations. It seems most unlikely that these could be disguised directions for encipherment or any kind of secret writing." *Spiritual and Demonic Magic*, Walker, p. 87. Walker heavily influenced Frances Yates, who echoed his assessment of the *Steganographia* in her *Giordano Bruno and the Hermetic Tradition*, p. 145.
18. He published his results in "Schwarzweisse Magie. Der Schlüssel zum dritten Buch der Steganographia des Trithemius," *Daphnis* 25, no. 1 (1996).
19. "Solved," Reeds, p. 14. Reeds discovered that the phrase was a pangram by typing it into an Internet search engine, which brought up a reference to a manuscript held in the library of the Benedictine Abbey in Melk, Austria, cataloged by Christine Glassner.
20. Cecil was certainly no materialist, and firmly believed in alchemy, as was shown by his repeated attempts to lure Dee's skryer, Edward Kelley, back from Bohemia when news reached England of his ability to transform base metals into gold at will.
21. *John Dee's Catalogue*, Roberts and Watson, pp. 9 and 76.
22. There is no evidence to link Dee directly with this aspect of government business, but there are some suggestive hints. One is an entry in his diary, in which he mentions a visit by a "Mr Bacon, Mr Phillips of the custom house." The former was probably Francis Bacon; the latter may have been Thomas Phillips or Phelippes, Walsingham's chief cipher expert. Alan Stewart, coauthor of a biography of Bacon and editor of Bacon's works, believes Phillips was more likely to have been Thomas's father, William, or possibly another of William's children, whose name is unknown.
23. The history of the Voynich MS, named after a collector who found it in 1912, is convoluted. A letter attached to the first page, written by the Prague scientist Johannes Marcus Marci in 1665, states that the MS was sold to Rudolf for 600 ducats, and in October 1586, when Dee is in contact with Rudolf, he records having 630 ducats, a significant

sum, particularly during a period when he was generally short of money. Also Arthur Dee reported to Sir Thomas Browne that while in Bohemia his father owned a book "containing nothing but Hieroglyphicks" (see Bod MS Ashmole 1788, ff151–152). Roberts and Watson consider the foliation to be in Dee's hand (*John Dee's Catalogue*, p. 172) but others have contested this. The volume is now in the Yale Library, ref MS Beinecke 408.

/ CHAPTER X

1. *MH*, pp. 115 and 117.
2. *CR*, chapter 3, section 6.
3. From the preface of *General and Rare Memorials*, Dee, ∈.j^v.
4. *MH*, p. 121.
5. Dee wrote in the *Compendious Rehearsal* that "if I would disclose unto her the secretes of that booke, she would *et discere et facere*," chapter 4.
6. *A Translation of John Dee's "Monas Hieroglyphica,"* Josten, Ambix, p. 119.
7. See *John Dee*, Sherman, p. 144. Others, e.g., "John Dee," Graham Yewbrey, linked Dee's concept of cosmopolitical with his magical philosophy.
8. *CR*, chapter 3, section 6.
9. *The Praise of Dancing*, vs. 16.
10. A full account of the episode, enacted at Woodstock, is contained in *At the Court of Queen Elizabeth: The Life and Lyrics of Sir Edward Dyer*, Sargent, pp. 30–34.
11. *CR*, chapter 4; *Diaries*, 10 October 1580.
12. *Astrological Discourse*, Harvey, A3^r.
13. *CR*, chapter 4.
14. *CR*, chapter 4.
15. See the British Library catalogue entry for Grudius's *Constitutiones clarissimi . . . Ordinis Velleris Aurei: e Gallico in Latinum conversae*, written under the auspices of the Order of the Golden Fleece.
16. *Richard II*, III, 2.

CHAPTER XI

1. *The Environs of London*, Lysons, volume 1, p. 364.
2. There are two versions of this story. This one comes from Ashmole, the other, in which Dee is said to have demonstrated the eclipse to a

Polish prince, is in Aubrey. The dating of this event comes from Dee's diary (entry for 25 February 1598), though he does not mention Faldo. See *Elias Ashmole*, Josten, pp. 1298–1300.

3. "Mortlake Revisited," Cousins, p. 109.

4. The earliest surviving reference to Mortlake by Dee is an inscription in a copy of his *Monas Hieroglyphica*, which is dated Mortlake 18 September 1566 (Hunterian collection, Glasgow, ref R 6.15), see *John Dee's Catalogue*, Roberts and Watson, p. 10.

5. Chancery Proceedings, series 2, bundle 49, no. 44. See *Tudor Geography*, Taylor, p. 107.

6. An eight-page scrawled and incomplete catalog of his collection drawn up by Dee between 1557 and 1559 lists around 320 books and 32 manuscripts. See *John Dee's Catalogue*, Roberts and Watson, p. 8.

7. *John Dee's Catalogue*, Roberts and Watson, pp. 238–243.

8. *John Dee*, Sherman, p. 41.

9. Miniature timepieces were precious rarities in Dee's day; a tiny clock mounted in a bracelet was given by the earl of Leicester to Queen Elizabeth as a New Year's gift in 1572, believed to be the first wristwatch.

10. *Diaries*, 9 February 1581, 1 August 1583, 5 April 1592, 3 June 1583.

11. *John Dee*, Sherman, p. 128. The *Synopsis* has never been published. In chapter 6 of his book, Sherman provides the first detailed study of this important document, which has lain more or less untouched since it was presented to the government. It is now in the British Library, MS Cotton Charter XIII, art. 39. It has suffered fire damage along its upper edge.

12. *John Dee*, Sherman, p. 160.

13. For drawing up the queen's "title royal" to foreign dominions, "I have refused an hundred poundes in money offred by some subjectes of this kingdome," *CR*, chapter V, §8.

14. Quoted in *John Dee*, Calder, chapter 6, §7.

15. *Annals*, Strype, volume 2, pt. 1, p. 520.

16. *Diaries*, 11 May 1592.

17. For the influence of Paracelsus on modern medicine, see *The Greatest Benefit*, Porter, pp. 201–205. Dee's alchemical notes for 1581 are at Bod MS Rawlinson D241. See "Paracelsian Medicine in John Dee's Alchemical Diaries," Szulakowska, pp. 29–30.

18. *CR*, chapter 4, §6.

19. The letter is now in BL MS Lansdowne 19 art. 38; see also *Annals*, Strype, volume 2, pt. 1, pp. 523–525.

20. *Richard Hakluyt*, Parks, p. xi.

21. "The Conditions of Life for the Masses," Rowlands, p. 53.
22. See *Religion*, Thomas, pp. 279–280.
23. *John Dee's Library Catalogue*, Roberts and Watson, #215 and #459.
24. See *A Collection of Letters*, Halliwell, pp. 15–16.
25. *Natural Magick*, 1589 edition, book 20, volume 8, pp. 405–406. Quoted in Calder, chapter 8, note 7.
26. BL MS Lansdowne MS 19 art 38.

CHAPTER XII

1. "The Cartographic Lure of the Northwest Passage," Richard I. Ruggles, in *Meta Incognita*, Symons, p. 181.
2. *Tudor Geography*, Taylor, p. 7.
3. *Voyages and Discoveries*, Hakluyt, p. 60; *CR*, chapter 7.
4. *Voyages and Discoveries*, pp. 62–66.
5. See *Tudor Geography*, Taylor, p. 91, for the links between Dee and Chancellor. She suggests that Chancellor, "the first great English pilot," worked with Dee on astronomy while both were in the household of Sir Henry Sidney, the duke of Northumberland's son-in-law.
6. *CSP*, East Indies, volume 2, p. 56.
7. "The voyage to Guinea in the year 1554. The Captain whereof was John Lok," *Voyages and Discoveries*, Hakluyt, pp. 66–68.
8. Both have a common root, "Atlas," the name of the god who, according to Greek legend, supported the world on his shoulders. "Atlantic" was by no means the only name given to the ocean. In various late medieval maps based on Ptolemy, such as that of Henry Martellus drawn in the early sixteenth century, it is identified as "Oceanus Occidental" (Western Ocean). In earlier maps, it is not defined as a single body of water, but rather as part of the seas that surround the three continents.
9. *Discourse*, Gilbert, ¶¶.iiij^r.
10. "John Dee's Role in Martin Frobisher's Northwest Enterprise," William H. Sherman, in *Meta Incognita*, Symons, p. 288. I am grateful to William Sherman for drawing my attention to this volume. Dee's copy of Fernando Columbus's book (under the title *Historie del S. D. Fernando Colombo; nelle quali s'ha particolare, & vera relatione della vita, & de' fatti dell'Ammiraglio D. Christoforo Colombo*) is now at BL 615.d.7.
11. "Michael Lok's Account of the Preparation. Written 1577," document 12, in *Tudor Geography*, Taylor, pp. 269–270.

12. *CSP*, East Indies, volume 2, p. 11. Estimates of the current value of Elizabethan sums of money are very hard to make, but a guide in this instance comes from the rates of pay sailors could expect. The master of a ship of this class could expect to earn just over £12 a year; nowadays a sailor of equivalent rank could obviously expect over a thousand times as much. See *The Safeguard of the Sea*, Rodger, p. 500.

13. *Tudor Geography*, Taylor, pp. 107–108.

14. A full inventory of the navigational charts and instruments bought for the expedition drawn up by Lok survives, see "The Navigation of the Frobisher Voyages," McDermott.

15. According to an anonymous tract published at the time, the distances involved in discovering the Northwest Passage meant such a mission would be "utterly impossible or not without extreme perils of life and expense of victuals." See "Cathay and the Way Thither: The Navigation of the Frobisher Voyages," J. McDermott and D. W. Waters, in *Meta Incognita*, Symons, p. 360.

16. Quoted in *Tudor Geography*, Taylor, p. 97.

17. *Diaries*, 17 May 1580. The entry reads: "At the Muscovy House for the Cathay voyage. I was almost provoked to anger by the haughty words of W. B., in the presence of the commissioners."

18. *Tudor Geography*, Taylor, document 9 (xi), pp. 262–263.

19. "John Dee's Role in Martin Frobisher's Northwest Enterprise," William H. Sherman, in *Meta Incognita*, Symons, pp. 292–293.

20. BL MS Cotton Otho E VIIII, f49. This document, which is damaged by fire, is Lok's account of the expedition, presumably drawn up after he had debriefed the crew on the *Gabriel*'s return. The only other account of the voyage is Hall's log book, which is contained in *Principal Navigations*, Hakluyt, volume 7, pp. 204–211. The Hakluyt version, which is mainly concerned with navigational issues, does not even mention the storm or the near sinking of Hall's ship.

21. The explorers later named it the Countess of Warwick Island, and has since come to be called by its Inuit name, Kodlunarn, situated in Countess of Warwick Bay, off Baffin Island.

22. *CSP*, East Indies, volume 2, pp. 55–56.

23. *Principal Navigations*, Hakluyt, volume 7, p. 210.

24. *CSP*, East Indies, volume 2, p. 14.

25. *CSP*, East Indies, volume 2, p. 14.

26. *A True Discourse*, Best, p. 51.

27. *CSP*, East Indies, volume 2, p. 18.

28. *Correspondence of Sir Philip Sidney*, Pears, pp. 118–119.

29. *Principal Navigations*, Hakluyt, volume 7, p. 211.
30. *CSP*, East Indies, volume 2, p. 20. The issue of taking prisoners was clearly a controversial one, as the plans were subject to continual change. A week before the fleet was due to set sail, the Privy Council announced that "no disordered person" was to be taken, but amended this to allow eight or ten "prisoners and condemned persons" to be taken.
31. BL MS Sloane 2442, f23ʳ. Quoted in "John Dee's Role in Martin Frobisher's Northwest Enterprise," William H. Sherman, in *Meta Incognita*, Symons, p. 295.
32. *Principal Navigations*, Hakluyt, volume 7, p. 214.
33. *Principal Navigations*, Hakluyt, volume 7, p. 218.
34. Schutz is described as an "Almain" in *CSP*, East Indies, volume 2, p. 34.
35. *Correspondence of Sir Philip Sidney*, Pears, p. 144.
36. See "Martin Frobisher, the Spaniards and a Sixteenth-Century Northern Spy," Bernard Allaire and Donald Hogarth, in *Meta Incognita*, Symons, pp. 575–588.
37. Allaire and Hogarth suggest the pseudo-sapphire may have been well-crystallized quartz, apatite, or white feldspar, and the false ruby red garnet. See "Martin Frobisher, the Spaniards and a Sixteenth-Century Northern Spy," p. 580.
38. For estimates of royal income during the Elizabethan period, see *The Later Tudors*, Penury Williams, p. 147.
39. Samples of the black stone are still visible in an Elizabethan wall lining Vicarage Lane in Dartford, London.

CHAPTER XIII

1. This is the reason that of all Latin American countries, Brazil is the only one with a Portuguese rather than Hispanic heritage.
2. Mercator's letter to Dee is now in BL MS Cotton Vitel. C. vii, f264ᵛ et seq. It has been translated and transcribed by Taylor in her paper "A letter dated 1577 from Mercator to John Dee."
3. See, for example, *Gloriana*, Roy Strong, p. 92.
4. *General and Rare Memorials*, Dee, Aiiijᵛ.
5. See *The Safeguard of the Sea*, Rodger, pp. 229 and 248.
6. *General and Rare Memorials*, Dee, Ciᵛ–C.ijʳ.
7. A sample of it, however, is apparently published in an appendix to *A Regiment for the Sea*, Taylor.
8. BL MS Cotton Vitellus C. VII, ff26–269.

9. See *Purchas his Pilgrims*, Purchas, volume 1, pp. 93–116.
10. BL Add. MSS 59681, f21. The original of the *Brytanici Imperii Limites* has been lost, but a copy made in c. 1583 has recently been acquired by the British Library. William Sherman was the first Dee scholar to study this manuscript in detail. See Sherman, pp. 182–192.
11. Ortelius's map of 1570 shows Norumbega as an area south of Hudson Bay and north of Virginia. See *The Mapping of America*, Schwartz and Ehrenberg, pp. 43 and 83. The word is thought to come from the Abnaki Indian term for quiet water between two rapids.
12. See *Diaries*, 28 March 1583, pp. 58 and 62.
13. See *Raising Spirits*, Wilding, p 43.
14. *Diaries*, 16 July 1582, p. 46.
15. *A Briefe Discourse of Royall Monarchie*, Charles Merbury, 1581. Quoted in *John Dee*, Sherman, p. 150.
16. *Diaries*, 22 September and 10 October 1580. In 1582, a "Murfin" was discovered to have forged documents he used to substantiate claims that he had uncovered a plot in Ireland to overthrow the queen; it seems possible that it was the same person. See *Annals*, Strype, volume 3, pt. 1, pp. 202–207.
17. *Diaries*, 17 September 1580, Fenton, p. 10.
18. *Diaries*, 7 October 1580.
19. *Diaries*, 10 October 1580.

CHAPTER XIV

1. *Diaries*.
2. In *Diaries*, Fenton suggests he may have been the Thomas Robinson who, according to *Alumni Cantabridgiensis*, Venn, matriculated from Caius College, Cambridge, in 1581 and wrote a poem about the philosopher's stone.
3. See *Athenae Oxoniensis*, Wood, volume 1, p. 279.
4. Bodleian MS Ashmole 972, a copy of Ashmole's *Theatricum Chemicum*, p. 479.
5. See "Revising a Biography," Bassnett.
6. There is a reference to Kelley having a "walking staff" in a lengthy note Dee wrote in one of his *Liber Mysteriorum*. See *T&FR*, p. 229 and *Diaries*, p. 140. Several times Dee refers to Kelley kneeling, though perhaps it was uncomfortable for him.
7. In a record of an action undertaken with Kelley on 4 May 1582, Dee wrote that Kelley (still under the assumed name of Talbot) refused to "put off his hat," which indicates on previous occasion he had done

so, which in turn suggests that even if he wore a cowl, he did not always do so in Dee's company.

8. This description appears in a letter from Christopher Parkins to Sir Robert Cecil, son of William Cecil, PRO SP 81/7, ff140 and 143–144. The letter is quoted in "Edward Kelley," Wilding, p. 17.

9. The story appears in *Histoire de la Philosophie Hermétique*, Paris, 1742, volume 1, pp. 306–307. See "Edward Kelley," Wilding, p. 2.

10. *Ancient Funerall Monuments*, Weever, pp. 45–46. The account is quoted in *T&FR*, postscript [fifty-fifth page of unpaginated preface]. Weever's lurid account is unconfirmed by other sources; however, it seems he was knowledgeable about Kelley, as in the same book he reveals that Kelley used the alias "Talbot." No other writer would make this identification until the publication of *The Private Diaries of Dr John Dee*, ed. James Orchard Halliwell, Camden Society, 1842. The accounts of Dee's séances with Kelley in *T&FR* do not use the name Talbot.

11. See *The Shakespeare Conspiracy*, Phillips and Keatman, p. 151. There appears to be no evidence to support the link between Kelley and Langton.

12. Bod MS Ashmole 1790, ff60–61; see also *Ashmole*, Josten.

13. *Diaries*, p. 46 and note, 16 July 1582.

14. It is possible Dee had heard of Kelley working as "Talbot" for Thomas Allen, the fellow scientist whose name was coupled with Dee's in a political pamphlet, as both were suspected of "figuring and conjuring" for Robert Dudley, earl of Leicester. The link between Kelley/Talbot and Thomas Allen is mentioned in only one source, *Athenae Oxoniensis*, Wood, volume 1, p. 639. The link between Dee and Allen is in *Leicester's Commonwealth*, 1641 ed., p. 71, from the expanded tract of 1585, *Discours de la Vie Abominable . . . (de) my Lorde de Lecestre Machaveliste*. Allen and Dee certainly knew each other, as Allen was appointed receiver for the Cathay Company once Lok was declared bankrupt.

15. *Religion*, Thomas, pp. 294–295.

CHAPTER XV

1. Brahe wrote about what he saw in *De Nova Stella*, published in 1573. What follows is mainly taken from *Tycho Brahe*, Dreyer, pp. 38–69.

2. "The Influence of Thomas Digges," Johnson, pp. 390–410.

3. *Opus Majus*, Bacon, volume 2, p. 582.

4. The apparition in Cassiopeia would now be recognized as a supernova, an exploding star, an astronomical event that is still regarded as a noteworthy rarity.

5. *Brahe*, Dreyer, pp. 38–71; *The Comet of 1577*, Hellman, p. 117.

6. "For the cosmos, [as] also the sun, is . . . the cause . . . without which nothing can be or come to be," *Hermetica*, Trismegistus, p. 30. Ironically, at around the same time as Copernicanism was confirmed, the status of Trismegistus as a contemporary of Moses was refuted by Isaac Casaubon, the father of Meric, the editor of Dee's mystical diaries.

7. Quoted in "Thomas Digges, the Copernican System," Johnson and Larkey, p. 111.

8. *Ephemeris anni 1557*, Dee.

9. The treatise was called *A Perfit Description of the Caelestiall Orbes according to the most aunciente doctrine of the Pythagoreans*, and was published as an appendix to a new edition of his father's work *Prognostication euerlasting*. Digges's contribution to modern astronomy, which was undoubtedly great and has been neglected, is discussed in "The Influence of Thomas Digges," Johnson, pp. 390–410.

10. *Polimanteia*, Covell, H3^r. The Puritan Clovell described astrologers as having "made themselves ridiculous to the whole world" through their prognostications concerning the new star and subsequent conjunctions.

11. The John Harvey quote appears in "The Fiery Trigon," Aston, p. 170. The conjunction of Saturn and Jupiter following that of 1583 would occur in 1603 in Aries. This was the year Elizabeth died and James VI of Scotland succeeded to the English throne.

12. *Ptolemy's Tetrabiblios*, trans. Ashmand, pp. 43–52.

13. *An Astrological Discourse*, Richard Harvey, p. 8. See "The Fiery Trigon," Aston, p. 167.

14. See *Brahe*, Dreyer, pp. 193–197.

15. *De Coniunctionibus magnis insignioribus superiorum planetarum*, Cyprian Leowitz, London, 1573, L3^r, quoted in "The Fiery Trigon Conjunction: An Elizabethan Astrological Prediction," Aston, p. 166.

16. Translation from the Latin quoted in *Catastrophe Mundi*, Holwell, pp. 86–89.

17. *Annals*, Strype, volume 2, pt. 2, p. 152.

18. *Annals*, Strype, volume 2, pt. 2, p. 152.

19. *CR*, chapter 5, §3.

20. *The Comet of 1577*, Hellman, pp. 194–195.

21. The method they used was parallax, the subject of Dee's paper on the new star of 1572. Parallax works on the principle that the distance of a single point can be measured by noting the angle between the lines of sight of the point as seen from two separate observation points. If the object is close, the lines of sight will converge. If it is infinitely distant,

or too far away to be measured, the lines of sight will be parallel. This is what Brahe, Dee, and Digges noted with both the new star and the comet of 1577.

22. *Comets*, Genuth, p. 47.

23. *Tomas Twyne's Discourse on the Earthquake*, Twyne; *A Chronological and Historical Account of the Most Memorable Earthquakes*, Grey.

24. Quoted in *Elizabeth the Queen*, Weir, p. 222.

25. *Diaries*, 11 February 1583, p. 53. *Biothanatos* usually denotes death by suicide, "self-murder," however, in a copy of a work by Julius Firmicus Maternus, Dee added notes on the term, which is defined in the text as referring to those who die a violent death. See Roberts and Watson, #251, p. 85.

26. The *Astronomica* is bound together with a collection of Roman astrological texts, including *Matheseos libri* by the Julius Firmicus Maternus. See *John Dee's Library Catalogue*, Roberts and Watson, #251, p. 85.

27. *General and Rare Memorials*, Dee, ε.*iiijʳ.

CHAPTER XVI

1. "1552 Natus Johannes davis die 3 Maij 1552 . . . per magiam eliciebatur W. Em. 1568 Maiij 22. in aedibus meis," Stöffler's *Ephemerides*, Bod MS Ashmole 423, f295.

2. BL Add MSS 36674: "Vision" dated 24 Feb. 1567, seen by "H.G." and his "skrier" John Davies. "Certaine strang visions or apparitions of memorable note. Anno 1567. Lately imparted unto mee for secrets of match importance. A notable journal of an experimental magitian."

3. *General and Rare Memorials*, Dee, Δij-E*iiij.

4. *Diaries*, p. 18.

5. See Dee's letter to Walsingham, 14 May 1586, *T&FR*, p. 423. Dee writes of God making of "*Saul* (E. K.) a *Paul*." The reference to Kelley as E. K. and to Kelley's irreligiousness shows that Walsingham must have been familiar with Kelley's role in Dee's household.

6. "Necessary Advertisement," Dee, §6.

7. *MP*, A.iiiiᵛ.

8. *Diaries*, 8 and 9 October 1581.

9. See *Mysteriorum Liber Primus*, BL MS Sloane 3188.

10. *Diaries*, pp. 21–22.

11. The other is Gabriel. Michael appears in Jude 9 and Revelations 12. An unnamed angel also appears to Daniel "like beryl, his face like the appearance of lightning, his eyes like flaming torches, his arms and legs like the gleam of burnished bronze" to report the rising of

"Michael, the great prince" (Daniel 10:12). There are many other angels identified in the "non-canonical" parts of the Bible, such as the Apocrypha and the Pseudepigrapha.

12. There were a number of ways of spelling the angel's name, all equivalent according to cabalistic principles: Haniel = Anael = Anfiel = Aniyel = Anafiel = Onoel = Ariel = Simiel. See *A Dictionary of Angels*, Davidson, p. xv.

13. The passage in the diary is barely legible and hard to interpret, being scattered with ambiguous pronouns. Fenton has "I would so flatter his friend the learned man [Talbot] that I would bereave him [Clerkson] of him [Talbot]," see *Diaries*, p. 24.

14. *Diaries*, 9 March 1582, p. 24.

15. This entry has been crossed over, and is very hard to read. Fenton's transliteration (*Diaries*, p. 25) seems to be as accurate as is possible.

16. See *Diaries*, p. 26.

CHAPTER XVII

1. *T&FR*, p. 18.

2. *Diaries*, 18 April 1583.

3. "The Devil's Looking Glass," Hugh Tait, pp. 195–212.

4. Vita Adae et Evae, chapter 48, vs. 4; Book of Enoch, chapter 10, vs. 1, *The Apocrypha and Pseudepigrapha of the Old Testament*, Charles.

5. Genesis 5:19; Jude, vs. 14.

6. *John Dee's Natural Philosophy*, Clulee, p. 208.

7. *John Dee's Library Catalogue*, Roberts and Watson, p. 94.

8. *Diaries*, 17 January 1582. The entry reads "Libri Soyga fumig." In his edition of the diaries, Fenton was not sure how to interpret "fumig." Another Dee scholar, John Henry Jones, suggested to Fenton that it referred to fumigation.

9. At the Bodleian, MS Bodley 908, at the British Library, MS Sloane 8.

10. *Diaries*, pp. 28–29.

11. A cabalistic word made up of the initials of the Hebrew phrase, "Athah gabor leolam, Adonai," "Thou art powerful and eternal, Lord." See *An Encyclopaedia of Occultism*, Spence.

CHAPTER XVIII

1. Bod MS Ashmole 1790, f39. The list of instructions appears among a transcription of a number of actions, possibly made by Elias Ashmole.

2. BL MS Sloane 3188, f14.

3. Bod MS Ashmole 1788, f143.
4. *Giordano Bruno*, Bossy, p. 5.
5. *Diaries*, 15 June 1583, 4 April 1583.
6. *Diaries*, 6 May 1582.
7. *Diaries*, 29 May 1582. This entry, like most relating to Talbot's behavior, has been mutilated and is hard to read.

CHAPTER XIX

1. *Diaries*, 19 July 1582; the chests of books are mentioned in a diary entry dated 8 October 1581.
2. *T&FR*, p. 28.
3. *T&FR*, p. 153.
4. *T&FR*, p. 91.
5. *Diaries*, p. 51.
6. *Diaries*, 22 November 1582, p. 51.
7. *Diaries*, 24 November 1582, pp. 51–52.
8. *Diaries*, 18 April 1583, p. 69.
9. *T&FR*, 10 July 1607, p. 34.
10. *Theatrum Chemicum*, Elias Ashmole, 1:481. See MSS Smith 95.
11. *Histoire de Philosophie Hermétique*, Nicolas Lenglet du Fresnoy, Paris, 1742, volume 1, pp. 307–310. The story is reproduced in *Edward Kelley*, Waite, pp. xvii–xix. See *John Dee*, Smith, p. 47.
12. Dee identifies Raphael with Medicina Dei in a diagram showing the relationship of Anael to the angels Michael, Gabriel, Raphael, and Uriel, see MS Sloane 3188, f1.
13. Bod MS Ashmole 1789 ff1–62.
14. *MP*, biii^v.
15. *John Dee*, Calder, chapter 8, §8.
16. *Annals*, Strype, volume 2, pt. 1, p. 526.
17. A full discussion of Dee's calendar reform proposals can be found in "John Dee and the English Calendar," Poole. The paper forms part of his *Time's Alteration*, London, 1998.
18. *Time in History*, Whitrow, p. 119; *The Calendar*, Duncan, p. 307.
19. *CR*, chapter 4, §10.
20. *Diaries*, p. 59
21. See "John Dee and the Secret Societies," Heisler.
22. *Diaries*, p. 66.
23. *Diaries*, p. 67.
24. *T&FR*, 4 July 1583, p. 31.

25. *Diaries*, p. 98.
26. *Diaries*, 22–23 January 1582, p. 23.
27. See "Revising a Biography," Bassnett, pp. 1–8.
28. *Diaries*, 28 April 1583, p. 75.
29. See *Diaries*, p. 84.
30. *Diaries*, 8 and 9 May 1583, pp. 80 and 82.

CHAPTER XX

1. *Diaries*, 15 June 1583, p. 92.
2. See *The Family of Love*, Hamilton, pp. 32–34.
3. Quoted in *Raising Spirits*, Wilding, p. 87.
4. *Chronicles of England*, Holinshed, volume 6, p. 507.
5. *Giordano Bruno*, Yates, p. 190.
6. "Bruno at Oxford," McNulty, pp. 300–305.
7. Quoted in *Giordano Bruno*, Yates, p. 207.
8. *Giordano Bruno*, Yates, p. 26.
9. *Diaries*, 23 May 1583.
10. *Diaries*, 28 May 1583. This is the first action featured in *True and Faithful Relation*, pp. 1–3.
11. *Diaries*, 3 June 1583 (*T&FR* gives the date as Monday, 2 June).
12. *Diaries*, 5 June 1583.
13. *T&FR*, p. 6.
14. Dee described Young as "my brother" in *Diaries* (21 November 1587) and in a letter to Walsingham (17 July 1587, *CSP*, Domestic, *Elizabeth and James I, Addenda 1580–1625*), which may have meant he was a brother-in-law by one of his earlier marriages.
15. *T&FR*, pp. 9–10.

CHAPTER XXI

1. In a letter sent from Bohemia to Richard Hesketh on 9 September 1593, Abraham Faulkon wrote that Kelley, just released from prison, "did fish a pond, and gave me good store of fish home with me."
2. See *The Reckoning*, Nicholl, pp. 113 and 234ff.
3. *Diaries*, 15 June 1583, p. 93.
4. *Diaries*, 18 June 1583, p. 93; *T&FR*, pp. 18–20.
5. *T&FR*, pp. 18–20.
6. See John 20:24.
7. *Diaries*, 9 June 1583.

8. See *Raising Spirits*, Wilding, p. 119.
9. *Defensative*, Howard. See *Giordano Bruno*, Bossy, pp. 99–100.
10. The records for the actions do not survive, though Dee mentions the appearance of Laski's guardian angel, Jubanladaech. See *Diaries*, p. 100.
11. *Diaries*, p. 100.

CHAPTER XXII

1. Sidney to Hubert Languet, 11 February 1574, *The Correspondence of Sir Philip Sidney*, Pears, p. 35. The phrase Sidney used was "ignotum Deum nostrum," a pun on Dee's name. He is clearly referring to Dee, as he refers to Dee's Welsh origins and of him "brandishing" his "hieroglyphic monad."
2. *Elizabethan Critical Essays*, Smith, volume 1, p. 89. The earliest surviving entry in Dee's private diary, dated 16 January 1577, mentions a meeting between Dee, Sidney, and Dyer with Sidney's patron, Robert Dudley, the earl of Leicester. See also *At the Court of Queen Elizabeth*, Sargent, p. 59.
3. See, for example, *Philip Sidney*, Stewart, p. 224. Stewart argues that Harvey was claiming an intimacy with Sidney and Dyer's literary activities to enhance his own standing.
4. *The Faerie Queen*, Spenser, Book II, Canto IX, 53–54.
5. *The Faerie Queen*, Spenser, Book II, introduction, 3.
6. For example, in a marginal note in his record of an action of 19 June 1583, Dee notes "A. L. poverty." Laski's financial difficulties were apparently well known and widely discussed; Charles de l'Ecluse wrote to Sir Philip Sidney of the Polish prince having "reached the bottom of his purse." See *Young Philip Sidney*, Osborn.
7. For example, in his 1590 *Discourse Apologetical* to the Archbishop of Canterbury he claimed that the voyage was "undertaken by her Majesty's good favour and licence."
8. In a letter to Walsingham sent 17 July 1587 he wrote, "I trust more will be glad of our coming home than were sorry of our going abroad" (*CSP, Domestic, Elizabeth and James I, Addenda 1580–1625*, p. 104). Sir Stephen Powel, while visiting the landgrave of Hesse Kassel at the same time that Dee was there, was told by a member of the landgrave's council that Dee had left England on account of the "hatred of nobles" (Bodleian MS Tanner 309, ff67b, 68).
9. *General and Rare Memorials*, Dee, Δij-E*iiij.

10. Roberts and Watson suggest this, on the basis of the way Dee marked the 1583 catalog of his library, which he updated with a series of marks following his return from the Continent.
11. *T&FR*, 26 October 1583, p. 42.
12. In 1582, Lord Emden and Cecil had exchanged letters indicating they were quite close, which included a reference to a large sum of money owed to Cecil. See *Annals*, Strype, volume 3, pt. 1, pp. 207–208.
13. *Diaries*, 6 November 1583.
14. *Diaries*, 13 October 1583.
15. *Diaries*, 15 November 1583.
16. *Diaries*, 18 February 1584. It was during this period that Dee started to date his diary entries using both the old Julian and the new Gregorian calendars, and so gives the date of this action 18 February "stilo veteri" (old style) and 28 Feb. "stilo novo" (new style). All following dates are given new style, unless otherwise specified.
17. *T&FR*, 10 April 1584, p. 76.
18. *T&FR*, 10 April 1584, pp. 73–75. Kelley's more explicit explanation concerning the two types of vision he beheld is set out in the action of *T&FR*, 14 April 1584, p. 88. The angels, he told Dee, he sees "with my external eye, not within my imagination."
19. *Diaries*, 17 and 19 April 1584.
20. *T&FR*, 7 and 14 May 1584, pp. 117 and 138.
21. *Diaries*, 28 May 1584.
22. In *Raising Spirits*, Wilding quotes a letter written from Arthur Champernowne to Walsingham reporting Zoborowski's arrest and execution, and Dee's connection with Laski, which had, he added, led the philosopher to quit "a certain estate for an uncertain hope. It is to be feared that he will repent of it at leisure." See p. 172.
23. *Diaries*, 13 March 1584, 25 April 1584.
24. *Diaries*, 21 May 1584.

CHAPTER XXIII

1. The term "robot" was coined by the Czech writer Karel Čapek in his play *R.U.R.* (1920), derived from the Czech word for work.
2. The first map of Europe even to attempt to draw state boundaries was not published until 1602. See "War, Religion, and the State," Gunn, pp. 102–103.
3. *Rudolf II*, Evans, p. 3. The tactic of dispensing with oppressive officials by throwing them out of windows has a long tradition in Czech

politics, there being two prior to the defenestration of 1618, in 1419 and 1493. Jerome K. Jerome commented that "Prague could avoid half of her problems if the windows were smaller and less tempting" (see *Prague Castle*, Dudák, p. 101).

4. *The Complete Words of Philip Sidney*, Feuillerat, volume 3, pp. 109–114.

5. *Magic Prague*, Ripellino, p. 103.

6. Both Hajek's house and the original Bethlehem Chapel have been demolished. The chapel was rebuilt after the Second World War. Hajek's house was numbered 252 on the square in the land registry. The following account of its history comes from *A Basic Description of the Geography of Old Prague*, volume 1, pt. 2, section XIIa–XXX, Prague, 1915.

7. *Zaklady stareho mistopisu Prazskeho*, Teige, volume 2, XIIa–XXX.

8. See *Diaries*, pp. 134–135. The text was originally in Latin (see *T&FR*, p. 212) and has been translated with the help of Barbara Prichard and Robin Cousins.

9. *The Comet of 1577*, Hellman, p. 184ff.

10. *T&FR*, pp. 215–217.

11. 1 Cor. 1:13 and 20.

12. The account of Dee's audience with Rudolf is contained in *T&FR*, pp. 230–231.

13. *Magic Prague*, Ripellino, p. 69.

14. See *Rudolf II and Prague*, Fucikova.

15. See "Giuseppe Arcimboldo, the Habsburgs' Leonardo," Thomas DaCosta Kaufmann, in *Rudolf II*, Konečný, pp. 169–176.

16. *Rudolf II and Prague*, Fucikova, and *Rudolf II*, Vurm, p. 46.

17. *T&FR*, pp. 230–231; Fenton, pp. 142–143. The "Great Turk" was Murad III, the sultan of the Ottoman Empire.

CHAPTER XXIV

1. *T&FR*, 5 September 1584, p. 233.

2. *T&FR*, 12 September 1584, p. 237.

3. *Rudolf II*, Evans, p. 120; *Tycho Brahe*, Dreyer, p. 300.

4. *Diaries*, 6 October 1584.

5. *Circulis horologi Lunaris*, Václav Budovec, Hanau 1616, p. 245, quoted in *Rudolf II*, Evans, p. 224. Budovec was a Czech noble who had worked as Court Master at the Imperial Embassy in Constantinople and written a history of Turkey attacking the Islamic faith. He knew Dee personally. See *Rudolf II*, Vurm, p. 104.

6. "An Unknown Chapter," Josten, pp. 223–257.
7. "An Unknown Chapter," Josten. This was not the doctorate that gave Dee his title. Digges refers to Dee as being a doctor as early as 1573.

CHAPTER XXV

1. *John Dee*, Fell-Smith, p. 88.
2. *Forma*, dated 1581, is an anonymous work, and was first attributed to Pucci by the Italian historian in 1937. The attribution was confirmed by Luigi Firpo. See "Secret Societies," Eliav-Feldon, p. 141.
3. The street is now part of Betlémská or Bethlehem Street, which runs down from Bethlehem Square. It is shown in a German map of Prague by J. Jüttner dated 1811–1815 as Salz Strasse. I am indebted to Robin Cousins for this information.
4. *Diaries*, 21 March 1585.
5. *Diaries*, 12 April 1585.
6. The reference to a Jesuit confession appears in "An Unknown Chapter," Josten, p. 231.
7. Dee added a comment to an astrological note regarding the Polish wife of a Florentine that it had been sent by Pucci on 12 July 1585, the earliest date linking Pucci with Dee. See *Raising Spirits*, Wilding, pp. 296–297.
8. For the following account of Dee's encounter with Malaspina, and the burning of his books, see "An Unknown Chapter," Josten. This document, discovered by Josten among Ashmole's papers in the 1960s, appears to be a deposition written in Latin, perhaps for presentation by Dee to one of his supporters in Prague.
9. 1 John 4:1–2.
10. The evidence concerning Dee's residence during this period is indefinite. Dee identifies the vineyard as belonging to "John Carpio," probably Jan Kapr, who came from a prosperous Prague family and owned property in the Old Town. There is no known connection between Kapr and the Faust House itself. Kelley is known to have occupied the property, though only after Dee's departure from Bohemia in 1588. However, the description of the surroundings in Dee's account of the burning and recovery of the books (see below) fits well with contemporary drawings. See *Kouzelník z Londýna*, Sviták, p. 63.
11. This reinforces identifying the venue for the book burning as the Faust House. A monastical college (since rebuilt) was on the same square.
12. *T&FR*, pp. 418–419.

13. These are the books of mysteries now held by the BL MS Sloane 3189 and 3191.

14. PRO SP 81/6 f65. Quoted in *Raising Spirits*, Wilding, p. 339.

15. See *T&FR*, p. 424.

CHAPTER XXVI

1. Letter from Pucci to Dee, transcribed in *T&FR*, p. 439; Pucci refers to Dee having to tolerate lodgings that were "sordido & angusto."

2. 11 July 1586. This is part of a series of memoranda written by Dee about his relations with Pucci, see *T&FR*, p. 430.

3. See "The Alchemical World of the German Court," Moran, and *The Comet of 1577*, Hellman, p. 115.

4. According to Sviták, Vilem enjoyed the income from more than 10,000 estates scattered across Bohemia; *Kouzelník z Londýna*, Sviták, p. 110.

5. *Rudolf II*, Evans, pp. 65–67.

6. The round tower at Český Krumlov is still vividly painted, but no longer in the original colors, and the alchemical allusions have been lost.

7. See *Extraordinary Popular Delusions*, Mackay, pp. 98–256.

8. See "Transmutation: The Roots of the Dream," Karpenko, pp. 383–385.

9. See *John Dee's Conversations with Angels*, Harkness, p. 200.

10. *T&FR*, 11 February 1584 and 14 January 1585, pp. 62–65 and 355–361.

11. For example, see entries for dates between 27 December 1586 and 29 January 1587, *Diaries*, pp. 204–205, and 5 and 14 July 1587, Fenton p. 229.

12. Now Zloty Stok, on the Czech/Polish border.

13. Dee's son Arthur would take up a similar if less lavish offer, being appointed physician to the emperor of Russia in 1627, on the recommendation of Charles I.

14. Dee's record of the recovery of the burnt books does not mention the powder. However, there is a reference to "the powder" in an action dated 4 April 1587.

15. *Kouzelník z Londýna*, Sviták, p. 144.

16. *Diaries*, 24 November 1587, p. 231. Dee refers to Krčín in his diaries as "Captain Critzin."

17. These legends are scattered through the manuscript records of Ashmole, and elsewhere, for example, Bod MS Smith 95.

18. *Diaries*, 8 Feb. 1588, p. 233.

19. Now Jindrichuv Hradec, just northeast of Třeboň.

20. *Diaries*, 21 May 1589, p. 239.
21. *Diaries*, 16 September 1589.
22. For example, see *Diaries*, 3 July 1580, 15 July 1582, 31 July 1591.
23. Quoted in "Paracelsian Medicine in John Dee's Alchemical Diaries," Szulakowska, p. 28.
24. The meaning of this symbol was first recognized by Edward Fenton. See *Diaries*, page 310, for his interpretation of this and other symbols used by Dee.
25. *Diaries*, 9 December 1579.
26. Luke 1:5–32.
27. *Diaries*, 2 October 1584.

CHAPTER XXVII

1. Luke 14:26.
2. 15 April 1583.
3. *T&FR*, 22 April 1587, pp. 17–18.

CHAPTER XXVIII

1. *Diaries*, 23 May 1587.
2. Others apparently took place. For example, on 5 March 1588, Dee noted in his diary "Sacrae Actionis finis 1.9," "the sacred action finished." See *Diaries*, p. 233.
3. *Diaries*, 26 May 1588. Dee uses the Latin for threats, "Minæ."
4. *Diaries*, 24 August 1588 and 12 September 1588, p. 236.
5. *Diaries*, 7 December 1588, p. 237.
6. *Diaries*, 20 January 1589, p. 238.
7. "Bohemian Nobility," Karpenko, p. 14.
8. *Rudolf II*, Evans, p. 226.
9. Burghley to Sir Henry Palavicino: "I pray you learn what you can, how Sir Edwd. Kelley's profession may be credited," PRO SP 81/6 ff7–8, quoted in "Edward Kelley, A Life," Wilding, p. 11. For Burghley's letters to Kelley, see, for example, BL MS Landsdowne 103, item 73 f211.
10. PRO SP 81/6, ff56–57, 65.
11. PRO SP 82/3, f134.
12. *Works*, Bacon, volume 1, p. 406.
13. "O paradox! Black is the badge of hell, / The hue of dungeons, and the school of night; / And beauty's crest becomes the heavens well," IV:3:250–252. For Roydon, see *The Reckoning*, Nicholl, p. 257ff.

14. BL MS Lansdowne 103, item 72. Michael Wilding suggested that Cecil's gout might be code, see "Edward Kelley: A Life," p. 13. If it is a code word, it is suggestive that he also used it in a letter of the earl of Emden; see *Annals*, Strype, volume 3, pt. 1, p. 207. He refers to it being his "chronical distemper . . . *his familiar disease.*"

15. *Annals*, Strype, volume 3, pt. 2, pp. 617–620.

16. The account is contained in MS Lansdowne 68, item 85, ff192–195, and *Annals*, Strype, volume 3, pt. 2, 1824, pp. 621–625. The report appears in a letter sent from Frankfurt to Edward Wotton. Wilding ("Edward Kelley: A Life," p. 14) shows that the author was probably Edward's half-brother Henry.

17. Thomas Webbe to Burghley, 26 June 1591, BL MS Lansdowne 68, item 93, ff210–211; *Fugger Newsletters*, pp. 221–222.

18. All these theories were reported in the letter sent to Edward Wotton.

19. PRO SP 81/7, ff140, 143–144. See "Edward Kelley: A Life," Wilding, p. 17.

20. Abraham Faulkon to Richard Hesketh, 9 September 1593; quoted in "Edward Kelley: A Life," Wilding, p. 17.

21. See *The Shakespeare Conspiracy*, Phillips and Keatman, London, 1994.

22. PRO SP 88/1, f221.

23. *Edward Kelly*, Waite, p. 5.

24. See "John Dee and Edward Kelley," Ivan Sviták, *Kosmas*, volume 5 (1986), p. 137.

25. *Rudolf II*, Evans, p. 227.

CHAPTER XXIX

1. It was 25 December, Christmas Day, new style. On his return to England, Dee reverted to using the old-style Julian calendar.

2. *CR*, chapter 9. On 31 January 1589, Dee's servant Edmund Hilton was sent to Prague with "300 dollars" to buy "ten or twelve coach horses, and saddle horses." On 12 February, Hilton returned with "nine Hungarish horses." He acquired the remainder from elsewhere. See Fenton, p. 238.

3. Dee called Bremen "Breme."

4. Sherman believes that the "great bladder" was an Inuit gift brought back from the second of Frobisher's expeditions. See his paper "John Dee's Role in Martin Frobisher's Northwest Enterprise," in *Meta Incognita*, Symons, p. 294.

5. *CR*, chapter 7.

6. This account of the library's destruction is contained in, among other sources, *Lists of Manuscripts*, James, p. 4. The mud was more likely a result of the manuscripts having been buried.

7. *Diaries*, 30 March 1592.

8. *John Dee's Library Catalogue*, Roberts and Watson, p. 50

9. *CR*, chapter 7.

10. See *The Reckoning*, Nicholl, p. 221.

11. *Gallathea* was published in 1591, but entered into the Stationers' Register on 1 April 1585.

12. *Works*, Thomas Nashe, ed. R. B. McKerrow, volume 1, p. 367. Quoted in *At the Court of Queen Elizabeth*, Sargent, p. 106.

13. Bodleian, MS Smith 95. Lopez was examined in the Tower and executed in the autumn of 1593. See *Memoirs of the Reign of Queen Elizabeth*, Thomas Birch, London, 1754, p. 38.

14. *An Advertisement written to a Secretary of My L. Treasurer*, Antwerp, 1592, p. 18.

15. *Acts of the Privy Council*, volume 5, 1554–1556, 5 June 1555. See "John Dee as Ralegh's 'Conjuror,'" Strathmann, pp. 365–372.

16. *To the Kings most excellent Maiestie*, Dee.

17. "O paradox! Black is the badge of hell, / The hue of dungeons, and the school of night," 4:3:250–251. In the opening lines of the play, the king mentions "a little academe," but whether or not Shakespeare was alluding to Raleigh's set in the play is disputed. See "The Textual Evidence for 'The School of Night,'" Strathmann.

18. *Diaries*, 9 October 1595.

19. A copy of *De orbe novo decades octo* by Petrus Martyr and of *El viaje que hizo Antonio de Espeio en el anno de ochenta y tres*, by Antonio de Espejo in Dee's collection was given to him by Harriot, "amici mei" 24 January 1590. They are cataloged in *John Dee's Library Catalogue*, Roberts and Watson as items D1 and D8, see pp. 155–156.

20. Quoted in *The Reckoning*, Nicholl, p. 257.

21. BL MS Lansdowne 103, item 72.

22. *CR*, chapter 8.

23. Private communication between Rev. B. J. Bennett and Robin Cousins.

24. *Diaries*, 14 and 20 December 1591.

25. See *Diaries*, p. 264 and note 31. Dee spelled Cavendish "Candish."

26. *Diaries*, 5 August 1590, 22 September 1591, 27 June 1591.

27. *Diaries*, 20 and 21 February 1594, 9 January 1592.

28. *Diaries*, 11 September 1593.
29. *Diaries*, 22 July–29 August 1590.
30. See Bod MS Ashmole 423, f295. Dee notes Hesketh's birth on 24 or 25 July 1552 between one and four in the afternoon at "Ayghton in Lancashire."
31. Hatton died in 1591.
32. For the Hesketh conspiracy, see *The Reckoning*, Nicholl, pp. 248–249.
33. See *Diaries*, 24 December 1593, 26 January 1594, 10 March 1594.
34. *Diaries*, 3 June 1594, 28 October 1594, 7 December 1594.
35. *Diaries*, 21 May 1594.

CHAPTER XXX

1. For example, see *Diaries*, 19 May 1588.
2. *Diaries*, 31 January–5 February 1601.
3. See *John Dee's Library Catalogue*, Roberts and Watson, p. 60.
4. Bod MS Smith 95.
5. *Diaries*, 2 August 1589, 6 August 1597.
6. *Brief Lives*, Aubrey, p. 210.

EPILOGUE

1. It is now called Addle Hill and only exists as a cul-de-sac. It is possible that another Addle Street, in the northern part of the City, is being referred to. The first names of the Joneses are contained in BL MS Sloane 3191, where the names were jotted down in the volume entitled *Liber Scientiae Auxili et Victoria Terrestris*. The rest of this account comes from BL MS Sloane 3188, ff2^v–3. *Elias Ashmole*, Josten, pp. 1270–1271.
2. Woodall would become surgeon to the King's Guards, see *CSP*, Domestic, *1664–1665*, London, 1863, p. 535.
3. *John Dee's Library Catalogue*, Roberts and Watson, p. 61.
4. The "Book of Enoch," also referred to as the "Liber Logaeth" and the "Liber Mysteriorum, Sextus & Sanctus." The only surviving copy is in Edward Kelley's hand and entitled "The Book of Enoch revealed to Dr. John Dee by the Angels." See BL MS Sloane 3189.
5. Bod MS Ashmole 1790, f47. See *Elias Ashmole*, Josten, p. 1272.
6. *T&FR*, Preface, p. 44, also Bodleian MS Ashmole 1788, letter from N. Bernard, f65.
7. *T&FR*, Preface, p. 1.
8. *Hudibras*, Canto 3, II, 238–241.

9. *John Dee*, Calder, chapter 2, §3.

10. *The Life of Dr. John Dee . . . Containing an account of his studies . . . his travels . . . his various prophecies, among which may be noticed an earthquake to destroy London in the year 1842*, London, 1842; *The Predicted Plague . . . Queen Elizabeth in Richmond. Her Majesty's Book of Astrology and the Diary of her astrologer, Dr. Dee . . . By Hippocrates Junior*, London, 1899.

11. *Giordano Bruno*, Yates, p. 150.

12. *John Dee*, Sherman, p. xiii.

13. *Diaries*, 26 March 1583, p. 56.

14. *MP*, *.i^v.

15. *MP*, *.i^r.

16. *The Elizabethan World Picture*, Tillyard, p. 61.

CHRONOLOGY

✤

13 July 1527	Birth
1535	Chelmsford Grammar School
Nov. 1542	St. John's College, Cambridge
Early 1546	Graduated BA
Dec. 1546	Elected Fellow and Under-Reader in Greek at Trinity College
1547	Produced Aristophanes' *Peace* (mechanical scarab)
June 1547	Louvain
July 1550	Lectures in Paris
Dec. 1551	Presented to Edward VI
Feb. 1552	Enters Pembroke's service
1553	Enters Northumberland's service
Aug. 1553	Roland Dee imprisoned in the Tower of London
1554	Rejected math post at Oxford
28 May 1555	Arrested for conjuring
29 Aug. 1555	Released from prison
15 Jan. 1556	Presents plans for national library to Mary
Late 1558	Wrote paper selecting date for Elizabeth's coronation
Jan. 1559	Coronation of Elizabeth
1559	Develops "Paradoxicall Compass"
1562	Returns to Low Countries
Feb. 1563	Discovers copy of *Steganographia*
Apr. 1563	Zurich, meets Conrad Gesner
Summer 1563	At Duke of Urbino's court, Italy
Sept. 1563	Attends coronation of Maximilian (1527–1576) in Pressburg/Bratislava
Summer 1564	Returns from Antwerp to London; presents *Monas Hieroglyphica* to queen
1566	First reference to living at Mortlake

Jan. 1568	Publication of *Propaedeumata Aphoristica* and presentation to the queen
Feb. 1568	Audience with queen discussing alchemical secret
Feb. 1570	Publication of "Mathematical Praeface" to English Euclid
Early 1571	Trip to Lorraine to buy laboratory equipment
Mid/late 1571	Ill; attended to by queen's physicians
Nov. 1572	Appearance of the nova in Cassiopeia
1573	Publication of book on the nova
Oct. 1574	Letter to Burleigh about treasure
1575	Second marriage
Mar. 1576	Wife dies; queen visits within hours of the event
May 1576	Departure of first Frobisher expedition
Oct. 1576	Return of Frobisher with sample of black ore
Jan. 1577	Meeting with Robert Dudley, Philip Sidney, and Edward Dyer
May 1577	Departure of second Frobisher expedition; slandered by Vincent Murphyn
Aug. 1577	Printing of *General and Rare Memorials*
Nov. 1577	Visits court at Windsor Castle
Feb. 1578	Marriage to Jane Fromonds
1578?	Consulted on wax effigy of queen
Mar. 1578	Dee attends test of Frobisher's ore
Apr. 1578	Slanders against Dee investigated
May 1578	Departure of third Frobisher expedition
June 1578	Meeting with Richard Hackluyt
Nov./Dec. 1578	Sent by Leicester and Walsingham to consult foreign doctors about Elizabeth's illness
July 1579	Birth of first son, Arthur
Aug. 1579	Reports secret visit by Elizabeth's suitor Alençon to court
Dec. 1580	Mother relinquishes ownership of Mortlake to Dee
Aug. 1580	Meeting with Sir Humphrey Gilbert
Oct. 1580	Death of mother; visit by queen and court to Mortlake
June 1581	Birth of daughter Katherine
Dec. 1581	First record of action, with Barnabas Saul
Mar. 1582	First actions with Edward "Talbot"
July 1582	Meeting with Sir George Peckham about Catholic colony in New World
Nov. 1582	Reconciliation with Talbot, now "Kelley"; received the sacred shew-stone

Feb. 1583	Consulted by queen about marriage to Alençon; submits plans for reform of the calendar
Mar. 1583	Emissary arrives from Count Laski of Poland; Kelley delivers coded treasure map
May 1583	Laski's arrival in London; first meeting with Dee at Greenwich
June 1583	Laski attends first action
Sept. 1583	Dee and household depart for Poland with Laski
Mar. 1584	Arrives in Kraków
Aug. 1584	Arrives in Prague
Sept. 1584	Audience with Emperor Rudolf
Apr. 1585	Returns to Kraków. Audience with King Stephen Báthory of Poland
Summer 1585	Dee meets Francesco Pucci
Mar. 1586	Burning of Dee's books in Prague
May 1586	Banished from Bohemia by order of Rudolf
May 1586	Letter to Sir Francis Walsingham
Aug. 1586	At court of Landgrace of Hesse in Germany
Sept. 1586	At Třeboň under patronage of Vilem Rozmberk
Dec. 1586	Invited to join court of Russian emperor
Apr. 1587	Kelley hands over skrying to Dee's son Arthur; "cross-matching"
May 1587	Last recorded action with Kelley; cross-matching pact fulfilled
Feb. 1588	Birth of Theodore Dee
July 1588	Arrival of Sir Edward Dyer in Třeboň
Nov. 1588	Letter to queen regarding Armada
Feb. 1589	Kelley leaves Třeboň
Mar. 1589	Departs Třeboň
Apr. 1589	Reaches Bremen
July 1589	Writes to Walsingham with reports about the Low Countries
Aug. 1589	Learns in letter from Walsingham of Kelley being knighted
Dec. 1589	Dees returns to Mortlake
Feb. 1590	Birth of daughter Madimia, named after an angel
Jan. 1592	Birth of daughter Frances
Aug. 1592	Dines twice with William Cecil, Lord Treasurer
Nov. 1592	Audience with queen's commissioners regarding damage to Mortlake
May 1594	Audience with queen

June 1594	Visits Archbishop of Canterbury at Croydon regarding St. John's Cross
Oct. 1595	Dined with Sir Walter Raleigh at Durham House
Nov. 1595	News of Kelley's death
Feb. 1596	Arrives in Manchester
Mar. 1598	Returns to London; stays until June 1600
Apr. 1601	Death of son Theodore
Mar. 1603	Death of Queen Elizabeth
June 1604	Petitions James to be cleared of "slander"
Spring 1605	Manchester hit by plague; death of Jane Dee and several children
Mar. 1605	More séances with the angels; Dee suffers hemorrhages
July 1607	Final angelic actions with Bartholomew Hickman
1608/9	Dies

SELECT BIBLIOGRAPHY

✧

ABBREVIATIONS

T&FR: Dee, John, *A True and Faithful Relation*
MP: Dee, John, "Mathematicall Praeface"
CR: Dee, John, *Compendious Rehearsal*
MH: Dee, John, "A translation of John Dee's *Monas Hieroglyphica*"
CSP: *Calendar of State Papers*
Diaries: Dee, John, *The Diaries of John Dee*
Bod: Bodleian Library, University of Oxford
BL: British Library
PRO: Public Record Office, London

Acts of the Privy Council of England. London, 1890—.
Aristophanes. "Peace," trans. Eugene O'Neill, Jr. *The Complete Greek Drama*, eds. Whitney J. Oates and Eugene O'Neill. New York, 1938.
Ashmand, J. M., trans. *Ptolemy's Tetrabiblios or Quadripartite*. London, 1822.
Aston, Margaret. "The Fiery Trigon: An Elizabethan Astrological Prediction." *Isis* 61 (1970).
Aubrey, John. *Brief Lives, chiefly of Contemporaries, set down by John Aubrey, between the Years 1669 & 1696*, ed. Andrew Clark. Oxford, 1898.
Bacon, Francis. *The Works of Francis Bacon*, ed. Basil Montague. London, 1825.
Bacon, Roger. *Opus Majus*, trans. R. B. Burke. Philadelphia, 1928.
Bale, John. *Index Britanniae scriptorum quos ex variis bibliothecis non parvo labore collegit Ioannes Baleus, cum aliis. John Bale's Index of British and Other Writers*, ed. Reginald Lane Poole. Oxford, 1902.
Barker, Felix, and Peter Jackson. *The History of London in Maps*. London, 1990.
A Basic Description of the Geography of Old Prague. Prague, 1915.

Bassnett, Susan. "Revising a Biography: A New Interpretation of the Life of Elizabeth Jane Weston (Westonia)." *Cahiers Élisabéthains* 37 (1990).

Best, George. *A True Discourse of the late voyages of discovery for the finding of a passage to Cathay by the Northwest, under the conduct of Martin Frobisher, General.* London, 1578.

Birch, Thomas. *Memoirs of the Reign of Queen Elizabeth.* London, 1754.

Bossy, John. *Giordano Bruno and the Embassy Affair.* New Haven, 1991.

Calder, I. R. F. "John Dee: Studied as an English Neoplatonist," unpublished Ph.D. thesis, University of London, 1953, www.johndee.org.

Camden, William. *Britannia*, trans. Philemon Holland. London, 1610.

Cameron, Euan, ed. *Early Modern Europe.* Oxford, 1999.

Capp, Bernard. *English Almanacs 1500–1800: Astrology and the Popular Press.* Ithaca, 1979.

Catholic Record Society. London, 1905–.

Chambers, E. K. *Elizabethan Stage.* Oxford, 1923.

Charles, R. H., ed. *The Apocrypha and Pseudepigrapha of the Old Testament.* Oxford, 1913.

Clulee, Nicholas. *John Dee's Natural Philosophy: Between Science and Religion.* London, 1988.

Cousins, Robin E. "Mortlake Revisited: John Dee's House and His Burial in Mortlake." In *The Heptarchia Mystica of John Dee*, ed. Robert Turner. Wellingborough, 1986.

Covell, William. *Polimanteia.* London, 1595.

Davidson, Gustav. *A Dictionary of Angels, Including the Fallen Angels.* New York, 1967.

Davies, Normal. *God's Playground: A History of Poland*, volume 1. Oxford, 1982.

Dee, John. "Compendious Rehearsal" (1593). In *Remains Historical & Literary Connected with the Palatine Counties of Lancaster and Chester published by the Chetham Society*, ed. James Crossley, volume XXIV, 1851.

———. *The Diaries of John Dee*, ed. Edward Fenton. Charlbury, 1998.

———. *Ephemeris anni 1557, currentis iuxta Copernici et Reinhaldi Canones ... per J. Feild ... ad meridianum Londinensem.* London, 1556.

———. *General and rare memorials pertayning to the Perfect Arte of Navigation.* London, 1577.

———. *A letter, containing a most briefe Discourse Apologeticall.* London, 1603.

———. "Mathematicall Praeface." In *The Elements of Geometrie*, Euclid, trans. H. Billingsley. London, 1570.

————. "Necessary Advertisement." In *General and rare memorials per-taynig to the Perfect Arte of Navigation*. London, 1577, Δij-E*iiij; reprinted in *Remains Historical & Literary Connected with the Pala-tine Counties of Lancaster and Chester published by the Chetham Soci-ety*, ed. James Crossley, volume XXIV, 1851.

————. "Propaedeumata Aphoristica." In *John Dee on astronomy "Propaedeumata aphoristica" (1558 and 1568)*, Latin and English, trans. Wayne Shumaker. Berkeley, 1978.

————. *To the Kings most excellent Maiestie*. [A petition from Dee to James I, asking "to be tryed and cleared of that horrible and damnable . . . Sclaunder . . . that he is, or hath bin a Conjurer, or Caller, or Invocator of divels."] London, 1604.

————. "A Translation of John Dee's 'Monas Hieroglyphica,'" trans. C. H. Josten. *Ambix* 12 (1964).

————. *A True and Faithful Relation of what passed for many years between Dr. John Dee and Some Spirits*, ed. Meric Casaubon. London, 1659.

Dictionary of National Biography . . . from the earliest times to 1900, ed. Sir Leslie Stephen and Sir Sidney Lee. Oxford, 1963–1965.

Dreyer, J. L. E. *Tycho Brahe: A Picture of Scientific Life and Work in the Sixteenth Century*. Edinburgh, 1890.

Dudák, Vladislav. *Prague Castle*. Prague, 1998.

Duncan, David Ewing. *The Calendar*. London, 1999.

Ecclesiae Londino—Batavae Archivum . . . Ex autographis . . . editit Johannes Henricus Hessels. Holland, 1887–1897.

Eliav-Feldon, Miriam. "Secret Societies, Utopias, and Peace Plans: The Case of Francesco Pucci." *Journal of Medieval and Renaissance Studies* 14 (1984): 139–158.

Ellis, Henry. *Original letters, illustrative of English History*. London, 1824.

Evans, R. J. W. *Rudolf II and His World: A Study in Intellectual History, 1576–1612*. Oxford, 1973.

Fauvel, John, et al. *Let Newton Be!* Oxford, 1988.

Ferguson, Kitty. *Measuring the Universe: The Historical Quest to Quan-tify Space*. London, 1999.

Finlay, R. *Population and Metropolis: The Demography of London 1580–1650*. Cambridge, 1981.

Firpo, Luigi, and R. Piattoli. *Francesco Pucci, lettere, documenti e testimo-nianze*. Florence, 1959.

Foxe, John. *Acts and Monuments of these Latter and Perillous Dayes*, ed. Josiah Pratt. London, 1877 (4th ed.).

Fraser, Antonia. *The Six Wives of Henry VIII*. London, 1996.

French, Peter J. *John Dee: The World of an Elizabethan Magus*. London, 1972.

Fucikova, Eliska, et al. *Rudolf II and Prague: The Imperial Court and Residential City as the Cultural and Spiritual Heart of Central Europe*. London, 1997.

Fugger News-Letters. Second series: being a further selection from the Fugger papers specially referring to Queen Elizabeth and matters relating to England during the years 1568–1605, ed. Victor von Klarwill, trans. L. S. R. Byrne. London, 1926.

Genuth, Sara Schechner. *Comets, Popular Culture and the Birth of Model Cosmology*. Princeton, 1997.

Gilbert, Sir Humfrey. *A Discovrse of a Discouerie for a new Passage to Cataia*. London, 1576.

Gratton-Guiness, Ivor. *History of the Mathematical Sciences: The Rainbow of Mathematics*. London, 1997.

Grey, Zachary. *A Chronological and Historical Account of the Most Memorable Earthquakes*. Cambridge, 1750.

Gunn, Steven. "War, Religion, and the State." In *Early Modern Europe*, ed. Euan Cameron. Oxford, 1999.

Hakluyt, Richard. *Principal Navigations Voyages Traffiques and Discoveries of the English Nation*. Glasgow, 1904.

———. *Voyages and Discoveries*, ed. Jack Beeching. London 1985.

Hale, John. *The Civilization of Europe in the Renaissance*. London, 1993.

Halliwell, J. O. *Rara Mathematica*. London, 1841.

———, ed. *A Collection of Letters Illustrative of the Progress of Science*. London, 1841.

———. *The Private Diary of Dr. John Dee, and the catalogue of his library of manuscripts*. London, 1842.

Hamilton, Alistair. *The Family of Love*. Cambridge, 1981.

Harkness, Deborah E. *John Dee's Conversations with Angels*. Cambridge 1999.

———. "Managing an Experimental Household: The Dees of Mortlake and the Practice of Natural Philosophy." *Isis* 55 (1986).

Harvey, P. D. A. *Medieval Maps*. London, 1991.

Harvey, Richard. *Astrological Discourse*. London, 1583.

Heisler, Ron. "John Dee and the Secret Societies." *The Hermetic Journal* (1992).

Hellman, Clarisse Doris. *The Comet of 1577: Its Place in the History of Astronomy*. New York, 1944.

Herbermann, C. G., et al., eds. *Catholic Encyclopedia*. New York, 1907–1918.

Hessels, J. H., ed. *Ecclesiae Londino-Batavae Archivum*. Cambridge, 1887.

Hippocrates Junior [pseud.]. *The Predicted Plague*. London, 1900.

Holinshed, Raphael. *Chronicles of England, Scotland and Ireland* (1577), ed. H. Ellis. London, 1807–1808.

Holwell, John ["Merlin"]. *Catastrophe Mundi*. London, 1683.

Howard, Henry. *A Defensative against the Poyson of supposed Prophesies, not hitherto confuted by the penne of any man*. London, 1583.

Hudson, Winthrop S. *The Cambridge Connection and the Elizabethan Settlement*. London, 1980.

Hurle, Pamela. *Upton, Portrait of a Severnside Town*. Chichester, 1988.

James, M. R. "Lists of Manuscripts owned by Dr John Dee." *Supplement to the Transactions of the Bibliographical Society's Transactions* 1 (1921).

Jesuite, Robert Parsons [pseud.]. *Leicester's common-wealth*. London, 1641.

Johnson, F. R. "The Influence of Thomas Digges on the Progress of Modern Astronomy in Sixteenth-Century England." *Osiris* 1 (1936).

———, and Sanford V. Larkey. "Thomas Digges, the Copernican System, and the Idea of the Infinity of the Universe in 1576." *Huntington Library Bulletin* 5 (1934).

Josten, C. H. *Elias Ashmole (1617–1692): His Autobiographical and Historical Notes, His Correspondence, and Other Contemporary Sources Relating to His Life and Work*. Oxford, 1966.

———. "An Unknown Chapter in the Life of John Dee." *Journal of the Warburg and Courtauld Institutes* 28 (1965).

Karpenko, Vladimir. "Bohemian Nobility and Alchemy in the Second Half of the 16th Century." *Cauda Pavonis* 15 (1996).

———. "Transmutation: The Roots of the Dream." *Journal of Chemical Education* 72 (1995).

Konečný, Lubomír, ed. *Rudolf II, Prague and the World*. Prague, 1998.

Leader, Damiean Riehl. *A History of the University of Cambridge*. Cambridge, 1988.

Letters and Papers, Foreign and Domestic, of the reign of Henry VIII, ed. J. Gairdner and R. H. Brodie. London, 1862–1932.

Lilly, William. *Christian Astrology*. London, 1647.

———. *Mr. William Lilly's History of His Life and Times*. London, 1715.

Lysons, Daniel. *The Environs of London: Being an Historical Account of the Towns, Villages, and Hamlets, Within Twelve Miles of that Capital; Interspersed with Biographical Anecdotes*. London, 1792.

Machyn, Henry. *The Diary of Henry Machyn: Citizen and Merchant-Taylor of London from AD 1550 to AD 1563*, ed. John Gough Nichols. Camden Society, 1848.

Mackay, Charles. *Extraordinary Popular Delusions and the Madness of Crowds*, ed. Bernard M. Baruch. New York, 1932.

Mattingly, Garrett. *Catherine of Aragon*. London, 1942.

McDermott, James. "The Navigation of the Frobisher Voyages." *The Hakluyt Society Annual Talk 2nd July, 1997*. London, 1998.

McLean, Antonia. *Humanism and the Rise of Science in Tudor England*. London, 1972.

McNulty, Robert. "Bruno at Oxford." *Renaissance News* 13 (1960).

Moore Smith, G. C. "The Academic Drama at Cambridge: Extracts from College Records." *Malone Society Collections* 2 (1923).

Moran, Bruce T. "The Alchemical World of the German Court: Occult Philosophy and Chemical Medicine in the Circle of Moritz of Hessen (1572–1632)." *Sudhoffs Archiv Heft* 29 (1991).

Morris, T. A. *Europe and England in the Sixteenth Century*. London, 1998.

Nicholl, Charles. *The Reckoning*. Chicago, 1992.

Niclaes, Henrik. *Evangelium regni. A ioyfull message of the kingdom*, trans. C. Vitell. [Amsterdam?], c. 1575.

North, J. D. "Horoscopes and History." In *Warburg Institute Surveys and Texts*, volume 13. London, 1986.

———. *Stars, Minds and Fate*. London, 1989.

Osborn, James M. *Young Philip Sidney*. London, 1972.

Parks, George Bruner. *Richard Hakluyt and the English Voyages*. New York, 1928.

Pears, S. A., ed. and trans. *The Correspondence of Sir Philip Sidney and Hubert Languet*. London, 1845.

Phillips, Graham, and Martin Keatman. *The Shakespeare Conspiracy*. London, 1994.

Poole, Robert. "John Dee and the English Calendar: Science, Religion and Empire." In *Electronic Seminars in History*. Lancaster, 1997.

———. *Time's Alteration*. London, 1998.

"The Population of London, 1550–1700: A Review of Published Evidence," *The London Journal* 15 (1990).

Porter, Roy. *The Greatest Benefit to Mankind*. London, 1997.

Prideaux, W. R. B. "Books from John Dee's Library." *Notes & Queries*, ser. 9, volume 8 (1901).

Prockter, Adrian, and Robert Taylor. *The A to Z of Elizabethan London*. London Topographical Society publication no. 122, 1979.

Reeds, Jim. "Solved: The Ciphers in Book III of Trithemius' *Steganographia*." *Cryptologia* 22: 4 (1998).

Ripellino, Angelo Maria. *Magic Prague*, trans. David Newton Marinelli. London, 1994.

Roberts, Julian, and Andrew G. Watson. *John Dee's Library Catalogue*. London, 1990.

Rodger, N. A. M. *The Safeguard of the Sea*. London, 1997.

Rose, Paul Lawrence. "Erasmians and Mathematicians at Cambridge in the Early Sixteenth Century." *Sixteenth Century Journal* 8 (1977).

Rowlands, Alison. "The Conditions of Life for the Masses." In *Early Modern Europe*, ed. Euan Cameron. Oxford, 1999.

Sargent, Ralph M. *At the Court of Queen Elizabeth: The Life and Lyrics of Sir Edward Dyer*. London, 1935.

Scarisbrick, John Joseph. *Henry VIII*. London, 1971.

Scholem, G. G. *Major Trends in Jewish Mysticism*. Jerusalem, 1941.

Schwartz, Seymour I., and Ralph E. Ehrenberg. *The Mapping of America*. New York, 1980.

Sherman, William H. *John Dee: The Politics of Reading and Writing in the English Renaissance*. Amherst, 1995.

Shumaker, Wayne. *Renaissance Curiosa: John Dee's Conversations with Angels, Girolamo Cardano's Horoscope of Christ, Johannes Trithemius and Cryptography, George Dalgarno's Universal Language*. Binghampton, 1982.

Sidney, Philip. *The Complete Works of Philip Sidney*, ed. Albert Feuillerat. Cambridge, 1923.

Smith, Charlotte Fell. *John Dee*. London, 1909.

Smith, G. G., ed. *Elizabethan Critical Essays*. Oxford, 1904.

Spence, Lewis. *An Encyclopaedia of Occultism*. London, 1920.

Stewart, Alan. *Philip Sidney: A Double Life*. London, 2000.

Stow, John. *Survey of London Written in the Year 1598*, ed. Henry Morley. Stroud, 1994.

Strathmann, Ernest A. "John Dee as Ralegh's 'Conjuror.'" *Huntington Library Quarterly* 10 (1947).

———. "The Textual Evidence for 'The School of Night.'" *Modern Language Notes* 56 (1941).

Strong, Roy. *Gloriana*. London, 1987.

Strype, John. *Annals of the Reformation and Establishment of Religion*. Oxford, 1709.

Sviták, Ivan. "John Dee and Edward Kelley." *Kosmas* 5 (1986).

———. *Kouzelnik z Londýna: John Dee v Cecach, 1584–1589*. Prague, 1994.

———. *Sir Edward Kelley: cesky rytir, 1555–1598*. Prague, 1994.

Symons, Thomas H. B., ed. *Meta Incognita: A Discourse of Discovery*. Canada, 1999.

Szônyi, György E. "My Charms Are All O'erthrown." In *Jacobean Drama as Social Criticism*, ed. James Hogg. New York/Salzburg, 1995.

Szulakowska, Urszula. "Paracelsian Medicine in John Dee's Alchemical Diaries." *Cauda Pavonis* 18 (1999).

Tait, Hugh. "'The Devil's Looking Glass': The Magical Speculum of John Dee." In *Horace Walpole: Writer, Politician, and Connoisseur*, ed. Warren Huntington Smith. London, 1967.

Taylor, E. G. R. "John Dee and the Map of North-East Asia." *Imago Mundi* 12 (1955).

———. "A Letter Dated 1577 from Mercator to John Dee." *Imago Mundi* 13 (1956).

———. *Tudor Geography 1485–1583*. London, 1930.

———, ed. *A Regiment for the Sea and Other Writings on Navigation by William Bourne*. Cambridge, 1963.

Teige, Josef. *Zaklady stareho mistopisu Prazskeho [1437–1620]*. Prague, 1915.

Thomas, Keith. *Religion and the Decline of Magic*. London, 1991.

Tillyard, E. M. W. *The Elizabethan World Picture*. London, 1990.

Trismegistus, Hermes [pseud.]. *Hermetica*, ed. and trans. Brian P. Copenhaver. Cambridge, 1992.

Trithemius, Johannes. *Steganographia*, ed. Adam McLean, trans. (Book III) J. W. H. Walden. Edinburgh, c. 1982.

Twyne, Thomas. *Tomas Twyne's Discourse on the Earthquake of 1580*, ed. R. E. Ockenden. Oxford, 1936.

Venn, J., and J. A. Venn. *Alumni Cantabrigienses: A Biographical List of All Known Students, Graduates and Holders of Office at the University of Cambridge*. Cambridge, 1922.

Vurm, Robert B. *Rudolf II and His Prague*, trans. Helena Baker. Prague, 1997.

Waite, A. E., ed. *Edward Kelley, The Englisman's Two Excellent Treatises on the Philosopher's Stone*. London, 1893.

Walker, D. P. *Spiritual and Demonic Magic from Ficino to Campanella*. London, 1958.

Watkins, Susan. *In Public and in Private, Elizabeth I and Her World*. London, 1998.

Weever, John. *Ancient Funerall Monuments*. London, 1631.

Weinreb, Ben, and Christopher Hibbert, eds. *London Encyclopaedia*. London, 1983.

Weir, Alison. *Children of England*. London, 1997.

———. *Elizabeth the Queen*. London, 1998.

Whitby, Christopher. *John Dee's Actions with Spirits*. New York 1988.

Whitfield, Peter. *Landmarks in Western Science*. London, 1999.

Whitrow, G. J. *Time in History*. Oxford, 1988.

Wilding, Michael. "Edward Kelley: A Life." *Cauda Pavonis* 18 (1999).

———. *Raising Spirits, Making Gold and Swapping Wives*. Beeston, 1999.

Williams, Penry. *The Later Tudors: England 1547–1603*. Oxford, 1998.

Williamson, J. A. "Introduction." In *Richard Hakluyt and the English Voyages*, George Bruner Parks. American Geographical Society, 1928.

Wood, Anthony à. *Athenæ Oxonienses: An exact history of all the writers and bishops who have had their education in the most ancient and famous University of Oxford*. London, 1721 (2nd ed.).

Wrigley, E. A., and R. S. Schofield. *The Population History of England 1541–1871: A Reconstruction*. London, 1981.

Yates, Frances. *Giordano Bruno and the Hermetic Tradition*. Chicago, 1964.

Yewbrey, Graham. "John Dee and the 'Sidney Group,'" unpublished Ph.D. thesis, University of Hull, 1981.

Zetterberg, J. Peter. "The Mistaking of 'the Mathematicks' for Magic in Tudor and Stuart England." *Sixteenth Century Journal* 11 (1980).

INDEX

✤

ABOUT THE AUTHOR

✦

BENJAMIN WOOLLEY, a writer and broadcaster, has written about subjects ranging from Renaissance mathematics through Victorian calculating machines to the Space Age. His previous books include *Virtual Worlds*, an exploration of virtual reality, and *The Bride of Science*, a biography of Byron's brilliant daughter. He lives in London.